STILLBORN CRUSADE

ILYA SOMIN

STILLBORN CRUSADE

THE
Tragic Failure of
Western Intervention
IN THE
Russian Civil War
1918 - 1920

TRANSACTION PUBLISHERS
New Brunswick (U.S.A.) and London (U.K.)

Library of Congress Catalog Number: 96-13273
ISBN: 1-56000-274-3
Printed in the United States of America

Library of Congress Cataloging-in-Publication Data

Somin, Ilya.
    Stillborn crusade : the tragic failure of Western intervention in the Russian Civil War, 1918–20 / Ilya Somin.
        p. cm.
    Includes bibliographical references and index.
    ISBN 1-56000-274-3 (alk. paper)
    1. Soviet Union—History—Allied intervention, 1918–1920. I. Title.
DK265.4.S66 1996
947.084'1—dc20   96-13273
                                                                                        CIP

Contents

Acknowledgments   vii

1. Introduction   1
2. The Development of British Policy   27
3. "Why Not Save Siberia?" The Development of US Policy   79
4. The Whites Reconsidered   135
5. Lost Triumphs: The Possibilities of Intervention   179

Epilogue: Conclusions and Implications   209

Bibliography   223

Index   229

To my parents,
Yefim and Sofya Somin
for everything

Acknowledgments

Many people helped to bring this project to fruition. I would especially like to thank my thesis advisor, Professor N. Gordon Levin, with whom I first conceived of this topic. Professor Levin's help and encouragement have been invaluable, both in the writing of the present work and generally throughout my time at Amherst.

I also owe a great debt to Professor Peter Czap and Professor William Taubman, who generously agreed to fill in as advisors during the spring 1995 semester, when Professor Levin was on leave, and who also served as readers. Their insightful comments and criticisms have led to numerous improvements in both the style and the content of *Stillborn Crusade*.

Professor Paul Hollander of the University of Massachusetts, and Dr. Constantine Pleshakov of the Institute of USA and Canada Studies (Moscow), kindly took the time to read the manuscript and made useful suggestions. Christopher Gabriel of the Federalist Society provided me with a copy of his unpublished Oxford University M. Phil. thesis on Colonel Edward M. House and generally helped to impress upon me the surprising extent to which House was able to dominate President Wilson's attention to the exclusion of other advisers. At Amherst, Professor Hadley Arkes gave me the benefit of his expertise in the moral theory of intervention and reviewed the section of chapter 5 devoted to the application of that theory to the case of the Russian Civil War. D. Daniel Sokol read the entire manuscript and offered helpful advice on various points, an invaluable service he has performed for countless Amherst College History Department thesis writers over the last three years. Along with Michael Rubin, who also took the time to read large portions of the manuscript, Danny conducted a mock thesis defense for me that helped clarify my thinking on a number of issues.

While each of the above has helped correct flaws in my analysis, all of the opinions expressed herein are solely my own, as are any errors of whatever kind.

For their support and understanding during difficult times, I would like to thank all my friends at Amherst.

My mother, Sofya Somin, graciously took time out from her busy schedule to print out the numerous copies of the manuscript that I needed. For all their love and understanding, my greatest debt is to her and to my father, Yefim Somin. The dedication after the title page is but an inadequate expression of all I owe to them.

Amherst College
May 1995

The Russian Civil War 1918 - 1920

IN SIBERIA:
AMERICANS
BRITISH
JAPANESE

Murmansk
BRITISH

Kem
White Sea
AMERICANS
Archangel
FINNS
BRITISH
Onega

FINLAND

FINNS
YUDENICH
Petrograd

Perm
CZECHS
KOLCHAK

Vologda

Baltic Sea
Estonia

Tver
Nizhni-Novgorod
Kazan
Ufa

Latvia
Lithuania

Vitebsk
Moscow
Samara

Tula

Minsk
POLES
Orel
Tambov

POLAND

Kiev
Kharkov
Gurev

DENIKIN

Astrakhan

Odessa
Rostov

Crimea
Caspian Sea
Novorossisk

WRANGEL
Black Sea
Tbilisi
Baku

Batum
BRITISH
BRITISH

Yerevan

Bolshevik controlled area, November 1918
▲▲▲▲ Maximum advance of the Whites, 1918-19
▦▦▦ Remnant of the anti-Bolshevik armies by 1920-21
– – – Established Soviet Borders, 1921-39

0   200
Miles

1

Introduction

*"We have fought to make the world safe for
democracy. Does that mean that it shall be safe
for democracy everywhere but in Russia?"[1]*
—*New York Times,* June 30, 1919

*"[T]he great Allied Powers will, each of them
and all of them, learn to rue the fact that they
could not take more decided and more united
action to crush the Bolshevik peril before it had
grown too strong."[2]*
—Winston Churchill, February 14, 1920

The triumph of the Bolsheviks in the Russian Civil War was the first
great crack in the system of international relations established by the victorious Allies at the end of World War I. As Winston Churchill and a few
other farsighted statesmen had foreseen, this event placed the entire
Versailles arrangement in jeopardy almost before it had begun to function. A system based on the enforcement of shared liberal values through
the League of Nations and other multilateral arrangements could not easily function effectively if one of the most powerful European states was
led by a political movement that not only rejected those values but openly
proclaimed its intention to actively undermine them.

Besides pursuing aggressive foreign policies of its own, the emergence
of a totalitarian, anti-Western Russia would eventually help stimulate the
rise of totalitarian movements of a different ideological stripe but equally
aggressive foreign policy orientation in Germany and Italy. Had the Bolsheviks been defeated in the Russian Civil War, it is quite possible that
Hitler and Mussolini might never even have come to power, and, if they
had, it would have been far easier to establish a common Western-Rus-

1

sian front against them had Russia been under the rule of almost any regime other than the Soviet.

Both Hitler and Mussolini, as they openly admitted, owed much to Lenin's example.[3] In the words of Nikolai Bukharin, one of the leading ideologists of the early Soviet regime, "It is characteristic of Fascist methods of combat that they, more than any other party, have adopted and applied in practice the experiences of the Russian Revolution.... [O]ne discovers in them a complete application of Bolshevik tactics, and especially those of Russian Bolshevism."[4] More concretely, both Hitler and Mussolini benefited from the division among their opponents engendered by the presence of Moscow-controlled Communist parties more interested in combating liberals and social democrats than fascists and Nazis.

Along with the baneful effects of the Bolshevik victory on the development of world politics, we must also consider the more immediate consequences of their victory for Russia itself. A long debate has raged between those who believe that Lenin's vision of communism was betrayed by Stalin and those who see Stalin's policies as logical outgrowths of Leninism. Since the fall of the Soviet Union, not surprisingly, several powerful new studies have reasserted the latter position.[5] Yet, strictly speaking, it is not even necessary to enter into this dispute to judge that the Bolshevik victory represented a human catastrophe of immense proportions, for millions of people were slain by the communists *even during the period of Lenin's rule itself.* By a conservative estimate, some 9 million people died during the Russian Civil War of 1918–20 and in its immediate aftermath.[6] Of these, at least 5 million died of famine, mostly as a direct consequence of Bolshevik agricultural policies that deliberately confiscated grain for the use of the Red Army and artificially lowered prices to the point where peasants were unwilling to sell their produce.[7] The Bolshevik leadership persisted in these policies in full knowledge of their consequences.[8] Another 2 million victims of the Civil War perished in epidemics,[9] mostly in Bolshevik-controlled areas where malnutrition caused by famine and the general disruption of society caused by Bolshevik policies made such outbreaks almost inevitable. That the famines and epidemics were largely the result of Bolshevik policies rather than "wartime conditions" is strongly suggested by the fact that those areas of Russia that were under White (i.e., non-Bolshevik) control during the Civil War not only avoided such demographic calamities but actually experienced *increases* in population,[10] even though a disproportionately large percentage of the fighting took place there. Moreover, the losses from the famine would have been much greater were it not for the efforts of Herbert Hoover's American Relief Administration, which the Soviets only grudgingly permitted to function.[11]

In addition to these vast losses, Robert Conquest, the leading scholar of the Soviet regime's crimes, has estimated that some 200,000 political executions took place during the first six years of Soviet rule in Russia (1917-23), and hundreds of thousands more died as a result of mistreatment in prisons and concentration camps.[12] In his authoritative study of the Cheka, Lenin's secret police and forerunner of the KGB, British historian George Leggett estimates a total of 140,000 executions carried out by *this agency alone* during the 1917-21 period, a figure *ten times* greater than the estimated total for all government agencies over the last *fifty* years of the czarist regime (14,000), then generally believed to be the most repressive government in Europe.[13]

The crimes of the Lenin era alone, not to mention those of the Stalinist period that flowed from it, greatly outweighed the putative benefits Soviet rule brought to selected portions of the Russian population. Like any other great social transformation, the advent of communism raised new people to positions of authority, thus making these rising elites better off than they were before, in some cases dramatically so. This "upward mobility," has sometimes been used to put a relatively favorable gloss on early Soviet rule.[14] Yet similar gains could be cited for the early years of Nazi rule in Germany, a fact which has somehow failed to improve that regime's image among Western intellectuals. Moreover, many of these people might have done equally well or better under any of a number of possible alternative regimes. The evils of Soviet totalitarianism, like those of the Nazi variant, cannot be excused on the grounds that this regime could hardly help but benefit at least a few people.

The issue of the extent to which the Soviet regime was truly totalitarian in its earliest stages is outside the scope of this work and has, in any case, been comprehensively addressed by others.[15] The key point to remember is that the adoption of forced labor, coercive requisition of agricultural produce, secret police repression, press censorship, tight state control of industrial production, and other typically totalitarian policies normally associated with "war communism" were underway by the spring of 1918, well before the rise of significant armed opposition to communist rule.[16] Any pretensions to democracy that the Bolsheviks may have had were exploded by their forcible dissolution of the freely elected Constituent Assembly on January 5, 1918, if not by the Bolshevik coup itself. In fact, the most authoritative recent history of the Russian Civil War, notes that "'proper civil war,' against the conservative Whites, would actually lead in the winter of 1918-19 to more tolerance for the other [socialist] parties" as the Bolsheviks desperately cast about for whatever support they could get.[17] Later, in the immediate aftermath of the Whites' defeat, the Terror and other totalitarian policies were actually intensified.[18] The view that repression was merely the result of war is further undermined by the fact that it extended even to those opposition parties, notably the Mensheviks, who made a point of supporting the Bolshevik regime against its foreign and White enemies.[19] Totalitarianism must therefore be considered an inherent element of early Bolshevik policy and not merely a wartime aberration.

Nor is it anachronistic to use the term "totalitarian" to describe early Bolshevism, even if the word had not yet been invented at the time. Social scientists often use modern terminology to describe past events. The American Founding Fathers, for instance, are usually described as "liberal" and antebellum southern slaveowners as "racists," even though these terms were not commonly used in the eighteenth and nineteenth centuries respectively. Moreover, despite the absence of a convenient term for it, some contemporary observers of the Bolshevik regime, notably Winston Churchill, were able to perceive its uniqueness and grasp the distinctive elements of a totalitarian system.

Even if the more extreme Bolshevik policies really did begin only at the time the Civil War heated up, the vast number of deaths these policies caused—and their lack of precedent in the long history of bloody European civil conflicts—suggest that something more was at work than mere "wartime conditions." No such conditions could account for Lenin's belief that "[e]ven if ninety percent of the people perish, what matter if the other ten percent live to see the Revolution universal?"[20] To say that Bolshevik totalitarianism was the result of the Civil War is much like saying that the Nazi Holocaust was a consequence of World War II.[21] It *may* be technically correct, but it fails to come to grips with the kind of mindset which concluded that such cruel policies were necessarily called for by the conflict in question.

The estimates for the number of deaths caused by early Bolshevik policies are, of course, conjectural; no one will ever know the true death toll attributable to Leninist policies just as no one will ever know the true number of deaths resulting from the decisions of Stalin, Hitler, Mao, or Pol Pot. But unless the best estimates of historians are entirely wrong, it is clear that the early years of Bolshevik rule inflicted a toll of deaths roughly equivalent to that of the Holocaust; some six to seven million, if the figures for famine, disease, and execution are combined. Even if we arbitrarily cut this figure in half, to offset any alleged anti-Soviet biases of Conquest and the other Western and Russian emigre scholars on whose work it is based, we are still left with a number about twice as large as the number of deaths attributed to the contemporary Turkish genocide of the Armenians or Pol Pot's more recent mass murders in Cambodia.[22]

Moreover, unlike the Holocaust, the crimes of Stalin, or those of Pol Pot, early Bolshevik atrocities were widely publicized in the West at the time they occurred and were well known to Western leaders such as British Prime Minister Lloyd George and U.S. President Woodrow Wilson.[23] As early as December 1917, US Secretary of State Robert Lansing demonstrated impressive prescience in predicting that "Russia is about to be the stage on which will be acted one of the most terrible tragedies of all history.... [T]he Russian 'Terror' will far surpass in brutality and destruction of life and property the Terror of the French Revolution."[24] Allied leaders were well aware of the prevalence of the Red Terror, and even filed numerous diplomatic protests against it.[25] They were likewise cognizant of the vast famine created and deliberately maintained by Bolshevik agricultural policy.[26]

In addition to the enormous atrocities inflicted in the first years of Lenin's regime, it is also worthwhile to consider the overall human cost of communist rule in Russia and elsewhere during this century, since it is highly unlikely that communism would have triumphed in any other major nation had it not prevailed in Russia in 1918–20; everywhere else where they managed to seize power, communist forces were aided by the Soviet example and, usually, by direct Soviet assistance. A highly conservative estimate puts the total number of deaths due to communist policies in the USSR, China, Eastern Europe, North Korea, and Indochina, at 50 million.[27] To this must be added the vast costs imposed on the survivors, in terms of lowered standards of living, loss of freedom, fear, and so on— not to mention the burdens that the presence of communist states in the international system imposed on the West. Nor is it entirely anachronistic to frame the issue in this way, since the potential for the expansion of

Bolshevism into other states was a major concern of Western statesmen at the time of the Paris Peace Conference of 1919.[28]

It is in light of this historical background that we must view the issue of Allied intervention in the Russian Civil War. Logically, we should consider the question of what options were available to destroy the Bolshevik regime, or at least diminish its geographic scope. Not even the staunchest left-wing critics of the Allied interventions in 1918–20 attempt to deny that the Western powers deployed only a small fraction of the forces potentially available to them. Even if we set aside the unrealistic option of a full-scale war against the Soviet regime, the Allies might well have sent significantly more troops than they actually did. Nor did they make full use of the diplomatic and economic leverage they had over the states bordering Russia to induce them to cooperate effectively against the Bolsheviks, as advocated by Winston Churchill at the time. As we shall see, Churchill and others also suggested a host of other measures that could have been undertaken at relatively little cost and with at least some substantial hope of success.

Historian Martin Malia identifies three key moments during the Civil War when the Soviet regime was in "mortal danger":

> The first...was the summer of 1918, when the Germans occupied the west and south and the Whites advanced from the east. The second was the spring of 1919, when Admiral Kolchak [the chief White leader in Siberia] advanced out of Siberia towards...Moscow. And the third occasion was the fall of that year, when General Denikin advanced from [the] Ukraine to within two hundred kilometers of the capital, and General Yudenich moved on Petrograd from Estonia.[29]

At each of these crucial points, the Western Allies had realistic options for stronger intervention available to them, options that they rejected for a complex combination of reasons that we shall have occasion to examine later. Given that the White armies came so close to victory even with the relatively modest intervention that was undertaken, it is not unreasonable to suggest that they might well have prevailed if the intervention had been stronger and better coordinated. Certainly, the fear that it might was present in the minds of the Soviet leaders themselves, who, in the spring of 1919, offered substantial concessions to the Allies—including allowing the White regimes to keep all the territory they had thus far occupied—in exchange for the cessation of intervention. Surely Lenin and Trotsky would not have been willing to yield so much territory to their enemies[30] unless they were genuinely worried that continued intervention, properly conducted, might deprive of them of all that they still had.

Could it have? And would not the world have been infinitely better off if it had? To ask these questions seriously is to run counter to almost the entire historiography of the intervention as it has developed over the last sixty years. Historians of the intervention disagree on a number of issues, but they are nearly unanimous in believing that intervention, in so far as it may have been anti-Bolshevik in nature, was a bad thing.[31] Ironically, those historians most sympathetic to Woodrow Wilson and U.S. policy in general have sought to defend him by arguing that American intervention was wholly untinged by anti-Bolshevism and only motivated by a desire to oppose the Germans and/or counter Japanese ambitions in Siberia.[32] Betty Miller Unterberger, one of the leading exponents of this view, even goes so far as to praise U.S. policy because "[a]t various times the United States prevented political action against the Soviet government...America's participation in Allied intervention...provide[d] a moderating influence which tended to curb the more extreme ideas of the Allies."[33] On this view, American policy deserves praise for, in essence, *defending* the Soviet regime! One wonders how the historical profession would have reacted to a leading scholar who argued, for example, that the isolationists of the 1930s deserve praise for the assistance they implicitly rendered to the foreign policy of Nazi Germany and Japan.

As we shall see, Unterberger's analysis is not a wholly accurate reflection of U.S. policy, which did have at least some anti-Bolshevik elements. Still, the implicit assumption of her argument—that anti-Bolshevik intervention was necessarily wrong—is an interesting reflection of historians' attitudes. These attitudes were so deeply rooted that neither Unterberger nor any of the other leading scholars of the intervention even saw any need to explicitly defend them against possible opposing arguments.[34] In fact, neither Unterberger nor George F. Kennan, arguably the single most distinguished analyst of the intervention, ever even explicitly states the moral reasoning underlying their stance, though Unterberger makes vague references to Wilsonian theories of "self-determination."[35] The wrongness of anti-Bolshevik intervention was not a conclusion arrived at through analysis but an a priori assumption on which all analysis was based.

If it achieves nothing else, the present work can at least subject this assumption to critical scrutiny. In attempting to do so, we shall focus on the British and American interventions to the relative exclusion of those of the French, Japanese, and Italians. This choice is subject to obvious challenge. After all, the Japanese sent more troops to Russia than all the other Allied powers combined. More than seventy thousand Japanese troops were present in Siberia at their peak strength in the fall of 1918,[36] a force some ten times the size of its companion American contingent. The French, in their turn, were the most staunchly anti-Bolshevik of all the Allied powers. Prime Minister Georges Clemenceau and Marshal Ferdinand Foch, the French Supreme Commander of the Allied forces in Europe, made repeated proposals for intervention in 1918-19.

Ultimately, there is no reason to censure the historian who prefers to focus on French or Japanese efforts, though such scholars, at least in the English-speaking world, have been remarkably few in number.[37] Still, the contrary decision to concentrate on the British and Americans is also defensible, and not just on grounds of division of labor between scholars. As nearly all analysts agree, the Japanese intervention was not primarily motivated by any desire to undermine the Bolsheviks or even to improve the Allied position in the World War. Their goal was to establish de facto control of eastern Siberia, thus strengthening their overall position in the Far East, which Japanese leaders saw as their special "sphere of influence" in the traditional imperialist sense.[38] Unlike the American leaders and, to a lesser extent, the British, Japanese elites did not see themselves as custodians of world order or defenders of liberal values. They had no quarrel with the Bolsheviks per se. To suggest that the Japanese should have intervened more forcefully—with the goal of eliminating the menace of Bolshevism—would be equivalent to suggesting that they change the entire political and ideological orientation of their society. It would be only marginally less absurd to suggest that the Bolsheviks should have given up power voluntarily. The British and Americans on the other hand, had a different set of values, and they each had their articulate advocates of principled intervention. Most Anglo-American opponents of intervention also framed their position in terms of liberal values. Unlike that of the Japanese, Anglo-American intervention clearly poses the general issue of the proper response of liberal democracies to incipient totalitarianism. Furthermore, the Japanese, whatever their intentions, could not have intervened anywhere other than Siberia, the theater of operations most removed from Russia's heartland and therefore least likely to yield decisive results.

The ideological orientation of the French was closer to American and British views than that of the Japanese. But, in spite of their very real desire to see the Bolsheviks defeated, the French leaders were unable to do very much to achieve this goal. Their actual military presence in Russia was largely confined to a small force sent to the Black Sea port of Odessa in December 1918 and withdrawn soon thereafter, after having done almost no fighting. French military and economic aid to the Whites was also extremely limited in scope. Of all the Allied nations, France had suffered most in World War I, and it was simply incapable of further significant exertions. Although the British had also suffered substantially, they were not so completely demoralized and, in fact, were able to provide the only aid that actually proved of substantial use to the Whites.

The approximately 100 million pounds worth of aid that the British provided to the Whites in 1918–19 dwarfed all other Allied contributions.[39] Moreover, British efforts were concentrated on the White army led by General Anton Denikin in Southern Russia. Denikin's Volunteer Army was the best led and most capable of the various White forces. It also had the most prosperous and best-positioned home base. For these reasons, Denikin came much closer to taking Moscow and destroying the Bolshevik regime than did any of the other White leaders. Since the British were the only one of the Allied powers to focus substantial efforts on his forces, their intervention deserves special attention for this reason alone. It is also noteworthy that British troops in northern Russia and in the Denikin area did more actual fighting against the Bolsheviks than any of the other Allied units, though even they did not do all that much. Finally, British policy is worthy of reconsideration because of the extraordinary debate between Winston Churchill, the most articulate defender of intervention, and Prime Minister David Lloyd George and other skeptical members of the cabinet. As we shall see, Churchill found himself contending against both Lloyd George's skepticism, philosophically rooted in the "liberal" view of international relations, and the conservative "realist" perspectives of other hostile Cabinet members, notably Lord Curzon. This three-way ideological clash prefigured Western debates on policy towards the Soviet Union throughout the entire period of its existence. Indeed, the three views of the world articulated by Churchill, Lloyd George, and Curzon, respectively, underlie most Western conceptions of international relations to this very day. Herein lies another important reason why British policy towards the Russian Civil War is of particular interest.

The special role of Winston Churchill also deserves reconsideration. Churchill has gotten a great deal of praise for his foresight with respect to Nazi Germany, but historians have generally either censured or ignored his equally impressive foresight concerning the Soviet Union. Unlike most other Western statesmen at the time, Churchill grasped that the Bolshevik regime was an entirely new force in international relations and he foresaw that it would be a difficult and dangerous adversary. He even predicted that Bolshevik Russia would be a natural ally for a resurgent Germany bent on revenge. In addition, Churchill developed a number of inventive tactical schemes for making Allied intervention in Russia more effective. A reconsideration of Churchill's views on the intervention is one of the primary goals of the present work.

Although it was much more limited in scope, duration, and anti-Bolshevik intent than the British, it is the American intervention that has attracted the lion's share of scholarly attention to date. Much of this undoubtedly reflected cold war imperatives rather than the intervention's intrinsic significance. A bitter debate emerged between radical scholars, led by William Appleman Williams, who, echoing official Soviet historiography, argued that America's alleged anti-Bolshevism in 1918–19 was responsible for poisoning subsequent U.S.-Soviet relations, and "cold war" liberals, notably George Kennan, who attempted to absolve the United States of this charge.[40] Even aside from this issue, however, U.S. policy towards Russia in 1918–20 was of great significance, albeit in a sense somewhat different from that understood by either Williams or Kennan.

Essentially, American intervention was the dog that did not bite, at least not very hard. Alone among the Western Allies, the U.S. had emerged from the war virtually unscathed, indeed, more powerful than ever. This power was not just military and economic. Through his eloquence and idealism, U.S. President Woodrow Wilson had emerged as the great champion of liberal values in the world, not just in American eyes but in those of many Europeans, Africans, and Asians as well. Indeed, historians of ideology see Wilsonian liberalism and Leninist Bolshevism as the two great new visions of international relations to have emerged from the First World War.[41] Had Wilson and the United States generally taken a strong and unequivocal stance against Bolshevism and in favor of forceful intervention, the moral and political—not to mention, military—effects might have been enormous. Instead, as even Williams grants,[42] Wilson hesitated at numerous points. At no time did he commit anything like the full potential power of the United States, even with respect to military and economic assistance to the Whites short of sending U.S. forces to fight the Bolsheviks in their own right. A considerable part of his thinking turned on the idea that Bolshevism might best be countered through economic assistance to the Russian people as a whole, as opposed to narrowly focused military assistance intended for the Whites.[43] Had the United States been as committed to overthrowing Bolshevism as was France, or even Britain, things might have turned out differently. At the very least, the possibility should be explored.

By 1918, the United States was clearly the most powerful nation in the world and the least exhausted of the major Allies. It is, by now, almost a truism that American leaders failed to properly exploit this position in their efforts to establish the kind of postwar order which they desired. In an influential 1951 critique of American foreign policy, George Kennan condemned the Treaty of Versailles as "a peace which had the tragedies of the future written into it as by the devil's own hand."[44] But scholars have largely ignored the possibility that the failure to adequately support anti-Bolshevik intervention in Russia was one of the main causes of the broader defeat of the American diplomatic strategy. In fact, as noted above, those historians most intent on defending Woodrow Wilson and his policies attempt to prove that he never had *any* intention of overthrowing the Bolsheviks at all.

Existing scholarly opinion on the American intervention in Russia in 1918-20 can be divided into two major camps.* On the one hand, William Appleman Williams and other radical scholars argue that the inter-

---

* Unfortunately, David S. Foglesong's interesting and provocative new book, *America's Secret War Against Bolshevism: U.S. Intervention in the Russian Civil War, 1917-20*, (Chapel Hill: University of North Carolina Press, 1995), became available too late to be considered here. Foglesong examines in detail a large number of covert U.S. government activities in Russia which he contends were motivated by anti-Bolshevik animus. While he has skillfully brought together a wide range of evidence unduly neglected in other works (including this one), I do not believe his argument overturns the broad general conclusions about U.S. intervention I reach in chapter 3. This is principally because (1) Foglesong grants (pg. 295) that Wilson opposed "full-scale military intervention in Russia," for more or less the reasons I posit; (2) he presents very little compelling evidence to back up his claim that U.S. intervention policy was primarily motivated by anti-Bolshevik as opposed to anti-German and other considerations prior to the partial recognition of Admiral Kolchak's government in June 1919; and (3) I find Foglesong's argument that Wilson and his top advisers were enthusiastic advocates of covert action somewhat overdrawn, particularly in light of his own conclusion (e.g., pp. 121-26), that they were not aware of most of the more provocative of the actions taken by U.S. agents in Russia.

vention "was anti-Bolshevik in origin and intent."[45] In the opposite camp are those scholars who contend, like Kennan and Unterberger, that it was due to other causes. Both groups, it must be stressed, agree that anti-Bolshevik intervention, to the extent that it did occur, was wrong. Their disagreement centers largely on the question of whether or not it did.

Kennan, Unterberger, and others who deny anti-Bolshevik intent do not agree among themselves as to what its true causes were. Kennan stresses the imperatives of the ongoing war against Germany, which had reached a crisis stage by mid-1918. On this view, Wilson's decisions to send American forces to Siberia and northern Russia were "closely linked with America's wartime concerns. Had there been no great European war in progress, neither expedition would ever have been dispatched."[46] Britain and France had long pressured the United States to agree to an intervention in Russia in order to reestablish the Eastern Front in the war against Germany. This front had been undermined by Russia's withdrawal from the war after the Bolshevik-initiated Treaty of Brest-Litovsk was signed in March 1918. Some one million German troops were shifted from Russia to the West and it was understandable, Kennan contends, that the Allies should be desperate to find a way to reestablish the Eastern Front and that Wilson should eventually agree to accommodate them.

Kennan also stresses the role of the Czech Legion, a unit of Chechoslovak POWs that had been formed in Russia to fight the Germans and, in mid-1918, was on its way out of now-neutral Russia to Vladivostok on the Pacific coast, from whence it was to be transshiped to the Western Front in Europe.[47] In the spring and summer of 1918, for reasons to be examined more closely later, fighting broke out between the Czechs and Bolshevik forces while the former were en route through Siberia. Kennan contends that the desire to rescue the Czech Legion from its apparent predicament was what finally tipped the scales of Wilson's mind in favor of intervention.[48] He is particularly concerned to stress that "[T]here is no suggestion more preposterous than that he [Wilson] was animated in these decisions by hostility toward the Russian people or by a desire to overthrow the Soviet regime with American forces."[49]

In contrast to Kennan's emphasis on the broader demands of the war and on the Czech Legion, Christopher Lasch focuses on the view, held by some at the time, that the Bolsheviks were German agents. Almost no one disputes the fact that this belief was widespread in many circles, but Lasch is original in arguing that it was fully endorsed by Wilson and other leading American officials and that it motivated the American intervention. According to Lasch, Wilson and Secretary of State Lansing believed that the revolutionary Bolsheviks were not revolutionary at all, "but secretly allied with the reactionary designs of imperial Germany. Nor were they in any sense spontaneous; on the contrary, they were planned, directed and financed by Germany herself."[50]

These suspicions were bolstered by the widely known fact that Lenin had returned to Russia in April 1917 with German assistance and had financed his party partly with German funds. They were also buttressed by rumors, partially true, that the Bolsheviks had armed German and Austrian prisoners of war in order to fight the Czechs.[51] In fact, a recent study by the Russian historian General Dmitri Volkogonov, based on previously unavailable Bolshevik records, reveals that in the period before they took power, the Bolsheviks were much more dependent on German money than previously thought. Volkogonov also argues that they may even have had a kind of de facto understanding with the Germans to the effect that they would withdraw Russia from the war upon seizing power.[52]

Lasch's argument is an interesting one, but like most other discussions of the "German agent" issue, it overlooks the fact that the concept of an "agent" can have two different meanings. In the more narrow sense of the term, an agent is solely a tool of his sponsor, having no purposes of his own other than, perhaps, material greed for the money he is being paid. It is this sense of the word which Lasch apparently has in mind when he attributes to Wilson and Lansing the belief that the Bolsheviks were German agents. However, there is also another, more sophisticated sense of the term. By this definition, an agent may serve the interests of his sponsor even though his own underlying goals, indeed his entire ideological view of the world, might be different. Despite their differences, the two parties recognize a common interest and so help each other. This was certainly Lenin's view of the matter. "Nobody ever asked the Germans for 'help,'" he explained in a secret August 1918 note to the Bolshevik representative in Sweden, "but we had an understanding.... There was a coincidence of interests. We would have been idiots not to have taken advantage of it."[53]

Although they did not have access to this note, which was only revealed to the world in General Volkogonov's recent book, top American officials in 1918 were nonetheless able to distinguish between the two types of agency; they tended to conclude, however, that the difference did not matter. "As to Lenin and Trotsky," Lansing wrote in December 1917, "I am in doubt. They may be acting entirely in Germany's interest, but I cannot make that belief harmonize with some things they have done."[54] However, this doubt did not alleviate his fear that, as a result of Bolshevik policies, "Germany and Austria could remove their military forces for use elsewhere and Russia's resources would be at their mercy."[55] Even David Francis, the U.S. Ambassador to Russia, whom Lasch and other historians cite as being particularly convinced that the Bolsheviks were German agents, wrote that "They [the Bolsheviks] felt justified in accepting money from Germany as they promote the chances for their world-wide social revolution for which they are constantly working, being willing to sacrifice *any* country therefor" (emphasis mine).[56] How much the fear of German-Bolshevik cooperation eventually influenced the American decision to intervene in Russia is a question which will be addressed in its proper place.[57] At this point, it is only necessary to make the crucial distinction between the crude view that the Bolsheviks were pure tools of the Germans and the more sophisticated argument that, though independent, they were serving German interests for their own reasons.

A third explanation of the American intervention offered by historians who reject the anti-Bolshevism theory is that Wilson sent troops to Siberia in order to offset the intervention of the Japanese. The Japanese and the Americans had a longstanding rivalry in the Far East and Wilson was, it is argued, deeply suspicious of their motives in sending troops to Siberia, where, it was feared, they might try to establish permanent control. This is the view of Unterberger, who argues that Wilson's decision to drop his earlier doubts and agree to intervention in July 1918 occurred only "after it became evident that intervention would take place despite his opposition and probably with Japan in charge of the expedition. He joined it, not because he believed in it, but because he thought he could 'impose greater restraint on Japan within rather than outside it.'"[58] Williams, who grants that anti-Japanese motives were present, rightly points out that the anti-Japanese theory isn't necessarily mutually exclusive with the view that intervention was anti-Bolshevik: "[I]ntervention was aimed at the Bolsheviks as well as Japan,"[59] he contends.

As a practical matter, however, the two goals, to the extent that they were both present, *did* conflict. It was not easy for U.S. troops in Siberia to simultaneously help the Whites oppose the Bolsheviks and stand ready to oppose any suspicious Japanese moves at the same time. No less a personage than Vladimir Ilyich Lenin argued that internal quarrels between the interventionist powers, notably that between the U.S. and Japan, were crucial to the eventual Bolshevik victory. "We have been able to win so far," he said in 1920,

> only because of the serious disagreements among the imperialist powers.... Let us take Japan as an example. She held almost all of Siberia[60] and, of course could have helped Kolchak whenever necessary. She did not do so, however, because her interests differed radically from America's interests and she did not want to draw chestnuts out of the fire for American capital. This being clear, we had only to make full use of these differences between America and Japan to strengthen ourselves.[61]

Therefore, even if it is true, as Williams argues, that both anti-Bolshevik and anti-Japanese motives were present, it is still be important to know the relative saliency of each, since this would determine the extent to which U.S. officials were willing to sacrifice one set of goals to the other when it came to the crunch. This issue is almost completely ignored by Williams. But, as we shall see in chapter 3, anti-Japanese motives did indeed, to some extent, crowd out anti-Bolshevik ones as the intervention progressed.

A final theory of the intervention is that of N. Gordon Levin, which tends to cut across the traditional debate between advocates of the anti-Bolshevik and anti-German interpretations. "[H]istorians have," Levin claims, "partly obscured the complex nature of American intervention in Siberia by attempting to portray it as motivated almost exclusively by *either* an anti-German *or* an anti-Bolshevik intent on the part of the Wilson Administration. The confusion arises from a tendency to view these two motives as mutually exclusive when, in reality, they were fused in a Wilsonian desire to oppose both Bolshevism and German imperialism on behalf of a pro-Allied and liberal-nationalist Russia."[62] According to Levin, Wilson sought to oppose both Bolshevism and the Germans because they were both threats to the establishment of a truly liberal and democratic order in Russia. "At the innermost heart of Wilson's Russian policy," he concludes, "there lay the implicit desire to find a way...to help Russia regain the lost liberal-nationalist order of the March [February][63] Revolution."[64] The liberal Russian regime of the Provisional Government, which ruled from the overthrow of the tsar in March 1917 until the Bolshevik coup in November was Wilson's ideal.

Levin's theory bears some similarity to Williams', in that both stress the importance of anti-Bolshevism. But it is distinctive in two crucial respects: first, Levin, unlike Williams,[65] does not discount the importance of anti-German motives; second, Levin argues that Wilson wished to promote liberalism in Russia, not "counter-revolution." "The Wilsonian definition of counterrevolution in Russia," he contends, "was a desire to reinstate Tsarism and not a desire to overthrow Lenin in favor of democratic-nationalism."[66] On this view, Wilson clearly differentiated between liberal and conservative-monarchist opponents of Bolshevism, being prepared to support the former but not the latter.[67] By contrast, Williams lumps all Russian opponents of Bolshevism together as "counter-revolutionaries" and implies that American leaders did likewise, describing American actions as "efforts at counter-revolution."[68] This claim of Williams' is deeply at variance with the historical record, as shall be argued in chapter 3. However, the attempt to equate anticommunism with counterrevolution is a key element of the traditional radical left critique of U.S. policy towards the USSR and its allies, with respect to both the intervention period and later events.[69] Levin's book is also unusual in that it carefully avoids taking a position on the merits of the intervention, the only major study of the subject to do so.[70]

Even many of those scholars who reject Williams' theory that the American intervention was purely anti-Bolshevik, still lament its effects on the later course of U.S.-Soviet relations. George Kennan's views are particularly interesting in this respect, since Kennan was the leading interpreter of Soviet foreign policy for an entire generation of Americans and remains a respected elder statesman to this day. While denying that the intervention had any anti-Bolshevik motives, Kennan nevertheless deplores its effects on Soviet perceptions of the West. "[T]he intervention..." he believes, "came as a profound shock to the Soviet leaders, confirming them in many of their ideological prejudices, convincing them of the inalterable hostility of the of the capitalist world, [and] providing an excellent excuse...for the maintenance of severe dictatorship within Russia."[71]

In fact, the intervention did not come as "a profound shock" to the Bolsheviks, since they were convinced of the "inalterable hostility of the capitalist world" from the very beginning; and, both before and after the intervention, the Soviet leadership did not lack for a wide variety of other excuses for "the maintenance of severe dictatorship within Russia." In a secret report to the Seventh Communist Party Congress delivered in March 1918, well before any significant Allied intervention occurred, Lenin stated unequivocally that "International imperialism...could not under any circumstances, on any condition, live side by side with the Soviet Republic, both because of its objective position and because of the economic interests of the capitalist class which are embodied in it.... In this sphere a conflict is inevitable."[72] The secret nature of this report, not published until 1923, suggests that it was a real statement of deeply held beliefs rather than mere propaganda; the context of the passage is such as to make clear that "international imperialism," following standard early Bolshevik usage, refers to both the Allies and the Central Powers. Detailed consideration of the limited Bolshevik attempts at cooperation with the Allies in early 1918 is deferred until later chapters; for now it, is sufficient to recognize that, in Lenin's view, no amount of ad hoc cooperation on specific issues could alter the basic reality of underlying conflict. In fact, temporary cooperation was seen as merely another means of undermining the West in the long run. As Lenin put it in 1920, in a report on economic cooperation with capitalist nations, "[T]he concessions which we are giving, which we are forced to give, are a continuation of war [against capitalism] in another form, using other means."[73] In light of such attitudes, it is difficult to believe that Soviet foreign policy would have developed much differently no matter what Western governments did, short of turning communist themselves.

In addition to arguing that intervention poisoned the Soviets' general attitude towards the West, Kennan laments the loss of specific diplomatic openings that were allegedly present in 1918.[74] His position on this point is puzzling, since he also argues persuasively that Lenin's unofficial negotiations with the Americans were not sincere, in that he only wished to use them to forestall intervention and had no real intention of collaborating with the Allies against the Germans; Kennan also stresses the Bolsheviks' ideological intransigence.[75] One can only conjecture that Kennan's belief in the power of reasoned negotiation was so great that it transcended what he himself saw as the clear evidence of the historical record. Against the evidence and arguments advanced in his own work, Kennan is able to assert that "[H]ad it been possible [in May 1918]...to wait out the very few remaining months of the World War without proceeding to the despatch of any American forces to Russia—the entire subsequent course of Soviet-American relations might have been changed."[76] It is indicative of American intellectual attitudes towards the Cold War that the most distinguished American scholar of Soviet foreign policy feels compelled to grasp at even the flimsiest possible indications that early

U.S.-Soviet relations could have been improved while completely neglecting the possibility that a firmer stance might have obviated the need to deal with the Soviet Union altogether.

Despite its greater importance to the actual course of the Russian Civil War, the British intervention has not received anything like the amount of attention that has been devoted to the American. To date, the outstanding analysis of British intervention policy is the massive three-volume study by Richard Ullman.[77] As Ullman argues, there can be little doubt that British policy was not initially dominated by anti-Bolshevik sentiment. Indeed, as late as May 1918, Prime Minister David Lloyd George and Foreign Minister Arthur Balfour hoped that the Allies could intervene to oppose the Germans in Russia *at the invitation of the Bolsheviks*.[78] Only after this hope faded did the British agree to intervention without Bolshevik consent, and, even then, they saw it primarily as a way to resuscitate the Eastern Front against the Germans rather than as an effort to overthrow the Bolshevik regime.

As Ullman goes on to point out, however, anti-Bolshevism gradually superseded wartime imperatives as a rationale for intervention, particularly after World War I ended in November 1918. Throughout 1919, the decisive year of the Russian Civil War, the British gave substantial military assistance to the Whites, especially General Anton Denikin's Volunteer Army in southern Russia. Small British expeditionary forces even took an active part in the fighting in both the Denikin area and around the ports of Murmansk and Archangel in the Arctic Circle. These two cities were actually occupied by Allied forces in 1918-19, and the weakness of the White Russian forces in this region forced the British contingent to do the bulk of the fighting for itself. Even so, Ullman contends,[79] this aid was accompanied by serious doubts about its usefulness on the part of Lloyd George and other Cabinet ministers. Of all the British leaders only Winston Churchill, the state secretary for war, was unequivocally convinced of the wisdom and viability of overthrowing the Bolsheviks by force. The others were, as we shall see in chapter 2, torn by doubts to such an extent that many observers questioned whether Britain had any coherent Russian policy at all in 1919.

In addition to its magisterial thoroughness, Ullman's study is exceptional for one other important reason: he is almost the only leading scholar to seriously consider, albeit very briefly, the possibility that a bigger intervention might have worked. He quickly dismisses this suggestion, however, on the grounds that "Several hundred thousand Allied troops, at a minimum, would have been necessary for 'success' in 1919.... Merely to state such a prospect, however, is to emphasize its impossibility. None of the Powers was willing to commit even a small fraction of this number of soldiers."[80] But, given that the Whites came very close to victory with even the very small intervention that was undertaken, it is not at all clear that victory would have required hundreds of thousands of additional Allied troops. A much smaller, specialized force might have sufficed. Also, Ullman does not give adequate consideration to the possibility that the Allies could have given the Whites greater assistance by an assortment of means short of actual military intervention, a possibility which Churchill emphasized throughout the Russian Civil War.

Ullman does grant that the Bolsheviks might have been overthrown by a relatively small Allied force in July 1918, at the very beginning of the intervention: "If the initial landings at Archangel could have been carried out by two or three divisions...instead of the 1200 troops who actually occupied the port at the end of July, there is little doubt that they could have forced their way to Moscow and overthrown the Bolshevik regime."[81] However, Ullman concludes that, in 1918, "so great a diversion of resources from the west was unthinkable."[82] The issue of "thinkability" will be taken up in detail later. Here, it is enough to point out that two or three divisions was an insignificant force by Western Front standards, since each side deployed well over 150 divisions there by the summer of 1918.[83]

Despite certain limitations, Ullman's study is still extremely impressive. Among students of the American intervention, only Kennan is equally meticulous in describing all the manifold twists and turns of policymaking.[84] Ullman's work is also praiseworthy in that he carefully considers the full range of sometimes contradictory motives that underlay British policy. By contrast, most studies of the American intervention attempt to stress one motive to the near-total exclusion of others. Nonetheless, Ullman gives only very brief consideration to the possibilities of greater intervention. He also implicitly endorses the moral outlook underlying most analyses of the American intervention, even going so far as to suggest that a victorious White regime might have been no better for the West and for Russia than were the Bolsheviks.[85] Neither he nor any of the other major analysts of Anglo-American intervention have been able to fully come to terms with the profound threat represented by Bolshevism to both its own people and the outside world.[86] The purpose of the present work is to reconsider the intervention from a standpoint that keeps this threat fully in mind.

Before moving on to consider the specifics of Anglo-American intervention, it is important to address two important theoretical objections that might be lodged against the format of this study. The first accusation is that of ideological bias. Certainly, I make no secret of my view that the Bolshevik regime was fundamentally malevolent and that it would have been better if it had never come to power or been destroyed in its infancy. This perspective, to put it mildly, is at variance with the view that historical analysis must be limited to strictly neutral consideration of the evidence.

One possible rebuttal to the charge is that this study's bias in favor of anti-Bolshevik intervention is no more egregious than Kennan's or Williams' or Unterberger's bias against it. Moreover, while their analyses consider the wrongness and futility of anti-Bolshevik intervention to be essentially axiomatic, I will at least try to defend my view that intervention was both viable and morally imperative against possible objections.[87] But it is not enough to rebut a serious potential criticism merely by citing the practices of others, even if they be scholars as eminent as George F. Kennan and William Appleman Williams. After all, if the objection is correct, their efforts must also be considered unduly biased. A better response to the charge of bias is that of Richard Pipes, in his preface to *The Russian Revolution*:

> [S]cholarship requires the historian to treat critically his sources and to render honestly the information he obtains from them. It does not call for ethical nihilism, that is, accepting that whatever happened had to happen and hence is beyond good and evil.... The Russian Revolution was made neither by the forces of nature nor by anonymous masses but by identifiable men pursuing their own advantages. Although it had spontaneous aspects, in the main it was the result of deliberate action. As such it is very properly subject to value judgment.[88]

What is true for the Russian Revolution is certainly also true of the efforts at intervention which might have altered its outcome. In addition, American and British leaders at the time certainly saw intervention as, at least in part, a moral issue. Even from the standpoint of simply understanding their views, ideological considerations cannot be excluded. It is precisely because important issues of principle were involved that the intervention attracted so much interest at the time and ever since.

The second charge which can be leveled against the structure of this work is that of counterfactualism. Inevitably, an analysis of the possibility of greater intervention must include speculation on the probable out-comes of actions which did not take place. This violates the great histori-ans' taboo against counterfactualism, which holds that only "real" events which actually occurred are fit subjects for historical study. In actuality, however, the taboo is routinely violated in eminently respectable studies of both the intervention and other issues. Much scholarship on the Ameri-can Civil War, for example, is devoted to the question of whether the war was an "irrepressible conflict" or whether it could have been avoided by a more cautious policy on the part of either North or South in the imme-diate prewar period. Similarly, the many works which condemn Western appeasement of Nazi Germany in the 1930s implicitly or explicitly work from the premise that there was another course available and that that policy would have brought better results. On the specific issue of West-ern intervention in the Russian Civil War, we have seen how George Kennan, among others, contends that a different American policy might have led to better U.S.-Soviet relations in the long run.

These examples are not mere aberrations, not just cases of scholars who have unthinkingly violated the essentially sound canons of their pro-fession. For any analysis of decisions taken in the past necessarily implies consideration of those options which were available to decision-makers but not adopted. And such consideration, in turn, would be meaningless in the absence of at least some consideration of the possible results of these alternative options. On a still deeper level, a strong case can be made that all causal analysis in history necessarily requires the use of counterfactuals. To determine whether X caused Y, one must ask—ex-plicitly or implicitly—if Y would still have occurred in the absence of X, an inquiry which inevitably leads us into the realm of counterfactualism.

In this study, analysis will be confined solely to those policy alterna-tives that were actually presented to American and British leaders in 1918-19, and particularly to those that might realistically been adopted. Thus, even though an intervention by hundreds of thousands of Allied troops would likely have been successful, this option will not be consid-ered since public opinion in the West would never have tolerated it. On the other hand, there were real alternatives that were politically viable, and these will be brought out in later chapters.

The study of history is, in large part, the study of past decisions. And, ultimately, the most important question that can be asked about a deci-sion is whether it was a *good* decision—or not.

Notes

1. "Enemies of Democracy," *New York Times,* June 30, 1919, p. 10.
2. Winston Churchill, "A Policy of Real Peace and Appeasement," speech before his Dundee constituents, February 14, 1920, in Robert Rhodes James, ed., *Winston S. Churchill: His Complete Speeches, 1897–1963,* vol. III, 1914–22, (London: Chelsea House, 1974), p. 2935.
3. See Richard Pipes, *Russia Under the Bolshevik Regime,* (New York: Knopf, 1993), ch. 5, hereafter cited as Pipes, *Bolshevik Regime*; Zbigniew Brzezinski, *The Grand Failure: The Birth and Death of Communism in the Twentieth Century,* (New York: Macmillan, 1989), pp. 6–8.
4. Bukharin, address before the Twelfth Party Congress, of the Communist Party of the Soviet Union [1923], Quoted in ibid., p. 253.
5. See ibid.; Martin Malia, *The Soviet Tragedy,* (New York: Free Press, 1994); Dmitri Volkogonov, *Lenin: A New Biography,* trans. Harold Shukman, (New York: Free Press, 1994).
6. Pipes, *Bolshevik Regime,* pp. 508–509.
7. Ibid.
8. See Richard Pipes, *The Russian Revolution,* (New York: Knopf, 1990), ch. 16.
9. Pipes, *Bolshevik Regime,* p. 509.
10. Ibid., p. 139.
11. See Ibid., pp. 416–19.
12. Robert Conquest, *The Human Cost of Soviet Communism,* prepared for US Senate Judiciary Committee, Sub-Committee to Investigate the Administration of the Internal Security Act and other Internal Security Laws, (Washington, DC: Government Printing Office, 1970), p. 11.
13. George Leggett, *The Cheka: Lenin's Secret Police,* (Oxford: Clarendon Press, 1981), p. 359. Lest it be argued that the two periods are not comparable because the early years of the Bolshevik regime were a time of crisis, it should be recalled that the 1867–1917 period included three wars, the Revolution of 1905 and the rise of an assortment of terrorist movements seeking to overthrow the tsarist government.
14. See, e.g., Sheila Fitzpatrick, *The Russian Revolution, 1917–32,* (New York: Oxford University Press, 1982), pp. 83–84, 97, 133–34.
15. See especially, Pipes, *Russian Revolution,* chapts. 15–16, 18; Pipes, *Bolshevik Regime*; Malia, *Soviet Tragedy,* chapts. 3–4; Volkogonov, *Lenin,* esp. chapts. 4, 6. The classic account of the Red Terror is Sergei Melgounov, *The Red Terror in Russia,* trans. anonymous, (London: J.M. Dent & Sons, 1925). For excellent analyses of the early origins of the Cheka, the Bolshevik secret police which was the key component of totalitarian rule, see Leggett, op. cit. and Leonard Gerson, *The Secret Police in Lenin's Russia,* (Philadelphia: Temple University Press, 1976). These two studies decisively demonstrate that the Cheka and its policies of "Red Terror" emerged well before the rise of organized armed opposition to Bolshevik rule.
16. See works cited in ibid.; Evan Mawdsley, *The Russian Civil War,* (London: Allen & Unwin, 1987), pp. 70–83; James Bunyan, *The Origin of Forced Labor in the Soviet State,* (Baltimore: Johns Hopkins Press, 1967).
17. Mawdsley, p. 78.
18. See works cited in note 14 above.
19. Leggett, pp. 316–23.
20. Quoted in Melgounov, p. 33.

21. In fact, the latter claim has somewhat greater validity than the former, since the Bolshevik Terror and totalitarian economic policies were begun before the Civil War and were outlined in theory even before the November 1917 coup. See Malia, op. cit. By contrast, although the Nazis had always intended to *repress* the Jews and possibly deport them, the decision to *exterminate* them en mass was not irrevocably taken until the notorious Wannsee Conference in January 1942. See William L. Shirer, *The Rise and Fall of the Third Reich,* (New York: 1960), pp. 1223–1293.

22. See Francois Ponchaud, *Cambodia: Year Zero,* (New York: Holt, Reinhart, & Winston, 1978).

23. In fact, even dubious reports of Bolshevik atrocities received wide circulation; see, e.g., Richard Ullman, *Britain and the Russian Civil War,* (Princeton: Princeton University Press, 1968), pp. 141–43, hereafter cited as Ullman, vol. 2; For public and private protests of Western diplomats against early manifestations of the Bolshevik Terror, see Foreign Relations of the United States, 1918, *Russia,* vol. 1, (Washington, D.C.: G.P.O. 1931), ch. 15; hereafter cited as FRUS, 1918, vol. 1.

24. Robert Lansing, memorandum, December 2, 1917, reprinted in Lansing, *War Memoirs of Robert Lansing,* (New York: Bobbs-Merrill, 1935), p. 342.

25. FRUS, 1918, vol. 1, ch. 15.

26. See, e.g., discussion of the Hoover-Nansen food relief plan in ch. 3. As the excerpted passages from Hoover's March 1919 memorandum to the President suggest, Hoover was well aware of the famine and of the fact that it was caused by Bolshevik policy.

27. Brzezinski, pp. 239–40; Brzezinski does not count the hundreds of thousands deaths caused communist rule in Cuba and in several African states. He also opts for lower-bound estimates of the death tolls in the USSR and China. As he notes (p. 27), upper-bound, but still credible, estimates for the Stalinist period in the USSR alone range as high as 40 million.

28. See John M. Thompson, *Russia, Bolshevism, and the Versailles Peace,* (Princeton: Princeton University Press, 1966); Arno Mayer, *The Politics and Diplomacy of Peace-Making, 1918–19,* (New York: Knopf, 1967). The latter work, however, probably exaggerates the importance of Bolshevism relative to other issues in the minds of the Allied leaders.

29. Malia, *Soviet Tragedy,* p. 121.

30. At the time, White forces occupied most of Siberia, the Crimea, the Caucasus, and large portions of southern, northern, and northwestern Russia.

31. This point was suggested to me by Professor N. Gordon Levin.

32. See, especially, Betty Miller Unterberger, *America's Siberian Expedition, 1918–20,* (Durham: Duke University Press, 1956), hereafter cited as Unterberger, *Expedition;* Unterberger, "Woodrow Wilson and the Russian Revolution," in Arthur S. Link, ed., *Woodrow Wilson and a Revolutionary World, 1913–21,* (Chapel Hill: University of North Carolina Press, 1982); Unterberger, *The United States, Revolutionary Russia, and the Rise of Czechoslovakia,* (Chapel Hill: University of North Carolina Press, 1989); George Kennan, *Soviet-American Relations, 1917–20,* vol. 2, *The Decision to Intervene,* (Princeton: Princeton University Press, 1958), hereafter cited as Kennan, *Decision.*

33. Unterberger, *Expedition,* p. 234.

34. Such arguments are noticably absent from the works of Kennan and Unterberger, cited above. They are equally missing from the studies of historians critical of what they considered to be American anti-Bolshevist intentions. See, e.g., William Appleman Williams, *American-Russian Relations, 1781–1947,* (New York: Rinehart & Co., 1952).

35. See Unterberger, "Woodrow Wilson and the Russian Revolution." However, these references generally occur in the context of discussing what she considers to be Wilson's views, rather than her own. It is nonetheless obvious that she sympathizes with the position she attributes to the president.

36. Unterberger, *Expedition*, p. 105.

37. For a notable exception, see James W. Morley, *The Japanese Thrust into Siberia, 1918*, (New York: Columbia University Press, 1957).

38. See ibid., esp. pp. 311-13, where Morley concludes that the internal Japanese debate over Siberian policy was eventually won by the relatively anti-Western "Asia first" faction in the Japanese government which wanted to consolidate Japan's position in the Far East by applying in Siberia "policies similar to those they were applying in China" (Morley, p. 312).

39. Winston Churchill, *The Aftermath*, (London: Thornton Butterworth, 1929), p. 256; For detailed figures on British expenditures and breakdown by categories, see Richard Ullman, *Anglo-Soviet Relations, 1917-21*, vol. 2, *Britain and the Russian Civil War*, (Princeton: Princeton University Press, 1968), pp. 365-68, hereafter cited as Ullman, vol. 2.

40. See Williams, op. cit., and Kennan, *Decision;* Kennan, *Russia and the West Under Lenin and Stalin*, (New York: Mentor, 1961), chaps. 3-8.

41. See, e.g., N. Gordon Levin, Jr., *Woodrow Wilson and World Politics*, (New York: Oxford University Press, 1968); Arno Mayer, *Politics and Diplomacy of Peace-Making.*

42. See Williams, op. cit., ch. 6.

43. See ibid.; ch. 3 below; Levin, pp. 191, 217. Although, as Levin correctly stresses (p. 217), this concept of food aid did not imply any recognition of the legitimacy of the Bolsheviks.

44. George F. Kennan, *American Diplomacy, 1900–1950*, (Chicago: University of Chicago Press, 1951), p. 69.

45. Williams, "American Intervention in Russia, 1917-20," Part II, *Studies on the Left*, Winter, 1964, p. 57.

46. Kennan, "American Troops in Russia," *Atlantic Monthly*, January 1959, p. 42; see also, Kennan, *Decision*, and Kennan, "The United States and the Soviet Union, 1917-76," *Foreign Affairs*, July 1976, pp. 671-72.

47. See Kennan, *Decision*, esp. chaps. 12-13, 28.

48. Ibid., ch. 28.

49. Kennan, "American Troops in Russia," p. 42.

50. Christopher Lasch, "American Intervention in Siberia: A Reinterpretation," *Political Science Quarterly*, June 1962, p. 223.

51. Ibid.

52. Volkogonov, pp. 109-28.

53. Quoted in ibid., p. 117.

54. Lansing, December 2 memorandum, op. cit., p. 341.

55. Ibid., p. 340.

56. Ambassador Francis to Secretary of State, February 13, 1918, in FRUS, 1918, vol. 1, p. 380.

57. See ch. 3.

58. Unterberger, *America's Siberian Expedition*, p. 88; in more recent works, Unterberger continues to stress the Japanese factor, but also stresses the importance of rescuing the Czechs. See Unterberger, "Woodrow Wilson and the Russian Revolution," p. 70; Unterberger, *The United States, Revolutionary Russia, and the Rise of Czechoslovakia.*

59. Williams, *American-Russian Relations,* p. 146.
60. This is not entirely true, as Admiral Kolchak's forces and the Americans between them controlled considerably more Siberian territory than did the Japanese. Lenin might have been deliberately trying to conceal this fact, as it would have made Kolchak seem more independent and less a pure puppet of the Allies.
61. Lenin, "Report on Concessions to the Communist Party Faction at the Eighth Congress of the Soviets of the RSFSR" December 21, 1920, in Xenia Eudin and Henry H. Fisher, eds., *Soviet Russia and the West, 1920–27: A Documentary Survey,* (Stanford: Stanford University Press, 1957), p. 45.
62. Levin, op. cit., p. 104.
63. The "March" Revolution of 1917, which overthrew the tsarist autocracy in favor of the liberal regime of the Provisional Government, is more usually referred to as the "February" Revolution, because that is when it occurred under the Russian Orthodox Church calendar, which was the primary calendar used in Russia until abolished by the Bolsheviks on January 1, 1918. In this study, all dates go by the Western calendar, unless otherwise noted.
64. Ibid., p. 220.
65. See Williams, "American Intervention in Russia, 1917–20," Part II, op. cit.
66. Levin, p. 109.
67. Ibid.
68. Williams, *American-Russian Relations,* p. 144; see also, p. 170, and ch. 6 passim. The quote on p. 144 refers to alleged earlier efforts by American diplomats to involve the U.S. in anti-Bolshevik intrigues rather than to the intervention itself. But it is clear that Williams sees these attempts and the intervention itself as part of a common pattern.
69. See, e.g., Richard J. Barnet, *Intervention and Revolution: The United States in the Third World,* (New York: New American Library, 1972).
70. Professor Levin who was my thesis adviser for this project, points out that he was, in fact, opposed to the intervention at the time he wrote *Woodrow Wilson and World Politics.* This view, however, was not reflected in the book. Since then, he has come to consider the idea of anti-Bolshevik intervention with at least somewhat greater sympathy.
71. Kennan, *Soviet Foreign Policy, 1917–41,* (New York: Van Nostrand, 1960), p. 30.
72. Lenin, "Report on War and Peace," March 7, 1918, in Robert C. Tucker, *The Lenin Anthology,* (New York: Norton, 1975), p. 542
73. Lenin, "Report on Concessions," op cit., in ibid., p. 628
74. See Kennan, *Decision,* esp. p. 302.
75. See ibid., pp. 131–33, 220–23.
76. Ibid., p. 302; Kennan draws this conclusion from the extremely weak evidence of a May 23, 1918 discussion between DeWitt Poole, the American Consul in Moscow and Bolshevik Foreign Minister Georgi Chicherin. But, as Kennan himself describes it (pp. 299–301), the meeting amounted to little more than an exchange of views and neither side seemed prepared to significantly alter its position.
77. Richard Ullman, *Anglo-Soviet Relations, 1917–21,* 3 Vols., (Princeton: Princeton University Press, 1961–73).
78. See ibid., vol. 1, *Intervention and the War,* (Princeton: Princeton University Press, 1961), ch. 5; hereafter cited as Ullman, vol. 1.
79. See Ullman, vol. 2.
80. Ibid., p. 357.
81. Ullman, vol. 1, p. 333.

82. Ibid.

83. A World War I division usually had a strength of roughly 10,000 men.

84. See Kennan, *Soviet-American Relations, 1917–20,* op. cit.

85. Ullman, vol. 2, pp. 351–52.

86. Among the few other brief mentions of the possibility that a more forceful intervention might have worked are George Brinkley, *The Volunteer Army and Allied
Intervention in South Russia, 1917–21,* (Notre Dame: University of Notre Dame
Press, 1966), p. 282, and Robert Conquest, "Reds," *New York Review of Books,*
July 14, 1994, p. 3. Neither of these works, however, makes a serious effort to
analyze the possibility in detail and both primarily concentrate on other issues. In
each case, the reference is only a brief aside.

87. See, esp., chs. 4–6 of this work.

88. Pipes, *Russian Revolution,* pp. xxiii–iv.

2

The Development of British Policy

The Bolshevik Revolution could hardly have come at a worse time for the British—and for the Allied cause in general. It was clear that the Bolsheviks, who had always opposed the war against the Central Powers more unambiguously than any other Russian political party, were likely to make a separate peace with Germany. It was equally clear that the resulting transfer of hundreds of thousands of German troops to the West might well spell defeat for the Allies. "The Germans," British Prime Minister David Lloyd George recalled, "had held the Western Front for two years against a combination which was 50 per cent. stronger than their own as far as numbers were concerned."[3] Having fought the Allies to a draw under conditions of marked inferiority, they might now, for the first time since 1914, get the chance to face them with an actual numerical advantage. At least until the arrival of large American forces, an event not expected for many months,[4] the prospect of outright defeat was a distinct possibility.

The day after their successful November 7, 1917 coup against the Provisional Government, the Bolshevik leaders issued a "Decree on Peace," drafted by Vladimir Lenin himself, that called for "an immediate peace without annexations...and without indemnities."[5] While the Bolsheviks claimed to seek "a general and not a separate peace"[6] and formally invited both sides to agree to an immediate general armistice, they soon signed a separate armistice with the Germans and Austrians and began peace negotiations on December 2, 1917. Simultaneously, they published and repudiated their predecessors' secret treaties with the Allies. Numerous Bolshevik pronouncements urged the working classes of the warring powers to overthrow their governments. For some time, the Bolsheviks truly believed that this eventuality would soon come to pass. Leon Trotsky, the newly appointed commissar for foreign affairs, joked that "I myself took this job so I would have more time for Party Work. All there is to do is to publish the secret treaties. Then I will close up shop."[7]

Despite such provocations, the British took a cautious line toward the new revolutionary regime. While they certainly disliked its ideology and feared its threats to sign a separate peace if the Allies did not accept Bolshevik proposals for a general peace conference, Lloyd George and his colleagues still hoped to salvage what they could from the Russian debacle. In a December 9 memorandum, Foreign Minister Arthur Balfour urged that "[W]e ought if, if possible, not...come to an open breach with the Bolsheviks or drive them into the enemy's camp."[8] He took it for granted that "for the remainder of this war, the Bolsheviks are going to fight neither Germany nor anyone else. But," Balfour continued, "if we can prevent their aiding Germany, we do a great deal, and to this we should devote our efforts."[9] The Foreign Minister worried that, if the Bolsheviks were unduly antagonized, they might allow the Germans to "us[e] the large potential resources of Russia to break the Allied Blockade."[10]

Although the Cabinet was not completely united on the issue,[11] Lloyd George endorsed Balfour's reasoning and its principles became official British policy. "[U]ltimately," he writes, "the Cabinet decided that His Majesty's Government was not primarily concerned with the composition of the Russian Government or with the local aspirations of the Bolsheviks or other political parties, except insofar as they bore on their attitude to our conflict with the Central Powers."[12]

While the Cabinet was not prepared to recognize the Bolsheviks as the legitimate government of Russia, they were willing to pursue informal contacts for the purpose of fostering potential cooperation against the Germans. On December 21, 1917, Lloyd George selected R.H. Bruce Lockhart, a junior member of the British foreign service with numerous contacts in Russia, to act as unofficial representative of the British government in Moscow.[13]

During the same period, however, the Cabinet also took the first steps towards establishing contact with the as yet weak anti-Bolshevik groups which were just beginning to form, notably the forces of General A.M. Kaledin, Ataman of the Don Cossacks of southwestern Russia.[14] In December, the British Cabinet decided to secretly provide Kaledin "[a]ny sum of money required for the purpose of maintaining alive in South East Russia the resistance to the Central Powers considered necessary by the War Office."[15] Thus, the British found themselves attempting to gain the support of both the Bolsheviks and the nascent White movement.

Historians have tended to consider the two strands of British policy contradictory. Richard Ullman, for example, refers to "the inconsistency of attempting to woo both the Bolsheviks and their enemies."[16] But there was not necessarily any "inconsistency" if we keep in mind the fact that both Russian factions were wooed only to the extent that they might be of use to the Allied war effort. From the British point of view, it was not contradictory to believe that the Whites could be persuaded to further Allied interests in the parts of Russia they controlled while the Bolsheviks, albeit to a lesser extent, might be persuaded to do the same in the regions where *they* held sway. Meanwhile, neither group would be directly supported in any effort to defeat the other. As Lloyd George explained it:

> The problem with which the British Government...were faced, was a purely military one. We were not concerned with the internal political troubles of Russia as such. What we had to consider as a war problem was how best to prevent Germany from revictualling herself afresh from the cornlands and the oilfields which would be laid open to her if she succeeded in penetrating to the Don and the rich provinces of the Caucasus. It was for this reason and not from any anti-Communist motives that we decided to give support to the loyalist Russians who were in control of these fertile areas.[17]

Thus, it is evident that wartime military considerations rather than anti-Bolshevism dominated British thinking at this point.

However, there was a latent element of anti-Bolshevik sentiment in the logic of the British position. In the first place, there was the obvious refusal of the British to recognize the Bolshevik regime's legitimacy. This refusal was not merely a formality, for its logic underpinned the entire policy of dealing with both the Bolsheviks and their enemies and reserving the option of supporting the latter against the new regime. The refusal to grant the Bolsheviks recognition was based on the weakness of their authority. In Lloyd George's words, "Had the whole of Russia been under Bolshevik rule our course would have been clear. We should have treated with them as the *de facto* Russian Government. *Had the Bolshevik leaders been the de facto Government, we could not have made war on them, or supported rebellion against their authority merely because they had made peace with Germany.* But outside the towns—and [even] they were not all Bolshevik—they had no authority" (emphasis mine).[18]

Here lay an important admission: while British policy was motivated by wartime military considerations, the reason why the Cabinet believed these military priorities could be pursued even against the will of the self-proclaimed government of Russia was that that government lacked sufficient legitimacy to be recognized on even a de facto basis. To be sure, the reason given for such non-recognition was not ideology but the narrow scope of the regime's authority. But the Provisional Government of 1917, which had been recognized by both the British and the other Allies, had been only marginally stronger. It is difficult, therefore, to avoid the conclusion that the decision to withhold recognition from the Bolsheviks was based, at least in part, on ideological hostility, even if only implicitly. Moreover, some elements of Bolshevik ideology inspired much less subtle negative reactions on the part of the British. For instance, the Cabinet was dismayed by the Bolshevik call for revolution in the Allied countries and Lloyd George hoped that Lockhart's mission "might prove a useful opportunity for getting certain conditions agreed to by the Bolshevik Government in regard to their noninterference in the internal politics of Allied nations."[19]

For about six months after Balfour's December 9 memorandum set forth the policy of refraining from a break with the Bolsheviks, the British continued to hold out hope that anti-German cooperation with the new Russian leadership might be possible. Even after the Bolsheviks signed the Treaty of Brest-Litovsk with the Germans on March 3, 1918, London still believed that they could be brought to reenter the war against Germany and aid in the reestablishment of the Eastern Front.[20]

Lockhart, who conducted Britain's negotiations with the Bolsheviks during this period, firmly believed that Lenin and Trotsky could be persuaded to accept Allied intervention.[21] "I can only repeat," he cabled Balfour on March 18, that "the Bolsheviks must fight Germany."[22] It is difficult to understand how Lockhart came to believe that the Bolsheviks might be willing to join the Allies in opposing the Germans. While Lenin and Trotsky repeatedly emphasized to him their willingness to accept Allied assistance in building up the new Red Army, never at any point did they promise to cooperate with them in setting up a new Eastern Front unless the Germans were to first reopen the fighting themselves. As Lenin told Lockhart on February 28, even before the Treaty of Brest-Litovsk was completed, "So long...as the German danger exists, I am prepared to risk a co-operation with the Allies, which should be temporarily advantageous to both of us. *In the event of German aggression*, I am even willing to accept military support" (emphasis mine).[23] As Lockhart himself put it in his memoirs, "Lenin...was for peace. Without peace he could not consolidate his position."[24] And, it should be added, the consolidation of the Bolshevik position against internal opposition to their radical policies was the most important item on the new regime's agenda throughout the entire period under discussion.

To be sure, Lockhart might have placed some hope in the attitude of Trotsky, who had opposed the Treaty of Brest-Litovsk, and seemed more amenable to the idea of Allied intervention to stimulate resistance to the Germans.[25] But Lockhart fully understood that Trotsky's position in the Bolshevik Party, which he had joined only in 1917, was not nearly as strong as Lenin's; Trotsky, he recalled, "was as incapable of standing against Lenin as a flea would be against an elephant.... There was not a Commissar who did not regard Lenin as a demi-god, whose decisions were to be accepted without question."[26] In any case, even Trotsky never went so far as to promise Lockhart and Raymond Robins, the unofficial American representative, that the Bolsheviks were willing to accept Allied intervention against the Germans without a prior German attack. In the absence of such an attack, the only form of cooperation with the Allies that he was willing to commit to was the acceptance of Allied military missions to help in the training of the nascent Red Army.[27] In the words of George F. Kennan, "The Soviet government...prizing this breathing space [created by the separate peace] had not the faintest intention of renewing military operations against the Germans."[28] Kennan is probably right to suggest that Bolshevik offers of cooperation with the British and Americans were largely motivated by a desire to forestall Japanese intervention in Siberia, then under serious consideration by the Allies, and by a mistaken fear that the Germans might break the peace and seek to conquer all of Russia.[29] As Lenin stated in a public speech on May 14—a speech strangely ignored by Lockhart and Robins—"[I]t is our duty to do everything that our diplomacy can do to delay the moment of war, to extend the respite period."[30] This theme was emphasized in all of Lenin's statements on foreign policy, both public and secret, throughout the spring of 1918.[31] He realized that any further advance by the Germans would likely mean the capture of Moscow and Petrograd, the centers of Bolshevik power in Russia, and the end of the Soviet regime. This view was clearly stated in his secret May 12–13 "Theses on the Present Political Situation":

> Although we do not in general reject military agreements with one of the imperialist coalitions against the other in those cases in which such a agreement could, without undermining the basis of Soviet power, strengthen its position...we cannot at the present moment enter into a military agreement with the Anglo-French coalition. For them, the importance of such a agreement would be the diversion of German troops from the West...which is an unacceptable condition since it would mean the complete collapse of Soviet power.[32]

Given this situation, it is possible to go beyond Kennan's evaluation of Bolshevik policy and point out that their willingness to accept military aid while abjuring any anti-German action may, in addition to the motives he cites, have been a cynical ploy to obtain Allied aid in building up forces whose primary purpose would be the repression of Russia's own people and the consolidation of Bolshevik power. In any case, it is clear that the Bolshevik leaders had no intention of cooperating with the Allies in any renewed fighting against the Germans unless the latter reopened hostilities themselves. Despite the later assertions of left-wing historians,[33] there was never any real chance for a Western-Soviet rapprochement during this period.

A few British officials recognized this fact and discounted the possibility of cooperation with the Bolsheviks. Sir William Wiseman, a key unofficial British representative in the United States, penned, on May 1, an analysis of the Russian situation which strikingly anticipates that of Lenin's "Theses" two weeks later. While believing that "Allied intervention at the invitation of the Bolsheviki...would probably be the most desirable course," he expressed "doubt whether this is feasible."[34] According to Wiseman, "If Trotzky invites Allied intervention the Germans would regard it as a hostile act and probably turn his Government out of Moscow and Petrograd. With this centre lost the best opinion considers that the whole Bolshevik influence in Russia would collapse. No one knows this better than Trotzky and for this reason he probably hesitates."[35] For this reason Wiseman tentatively urged that the Allies intervene without Bolshevik consent, in cooperation with the leaders of the ousted Provisional Government.[36] Ironically, Wiseman, sitting in the U.S. and lacking any special knowledge of Russia, had a much clearer view of the situation than Lockhart, whose extensive experience in Russia and alleged understanding of the situation there had been the main reason for his appointment. Some other officials agreed with General Alfred Knox, the former British military attache in Russia, in his view that "[t]he policy of flirtation with the Bolsheviks is both wrong as a policy and immoral."[37]

Nonetheless, Lloyd George and Foreign Minister Balfour continued to cling to the chimera of intervention by Bolshevik invitation. After becoming somewhat pessimistic in early April, Balfour renewed his faith in this prospect later in the month, after an ambiguous message from Trotsky.[38] "[I]n my view," he cabled the British ambassador to the United States on April 24,

> situation is entirely altered by apparent willingness of Trotsky to invite Allied assistance against German aggression. Allied troops would be able to traverse Siberia at a great speed provided Russians are friendly, and if joined by Bolsheviki and other Russian contingents would certainly constitute such a menace to the Germans in the East that the latter could hardly withdraw further divisions and might even be compelled to strengthen the forces already there.[39]

The persistent desire to cling to such forlorn hopes can only be explained by the desperate nature of the Allied situation on the Western Front where the Germans, reinforced by some one million troops transferred from Russia, had begun a massive offensive on March 21.[40] The goal of the onslaught, which German soldiers soon dubbed the "Peace Offensive" was to break Allied resistance once and for all. Over the next four months, the Germans drove the Allies back to within forty miles of Paris and inflicted over one million casualties on them.[41] The main burden of the German attack fell on the British army,[42] so the British were naturally desperate for any means of diverting German forces away from the West. The entire Allied cause and, even more immediately, the fate of the British army, seemed to depend on it. British hopes hinged upon the reestablishment of the Eastern Front by the insertion of Allied forces into Russia through Siberia and the northern Russian ports of Murmansk and Archangel. It was recognized that the bulk of the forces for the former expedition would have to be provided by the

Japanese, a formal member of the Allies whose large and competent army had thus far seen little action in the war.[43] "Unless Allied intervention is undertaken in Siberia forthwith," a British War Office memorandum warned in June, "we have no chance of being ultimately victorious, and shall incur serious risk of defeat in the meantime."[44]

With this fear in mind, the British had continued their early contacts with anti-Bolshevik forces throughout the winter and spring of 1918, even though their initial ally, General Kaledin, soon suffered a defeat at the hands of the Bolsheviks and committed suicide in February.[45] As we have seen, this policy was motivated by a desire to win the support of as many Russian factions as possible to the cause of reestablishing the Eastern Front against Germany and denying them the use of Russia's resources. As hopes for intervention by Bolshevik invitation faded, the possibility of intervention without their consent increasingly came to the forefront.[46]

In addition to the desire to reestablish the Eastern Front, British action was motivated by the need to safeguard precious war supplies—originally intended for Russian use against Germany—stockpiled at the ports of Vladivostok in Siberia and Murmansk and Archangel in northwestern Russia, on the Arctic Ocean. By early 1918, there were some 800,000 tons of Allied war supplies at Vladivostok,[47] 160,000 at Archangel,[48] and about 450,000 at Murmansk.[49] There were also large quantities of coal at these sites.[50] In February 1918, the Bolsheviks began transporting these extremely valuable stores, which had not even been paid for yet, to the interior of Russia.[51] It became increasingly clear that they had no intention of using the supplies for their originally intended purpose of fighting Germany.

The British were certainly displeased by this development. They were even more unhappy about the possibility that the supplies might be captured by the advancing Germans or, in the case of those at Vladivostok, turned over to them by the Bolsheviks.[52] Concern over the fate of the supplies strengthened the British desire for intervention, with or without Bolshevik consent. By June, plans for intervention in both the Murmansk-Archangel area and Siberia had already been developed. The primary stumbling block was the need to gain the approval of the United States, whose leaders had considerable doubts about the usefulness of these projects.[53]

Nonetheless, on March 6, the British landed a small force of Royal Marines to help protect the stores at Murmansk,[54] where the local Soviet, only partially under the control of the Bolshevik leadership in Moscow, was very receptive to the Allies.[55] They also repeatedly pressed the Japanese and Americans to send forces to Siberia. On May 17, the tiny British force at Murmansk was reinforced by a new 500-man contingent under General F.C. Poole,[56] and by 600 more troops on June 23.[57] Meanwhile, small British and Japanese contingents landed in Vladivostok on April 9 and took control of that city, where Allied warships had already been anchored offshore for months. The decision was taken by the military commanders on the spot, who were worried by Bolshevik attempts to ship Allied war supplies located in the city to the interior of Russia.[58] Neither of these actions, however, were motivated by any high-level decision to seek the overthrow of the Bolsheviks and both were influenced by extremely complicated factors of purely local significance.[59] In fact, the British actually sought to *avoid* armed clashes with Bolshevik forces during this period,[60] although the British forces at Murmansk did forcibly disarm 1,000 Red Guards which were sent to oppose them from Petrograd.[61]

Throughout the spring and summer, the British government maintained contact with various anti-Bolshevik forces in Siberia, southern Russia, the Murmansk-Archangel area, and even, clandestinely, in Bolshevik-controlled Russia.[62] However, these various forces were, as yet, too weak to offer a serious military challenge to the Bolsheviks, much less aid in Allied plans to reestablish the Eastern Front against Germany and Austria.

This situation was radically altered by the uprising of the Czechoslovak Legion against the Bolsheviks on May 25, 1918, the date that is often seen as the true beginning of the Russian Civil War.[63] The Czech Legion was a corps of approximately 70,000 men[64] which had been formed from Czech and Slovak prisoners captured by the Russians in earlier campaigns against the Austro-Hungarian army.[65] With the collapse of Russian resistance to the Germans, the Legion was left in a precarious position. The Czechs could no longer rely on the support of Russian forces, and they knew that they would likely be executed as traitors if captured by the advancing Germans and Austrians.[66] On March 26, 1918, they signed an agreement with the Bolsheviks in which the latter granted them safe passage through central Russia and Siberia to Vladivostok, a port on the Pacific Ocean from whence, it was hoped, the Czechs could be transported to Europe by Allied ships. In exchange, the Czechs agreed to give up some of their arms to the Bolsheviks, to leave as quickly as possible, and to remove "counterrevolutionary" Russian officers serving with the Legion.[67]

As the Czechs passed in transit through western Siberia, small-scale fighting broke out between their troops and local Bolshevik authorities, beginning with an incident on May 14 at Chelyabinsk, in which a Czech detachment clashed with a group of Hungarian war prisoners on their way to be repatriated.[68] Already suspicious of the Czechs, Moscow reacted to this relatively minor incident by ordering the Siberian Soviets to "detrain the Czechoslovaks and organize them into labor artels [detachments] or draft them into the Red Army."[69] Predictably, the Czechs refused to surrender and began to fight the Bolsheviks in earnest all along the Trans-Siberian Railway.

The Czech Legion was a well-disciplined, capable force made up of highly motivated volunteers. With the collapse of the old Russian army and the as yet disorganized state of the Red Army and its nascent White opponents, it was easily the most potent military force in all of Russia, with the obvious exception of the Germans. Over the next few weeks of fighting the Czechs seized control of most of Siberia and the Ural Mountains, and even considerable territories to the west of that range. Several anti-Bolshevik governments, mostly led by members of the Socialist-Revolutionary (S-R) Party, were quickly set up in the wake of the Czech victories. The most important of these regimes was the Committee of the Constituent Assembly (Komuch) government in Samara, made up of members of the Constituent Assembly, and the S-R -led Directorate in Omsk.[70]

Siberia and the Urals were regions where Bolshevik support was particularly weak and much of the local population was just waiting for a chance to remove them from power.[71] The S-Rs had gained more votes than any other party in the elections to the Constituent Assembly and they set out to recapture the mandate which they believed the Bolsheviks had unjustly denied them. Local White Russians soon formed their own detachments to fight alongside the Czechs. The Legion was also aided by the poor quality of the Red Army troops facing them. "The training of the Red Army at this time," as Winston Churchill caustically put it, "had not progressed beyond a knowledge of Communism, the execution of prisoners, and ordinary acts of brigandage and murder."[72]

Despite Soviet charges to the contrary, the British and the other Allies had done nothing to instigate the Czech uprising and were almost as surprised as the Soviets.[73] Nonetheless, they could not fail to notice the opportunities this new development created. In the words of Churchill, then serving as Lloyd George's minister of munitions, "by a series of accidents and chances…the whole of Russia from the Volga River to the Pacific Ocean, a region almost as large as the continent of Africa, had passed as if by magic into the control of the Allies."[74] On June 3, 1918, the Allied Supreme War Council in Paris decided to retain part of the Czech Legion in Russia and reroute a large part of the rest to Murmansk and Archangel, from whence they were to be shipped out to France. At the same time, additional Allied forces were to be dispatched to insure control of these Arctic ports.[75] French and British leaders were anxious to provide support for the Czechs against the Bolsheviks, and they also hoped to use them as the nucleus of a new Eastern Front. On July 2, 1918, the Allied Supreme War Council in Paris concluded that "Allied intervention [in Russia] is essential in order to win the war."[76] Likewise, as we shall see in chapter 3, it was the Czech uprising that finally broke the resistance of President Wilson to the idea of Allied intervention in Siberia. Both there and in Murmansk and Archangel, intervention was now to begin in earnest.

The revolt of the Czechs thus drastically altered not only the entire balance of power in Russia but the perceptions of the Allies. According to Lloyd George, "It is not too much to say that the presence of the Czech Legion was the determining factor in our Siberian expedition."[77] The hope of linking up with the Czechs was also one of the factors behind the British decision to send troops to Murmansk and Archangel.[78] Lloyd George and his colleagues intended not only to "protect and succour" the Czechs but also to "by means of them establish something like an anti-German front in South-East Russia and along the Urals."[79]

Even at this point, British policy was not primarily motivated by a desire to overthrow the Bolshevik regime per se, but by the hope of supporting the Czechs and possibly using them to help reestablish the Eastern Front. Nevertheless, the Cabinet now recognized that the Bolsheviks were unlikely to cooperate with them and was prepared to support any other Russian factions which were willing to fight the Germans, regardless of the effect which such action might have on Bolshevik regime's prospects. A July 16 memorandum by Balfour set out this new understanding:

[H]owever strong and genuine be our desire to keep out of Russian politics, it will probably be in practice almost impossible to prevent intervention having some (perhaps a great) effect on Russian Parties. The intervening force must necessarily work with those who are prepared to work with it. Indirectly it will strengthen those parties who are prepared to fight the Germans. We can do no more than attempt to the best of our ability to keep aloof from these internal divisions.[80]

The anti-Bolshevik implications of this view were set out more clearly in a July 17 telegram from Lloyd George to Lord Reading, the British ambassador to the United States:

> I do not believe that the Russian people, suffering...from the effect of both of autocracy and Bolshevism, can liberate themselves from Germanic penetration and domination unless the Allies can bring effective assistance to bear at once.... If we once do that we create [a] rallying point close at hand for all liberal and democratic forces in Russia.[81]

This statement is significant in its avowal of an intent to support the establishment of a new, non-Bolshevik, government in Russia.[82] It is clear from the context that the Bolsheviks were hardly to be counted among the "liberal and democratic forces" whom Lloyd George hoped to rally. In another part of this message, the prime minister even went so far as to say that Britain's war aims would not be fulfilled "unless by the end of the war Russia is settled on liberal, progressive and democratic lines.... I am an interventionist just as much because I am a democrat as because I want to win the war."[83] Too much should not be made of this last point. It does not seem to recur in any other important documents of the period in question and its inclusion in the telegram to Reading was partly motivated by Lloyd George's desire to help the ambassador reassure the Americans that intervention would not serve to promote reaction.[84] Even so, it is at least somewhat indicative of the prime minister's thinking, though he would later reiterate, time and again, the principle of nonintervention in Russian internal affairs.

Lloyd George also disavowed any desire to reestablish tsarism: "The last thing I would stand for would be the encouragement of any kind of repressive regime under whatever guise."[85] This latter sentiment was more than mere ritualistic talk. Both Balfour and Lloyd George expressed fears that the "reestablishment of the Russian autocracy would...be a misfortune for the British Empire."[86] A restored autocracy would, Balfour believed, probably become a, "purely military Empire...inevitably a danger to her neighbours; and to none...so much as ourselves."[87] Here was resurrected the traditional British imperial fear of a Russian move against British interests in India and the Near East. In addition, Balfour continued, a reconstituted tsarist regime would be a natural ally for Germany.[88] Though they were now willing to countenance the overthrow of the Bolshevik regime, the fear of reaction would continue to influence the two ministers' views of developments in Russia. Moreover, the primary goal of intervention was still to help win the war against Germany.

With this rationale in mind, the Allies did indeed begin their intervention. But its scale was totally incommensurate with the ambitious nature of its purposes. On August 1, a British-led force of only 1200 men, including a French battalion and fifty Americans, landed in Archangel.[89] Under the command of General Poole, these troops quickly seized control of the city and the surrounding area, supported by a White Russian coup planned to coincide with the landing.[90] A government for the northern Russian region controlled by the Allies was established under the leadership of N.V. Chaikovsky, a distinguished socialist member of the Constituent Assembly.[91] However, despite the arrival of reinforcements in the fall, which eventually raised the total number of Allied troops to over 10,000 at Murmansk[92] and about 8500 at Archangel by the end of the year,[93] the Allied forces in northern Russia did little more than hold the territory initially seized, right up until the time they were finally withdrawn in September 1919.

Not only was the Allied force in northern Russia extremely small, but many of its troops were of very poor quality. Most of the British troops, for instance, had low physical fitness ratings.[94] In Moscow, Lockhart, by now a committed interventionist,[95] could not believe that "[w]e had committed the incredible folly of landing at Archangel with fewer than twelve hundred men."[96] He had warned the British Cabinet that any intervening force must be strong enough to crush the Bolsheviks quickly and that "the support we would receive from the Russians would be in direct proportion to the number of troops we sent ourselves."[97] When, for a brief time, the Bolsheviks in Moscow believed that the Allies had actually landed in substantial force, they, according to Lockhart, "lost their heads and, in despair, began to pack their archives."[98] L. M. Karakhan, a high-ranking official in the Bolshevik Commissariat for Foreign Affairs, "spoke of the Bolsheviks as lost."[99] The party, he said, would be forced to go underground.[100] The Bolshevik leaders were well aware of the weakness of their position, which had just suffered a severe blow from the victories of the Czech Legion. In all of Russia, "the only military force on which the Bolsheviks could rely were three brigades of the Latvian Rifles, 35,000 strong."[101] And most of this force had been shifted to the Volga-Ural front to oppose the Czechs and their White allies, where it was fully engaged.[102] The only other troops available to the Bolsheviks were poorly trained re-

cent conscripts who were simply not capable of facing down serious opposition, as the Czech Legion's rapid conquest of Siberia and the Urals
graphically demonstrated. Moscow and Petrograd, the heart of Bolshevik power and the major repositories of such popular support as the Bolsheviks possessed,[103] were virtually wide open to any even moderately
sized Allied force. Two or three divisions, Lockhart and the Allied military attaches in Russia believed, would probably have sufficed.[104]

Unfortunately, despite the counsel of Lockhart and the example of the
Czech victories, the British government failed to grasp the golden opportunity that presented itself. Not only did they neglect to provide adequate
troops, but Poole's instructions did not even include an explicit order to
march on Moscow and overthrow the Bolshevik regime. Instead, Poole
was to "co-operate in restoring Russia with the object of resisting German influence and penetration" and encourage the Russians to "take the
field side by side with their Allies."[105] To call this "hopelessly vague lan-
guage," as Ullman does,[106] is to understate the point.

On August 8, Balfour instructed Lockhart to "as far as possible, maintain existing relations with [the] Bolshevik Government. Rupture, or declaration of war should come, if come it must, from Bolsheviks, not from
Allies."[107] Although the British Cabinet had finally reached the conclusion that cooperation with the Bolsheviks was fruitless and that things
would be much better if they could be overthrown, it failed to act on this
conclusion in anything even resembling a decisive manner. "To have intervened with hopelessly inadequate forces," Lockhart concluded in retrospect, "was an example of paralytic half-measures, which in the
circumstances amounted to a crime."[108] Actually, to paraphrase Talleyrand,
it was worse than a crime—it was a mistake.

The Americans and Japanese had finally bowed to Anglo-French pressure and agreed to a joint intervention in Siberia in July. In early August,
some 12,000 Japanese troops[109] and 8,763 Americans[110] arrived in
Vladivostok. The Japanese contingent helped the Czech troops in the area
to defeat some weak Bolshevik forces on August 25, but did little fighting thereafter.[111] The Americans, for reasons to be analyzed in chapter 3,
did virtually no fighting at all.

With the American and Japanese forces was a British battalion, the 25th
Middlesex, which had been transferred to Vladivostok from Hong Kong
earlier. Like many of the units sent to northern Russia, it was "a garrison
battalion composed of men physically unfit for duty in France."[112] Part of

the battalion was sent to the nearby Ussuri front, where fighting continued between the Czechs and the remnants of local Bolshevik forces, but Colonel T.A. Robertson, the British military representative in Vladivostok made an agreement with the Czech commander that these troops would be "used only defensively and in reserve." "As a result," Ullman notes, "they did little actual fighting, most of the time remaining idle spectators of the action between the Czechs and the Bolsheviks."[113] No attempt was made to move these British troops or the other Allied contingents to the Volga River area and the Ural Mountains, where most of the real fighting between the Czechs, the Russian Whites, and the Bolsheviks was taking place, some 5000 miles to the west. Such a move was not impossible, since the Czechs and White Russians had seized control of the Trans-Siberian Railway.[114]

Thus, the British failed to mount a truly credible challenge to the Bolshevik regime at what was perhaps the moment of its greatest weakness. Though the intervention forces in both Siberia and northern Russia were gradually increased during the fall of 1918, they accomplished little after their initial gains. Meanwhile, the Red Army was rapidly being built up under the ruthless supervision of Trotsky, newly appointed to the post of war commissar. By the end of the year, the Bolshevik forces had a paper strength of 800,000 men.[115] Though most of these troops were unreliable, poorly trained, ill-equipped, and prone to desertion, it was clear that the Red Army was now a force to be reckoned with. During September and October, the Red Army steadily drove back the Czechs and Siberian Whites, capturing the Komuch regime's headquarters in Samara on October 7.[116] After this point, the demoralized and homesick Czechs no longer took an active part in the fighting, though they remained in Siberia until early 1920. They were gradually replaced by White Russian units.

The already ineffective Komuch regime virtually collapsed under the weight of its defeats and submitted itself to the authority of the Omsk Directorate. On the night of November 17-18, the latter almost equally incompetent government was overthrown by a group of more conservative army officers and politicians. These men invited Admiral Alexander Kolchak, a distinguished naval officer and Arctic explorer who had served the Omsk government as minister of war, to become "Supreme Ruler" of Russia until such time as the Bolsheviks were defeated and the Constituent Assembly reestablished. However difficult it is to believe, Kolchak was apparently not involved in the planning for the coup and he assumed power reluctantly.[117] In a letter to his wife written soon after he became dictator, Kolchak complained of "the terrifying burden of Supreme Power," and called himself "a fighting man, reluctant to face the problems of statecraft."[118] Unfortunately, Kolchak's lack of skill in "statecraft" would become a significant liability to the Siberian Whites.

Although many British officials in Siberia welcomed Kolchak's ascension to power, hoping that he could restore order and stabilize the deteriorating position of the White armies at the front, there is no evidence to suggest that they knew of the coup in advance or had encouraged its leaders.[119] Indeed, the British Cabinet had tentatively decided to recognize the Omsk Directorate as a de facto government on November 14, just three days before its overthrow.[120] By the end of the year, the position of the Siberian Whites, though beginning to improve, was still a precarious one.

There was better news for the Whites and Allies in southern Russia. There, a group of former Imperial Army generals headed by General Lavr Kornilov and General Mikhail Alekseev, the army's chief of staff in 1915–17 and commander in chief under the Provisional Government, had raised a unit known as the Volunteer Army, which would become the most powerful of all the White forces. Originally, the Volunteer Army was just that, a force of willing recruits, most of them experienced soldiers. In an environment in which both Reds and Whites were usually forced to rely on unwilling, poorly trained conscripts, this made the Volunteers far more potent than numbers (the Army had just 5000 men as late as May 1918[121]) alone would suggest.

During the spring and summer of 1918, the Volunteer Army and an assortment of Cossack allies fought a series of running battles against the Bolshevik forces in southern Russia. From February to April, the Volunteers made the difficult trek from Rostov to Ekaterinodar, in the Kuban Province of southern Russia. In this almost epic campaign, which came to be known as the "Ice March,"[122] and after, they repeatedly defeated vastly superior Bolshevik forces. Indeed, the leading historical study of the Volunteer Army concludes that "[T]he soldiers performed miracles of military accomplishment; the world had seen few armies of comparable size with greater fighting ability."[123]

After General Kornilov, the Army's original commander was killed in battle on April 13, he was succeeded by General Anton Denikin.[124] During the fall of 1918 the Volunteer Army fought several additional successful campaigns against the Bolsheviks and formed tenuous agreements with the autonomous Don and Kuban Cossack governments, in which the latter subordinated themselves to Denikin's command and agreed to provide him with troops. By September, these alliances and the introduction of conscription had increased the size of the army to some 40,000 men.[125] As World War I came to an end on November 11, the Volunteers were in control of substantial portions of southern Russia. They were still too weak to march on Moscow unaided, but had already become a major factor in the unfolding Russian Civil War.

The end of the World War presented the British and the other Allies with a major dilemma with respect to Russia. They could no longer claim that the intervention was strictly a war operation and thereby sidestep the issue of the future government of Russia. On November 14, the same day as it decided to recognize the Omsk Directorate, the War Cabinet agreed to provide military assistance to Denikin and increase that provided to the Siberian Whites, who had already received 100,000 rifles and 200 guns from the British.[126]

However, these moves, though significant, did not imply a whole-hearted commitment to the overthrow of Bolshevism. In a November 29 memorandum endorsed by the War Cabinet, Foreign Minister Balfour set forth the ambivalent nature of British policy. "This country," he contended, "would certainly refuse to see its forces, after more than four years of strenuous fighting, dissipated over the huge expanse of Russia in order to carry out political reforms in a state which is no longer a belligerent Ally." Balfour believed that the Britain did not "have any mission to establish or disestablish any particular political system among the Russian people."[127] On the other hand, however, he was unwilling to "disinterest ourselves wholly from Russian affairs."[128] Balfour claimed that Britain had "obligations" to the Russian Whites, the Czechs, and the nascent governments set up under British auspices in the Caucasus and Transcaspia, "which last beyond the occasions which gave them birth."[129] Thus, he advocated a policy of limited military aid to these groups, leaving open the question of how extensive this aid should be and how long it should last.[130]

Some of the commitments listed by the British had few or no anti-Bolshevik elements to them. The governments of the Caucasian states of Georgia and Azerbaidjan, as well as those supported by Britain in Russian Central Asia, had little desire to participate in the Russian Civil War and were often almost as hostile to the Whites as to the Bolsheviks. Although British interest in these governments was vaguely connected to traditional imperial concerns about the security of India, Churchill was at least partially right to claim that "[w]hat the British government was going to do" in these areas "was never clearly thought out."[131]

At an Inter-Allied Conference on Russia in early December, Lloyd George first broached the idea of making peace with the Bolsheviks and inviting them to the upcoming Paris Peace Conference. "It was not possible to say," the prime minister said at the meeting, "that the Tartars , the Finns, the Letts, should come to the Peace Conference and not the Bolsheviks, who stood for two-thirds of the whole population. The Bolsheviks, whatever might be thought of them, appeared to have a hold over the majority of the population."[132] This statement is important not only for its call for accomodation with the Bolsheviks, but for its evidence that, even at this early stage, Lloyd George believed that the Bolsheviks commanded the support of the bulk of the Russian population.

In his memoirs, he would claim that "[t]he evidence that came home from our own most trusted and best informed agents in Russia convinced me that although the vast majority of the people were not Communists, they preferred Bolshevik rule to that of the supporters of the old regime."[133] In fact, however, most of the British officials stationed in Russia were strong supporters of intervention, including even the belatedly converted Lockhart.[134] And while the Whites had great difficulty attracting mass support, it is not correct to say that the majority of the people supported the Bolsheviks against them.[135] Finally, it was certainly not correct to describe the Whites, all of whose leaders had declared the resummoning of the February Revolution's Constituent Assembly to be their chief war aim, as uniformly "supporters of the old [tsarist] regime."[136]

While Lloyd George had already begun to form the attitudes that would eventually lead him to terminate the intervention, munitions minister Winston Churchill began his push for a much more aggressive anti-Bolshevik policy. At a December 31 War Cabinet meeting, he warned that "the more the Allies attempted to get away from this problem the more it would stick to them."[137] Churchill urged "joint action by the five great Powers, or if America refused to act, by the rest." The Munitions Minister did not oppose Lloyd George's call for negotiations outright, but he presciently pointed out that a "satisfactory settlement" could not be achieved "unless it was known that we have the power and will to enforce our views." He therefore concluded that "[w]hat we should say to the Russians was that if they were ready to come together we would help them: and that if they refused, we would use force to restore the situation and set up a democratic government."[138] Unlike Lloyd George, Churchill correctly recognized that "Bolshevism represented a mere fraction of the population."[139]

Lloyd George rejected Churchill's suggestions almost totally. He avowed that he was "definitely opposed to military intervention in any shape," justifying his position on the grounds that it would require too many troops to subdue the Bolsheviks.[140] At this point, too, he became one of the first to raise the argument that intervention would backfire by inspiring a nationalistic pro-Bolshevik backlash. "The one sure method of establishing the power of Bolshevism in Russia was to attempt to suppress it by foreign troops," he contended, "[T]o send our soldiers to shoot down the Bolsheviks would be to create more Bolsheviks there."[141] This argument was to become one of the standard claims of anti-interventionists, both at the time and after.[142] It has continued to color our perception of the intervention, even though no one has ever been able to identify any substantial group of Russians which came to support the Bolsheviks because of intervention and otherwise would not have.[143]

Churchill was not prepared to accept defeat, and he continued his efforts to promote the cause of intervention throughout 1919. In this endeavor, he was helped by the greater influence he achieved after his appointment to the post of war minister in January. Almost alone among the top British officials, he understood the true nature of Bolshevism and the challenge it posed to the West. He realized that Bolshevism was a new and unprecedented threat, and not, as Lloyd George often claimed, some sort of modern-day rehash of the French Revolution.[144] "Of all the tyrannies in history," Churchill avowed, "the Bolshevist tyranny is the worst, the most destructive and the most degrading. It is sheer humbug to pretend that it is not far worse than German militarism."[145] In the environment of 1919, there could be no stronger condemnation of a regime than to call it "worse than German militarism," the hated enemy that had just been finally defeated at such great cost. To a limited extent, Churchill even understood what we would now call the totalitarian implications of the Bolshevik program. "The political, economic, social, and moral life of the people of Russia," he pointed out, "has for the time being been utterly smashed. Famine and terror are the order of the day."[146] Churchill thus understood that the Bolsheviks had deliberately sought to destroy *all* aspects of the existing social order, though he did not fully grasp the comprehensive nature of the system with which they sought to replace it.

Unlike many other observers, Churchill took the Bolshevik calls for world revolution seriously. He warned that "[t]he Russian Bolshevist revolution...is assuming an aggressive and predatory form."[147] He greatly feared that the Bolsheviks, if they managed to prevail over their internal opponents, would seek to impose their system by force on the weak nations of Central and Eastern Europe.

This fear interacted with Churchill's broader concern for the future of the entire new order of international relations that he hoped the victorious Allies would now be able to create. For a brief moment in history, these powers, with their almost unchallengeable authority, had an opportunity to change the whole course of world history for the better. Churchill ardently hoped that the opportunity would not be wasted. "This is the moment," he said in a speech on February 22, 1919, "to consolidate the hard-won position gained in the war and to secure it for all time."[148] In addition to the fear of expansion by the Bolsheviks acting alone, Churchill also presciently worried about the possibility of a Bolshevik alliance with a revanchist Germany. He constantly reiterated this position throughout 1919,[149] but the clearest and most complete statement of Churchill's views on this point was his May 14 speech at Dundee:

> Our policy must be directed to prevent a union between German militarism and Russian Bolshevism, for if that occurred these tyrants and tyrannical masses would swiftly crush the little weak States which lie between, and they would then form a combination which would stretch from China to the Rhine, which would be unspeakably unfriendly to Britain and to the United States and France, and to all that those free democracies stand for. There are three great lines of policy which we can pursue by which these dangers can be warded off—the first is to make peace with the German people after they have paid their forfeit for their offences, the second is to aid those forces in Russia which are making war successfully upon the Bolshevist tyranny, and the third is to keep firm friends with France and the United States.[150]

It is hardly necessary to point out that the failure, in different degrees, to achieve these three goals was the main cause of the catastrophic decline in Britain's foreign policy fortunes during the interwar period. Churchill was even sufficiently insightful to recognize the danger that Japan might adhere to the German-Russian alliance he foresaw.[151]

As the Paris Peace Conference commenced in January, Churchill urged an increase in assistance to the Whites and suggested that the Allies work to "combine all the border States hostile to the Bolsheviks into one system of war and get everyone else to do as much as possible."[152] This latter suggestion was one of the most vital components of Churchill's anti-Bolshevik strategy. He realized that Poland, Finland, Romania, and the various smaller states bordering Russia all greatly feared Bolshevik expansionism and that, with the right set of promises and inducements, they could be persuaded to make a substantial contribution to the anticommunist cause.

Churchill also suggested that Britain should "wind up the Batum-Baku adventure in the Caucasus,"[153] where some 20,000[154] British troops were stationed, so that these forces could be used elsewhere. Eventually, he would argue that these forces could be best employed fighting the Bolsheviks rather than guarding the Caucasian republics, which would in any case inevitably be swallowed up by the Bolsheviks if the latter were to inflict a decisive defeat on Denikin.[155]

In contrast to Lloyd George, who supported very limited intervention primarily for the sake of living up to prior "obligations" to the Whites and Churchill, who saw successful intervention as a major priority for British policy, was the position of Lord Curzon, chairman of the British Cabinet's Eastern Committee and Balfour's successor as foreign minister in October 1919. Curzon, Lloyd George recalled, had a "special affection for the Caucasus."[156] Though staunchly anti-Bolshevik, he was opposed to any extensive policy of intervention in Russia proper, but wanted to preserve the independence of the Caucasian states under British tutelage, so that the latter could act as a buffer between Russia and India. Curzon's way of thinking was in the tradition of classic British imperialist strategy in the East. He feared that the Whites, with their program for reunifying the Russian empire would pose a threat to his plans for the Caucasus. "It must not be forgotten," he warned Churchill on March 6, "that the only place where a renascent Russia had any real chance of early success was the Caucasus. Denikin [is]...an Old Russian, an Imperialist, and a Monarchist."[157] In the words of Richard Ullman, "this attitude reflected a British tendency to discount ideology and to emphasize concrete interest: those who ruled in Moscow...would behave in roughly the same manner regardless of the political labels they wore.... [S]o far as the British Empire was concerned, more important than who ruled Russia was the precise extent of the territory they controlled."[158] By this reasoning, a strong, united Russia under White rule was more of a threat to British interests than a weak, divided one under the Bolsheviks, who had promised self-determination to the non-Russian states.

Whereas Lloyd George's views on the importance of nonintervention, the likelihood of Russian nationalist backlash against foreign interference, and the reactionary nature of the Whites, can be linked to the "liberal" theory of international relations then made newly prominent by U.S. President Woodrow Wilson, Curzon's position reflected the traditional "realist" emphasis on geography and power over ideology. Among the top British officials, only Churchill was able to combine Curzon's appreciation of the importance and utility of power with Lloyd George's understanding of the determinative impact that ideology can often have on a state's foreign policy.

Curzon's views were not quite as doctrinaire as is suggested by historians such as Ullman.[159] He supported some of Churchill's projects for intervention. In October 1919, he sternly instructed Oliver Wardrop, the British high commissioner for Transcaucasia to cool the anti-White ardor of the Caucasian governments at a time when Denikin was close to capturing Moscow. "It is most important," he admonished Wardrop, "that at this moment when Denikin's progress against the Bolsheviks promises great success he should not be hampered by fear of attack in the rear. Defeat of Bolshevism...is [in] the interest of this country."[160] Nonetheless, Curzon was unwilling to invest nearly as much in the anti-Bolshevik cause as Churchill. For example, he opposed Churchill's efforts to obtain British aid for the White General Yudenich's efforts to capture Petrograd in the fall, and he was "opposed to sending British troops to any part of Russia except Georgia."[161] Ultimately, "[F]or Curzon, with his Asian and imperial preoccupations, the great boon of the Bolshevik upheaval was that it seemed to eliminate Russia as a rival to the British Empire along thousands of miles of once contested frontier; the great defect of Churchill's policies was precisely that they threatened to re-create a Great Russia."[162] On this view, limited anti-Bolshevik intervention was just one of many tools that could be used to advance the British national interest, narrowly defined, and should not be pursued to the point of undercutting other, more important, imperial concerns.

Churchill developed a number of ingenious responses to Curzon's realist arguments. The most telling, as we have seen, was his recognition that a Bolshevik victory would mean the end of Caucasian independence just as surely as a White one, perhaps, he could have added, even more surely given the more centralized nature of the Bolshevik state relative to the plans for regional "autonomy" advanced by Denikin.[163] He also believed that increased British aid could be used as a lever to moderate Denikin's attitudes, making it possible, "on the one hand to enable him to fight the Bolsheviks, and on the other, to prevent him from maltreating the Southern States."[164] Finally—and most importantly—Churchill simply did not share Curzon's implicit belief that the Bolsheviks, despite their distasteful doctrines, would ultimately act much like any other Russian government would in their stead. "Theirs" he wrote on June 22, "is a war against civilised society which can never end. They seek as the first condition of their being the overthrow and destruction of all existing institutions and of every State and Government now standing in the world.... [B]etween them and such order of civilisation as we have been able to build up since the dawn of history there can, as Lenin rightly proclaims, be neither truce nor pact."[165]

Curzon never really made a serious attempt to rebut Churchill's criticisms, but he continued to hold to his own views. He had so much emotion and interest invested in the traditional imperial foreign policy to which he had devoted almost his entire career that he could hardly countenance a drastic change of perspective at so late a date.[166] Curzon's natural inclinations may also have been strengthened by his personal suspicion of Churchill, whose return to the Cabinet in 1917 he had bitterly opposed, predicting that "he will as a member of the Govt be an active danger in our midst."[167]

When the Paris Peace Conference began, Lloyd George, supported by President Wilson, put forward his proposal for an Allied sponsored peace conference between the Bolsheviks and their various enemies. In fact, they wanted to go even further than this. "Personally," the prime minister recalled, "I would have dealt with the Soviets as the *de facto* government of Russia. So would President Wilson. But we both agreed that we could not carry to that extent our colleagues at the Congress, nor the public opinion of our own countries which was frightened by Bolshevik violence and feared its spread."[168] This revealing statement should help lay to rest the traditional notion that the option of broader intervention was rejected primarily because of the opposition of Western public opinion to new military involvements.

By January 21, Lloyd George and Wilson had succeeded in persuading the Conference to adopt their proposal despite the skepticism of Clemenceau and Vittorio Orlando, the Italian leader. On January 22, the Conference adopted a draft proclamation to the various Russian factions drawn up by President Wilson. The message invited White and Bolshevik representatives to a February 15 conference at Prinkipo, an island in the Sea of Marmara, which lies between the Dardanelles and the Bosporus straits, and urged them to establish a cease-fire for this purpose. The text of the invitation stated that the Allies did not "wish or purpose to favour or assist any one of those organized groups now contending for the leadership and guidance of Russia against others."[169] In terms reminiscent of Lloyd George's and Wilson's private fear of aiding reaction in Russia, it also announced that the Western powers "will in no way, and in no circumstances, aid or give countenance to any attempt at counter-revolution."[170] The "counter-revolution" they had in mind was an attempt to restore tsarism rather than attempt to overthrow the Bolsheviks per se. Still, it is significant that Wilson and Lloyd George saw fit to include in the invitation a statement of their unequivocal opposition to "counter-revolution" but did not include a similar assertion of their distaste for the Bolshevik dictatorship. Even more importantly, the Prinkipo invitation was the first major declaration by the Allied governments that placed the Bolsheviks on an equal plane with the Whites.

As it turns out, the Prinkipo proposal is historically more important as an indicator of Lloyd George's and Wilson's attitudes than for any effect it had on the situation in Russia. The White leaders unequivocally refused to have anything to do with the Bolsheviks.[171] The Soviet government, for its part, sent an ambiguous reply which offered to make various economic and territorial concessions to the "Entente Powers...its only real adversaries" in exchange for an end to intervention, but did not grant any legitimacy to their Russian opponents or even offer to make any accomodation with them at all.[172] Fundamentally, as George Kennan has argued, the Prinkipo proposal was doomed to failure because "[w]hat the Bolsheviki and their Russian opponents were interested in was each other's total destruction. There was no room here for amicable discussion."[173] The determination of the Whites to reject negotiations with the Bolsheviks was also strengthened by French assurances that aid would continue regardless.[174] The Bolsheviks, on the other hand, were given no reason to believe that intervention would increase beyond its present limited level if they failed to moderate their stance towards the Whites. In sum, neither faction was given anything like sufficient incentive to alter its deeply held goals. The resulting failure merely underlined the justice of Churchill's December 31 warning to Lloyd George that "there was no chance of securing...a settlement unless it was known that we had the power and the will to enforce our views."[175]

The collapse of the Prinkipo plan presented Churchill with a new opportunity to push for an alternative to Lloyd George's policy. In January, before the Prinkipo plan was adopted, he had supported French Marshal Ferdinand Foch's proposal to fight the Bolsheviks by strengthening Polish forces opposing the Reds in a struggle over disputed territory in the Ukraine and by repatriating the 1.2 million Russian POWs still held in Germany to White-controlled areas, where the latter could use these trained troops to fight. This proposal was rejected by Lloyd George and Wilson and did not even fit in fully with the ideas of Clemenceau, whose policy was primarily to form a *cordon sanitaire* of hostile states around Bolshevik Russia rather than to work to overthrow the Bolsheviks directly.[176]

On February 14, Churchill arrived at the Peace Conference during a time when Lloyd George was away. In the wake of the failure of the Prinkipo proposal, he began to argue for a stronger anti-Bolshevik policy. While he "agreed that none of the Allies could send conscript troops to Russia" because of popular opposition to such a move, Churchill "thought that volunteers, technical experts, arms munitions tanks, aeroplanes, etc., might be furnished."[177] Churchill's suggestion was bitterly opposed by President Wilson,[178] but this did not prevent the former from pressing his proposals once more the next day, when Wilson had left.

On this occasion, Churchill made a fuller statement of his ideas. He proposed that the Bolsheviks should be sent an ultimatum requiring them to comply with the Prinkipo conditions within ten days.[179] He also suggested the establishment of "an Allied Council for Russian affairs," which would ensure "continuity of policy, unity of purpose, and control" of Allied policy towards Russia.[180] Most importantly, Churchill argued that "[t]he military section of the proposed Council should...be asked at once to draw up a plan for concerted action against the Bolsheviks."[181] Here, as throughout 1919, Churchill stressed the need for a unified anti-Bolshevik effort using all available resources, in contrast to the haphazard, contradictory policies which the Allies actually pursued. He warned the assembled delegates that there were only two options: "either to prepare some plan of military action in Russia, consistent with the resources available, or to withdraw the armies and to face the consequences of abandoning Russia to her fate."[182] He then outlined his oft-stated reasons for choosing the former.

Churchill's proposals were supported by Clemenceau, who "agreed with all that Mr. Churchill had said,"[183] and even Lord Balfour, who generally supported Lloyd George's position, did not criticize Churchill directly. For a brief moment, it almost seemed as if Churchill had won.

But the appearance was deceptive. As soon as Lloyd George found out about what Churchill had done, he immediately set out to ensure that the war minister's proposals would not be carried out by the Conference. On February 16, he sent a telegram to Philip Kerr, one of the British officials in Paris, in which he instructed the British delegation "not to commit this country to what would be a purely mad enterprise out of hatred of Bolshevik principles."[184] Under Lloyd George's prodding, the other members of British delegation came out in opposition to Churchill's schemes. This resistance, combined with that of President Wilson upon his return, was enough to sink them, and no Allied Commission on Russia was ever established.[185] In his memoirs, Lloyd George even claimed that Churchill had deviously "seized the opportunity created by the absence of President Wilson and myself to go over to Paris and urge his plans with regard to Russia upon the consideration of the French, the American and the British delegations,"[186] even though Churchill had gone to Paris on the instigation of Lloyd George himself.[187]

Churchill was incensed by Lloyd George's efforts to undercut him and he was even more troubled by the overall state of Allied policy towards the war in Russia. In a February 27 report to the Prime Minister, he reasserted his position:

> British assistance to Russia...is related to no concerted policy, and...while it constitutes a serious drain on our resources it is not backed by with sufficient vigor to lead to any definite result. *There is no 'will to win' behind any of these ventures. At every point we fall short of what is necessary to obtain real success.* The lack of any 'will to win' communicates itself to our troops and affects their morale: it communicates itself to our Russian Allies and retards their organization, and to our enemies and encourages their efforts. (Emphasis mine)[188]

On March 14, he pointed out that the precipitous Allied decision to order the Germans to "withdraw from the Ukraine without any provision being made to stop the Bolshevik advance, has enabled large portions of this rich territory full of new supplies of food to be overrun."[189] This was a serious oversight that was to make Denikin's effort to capture Moscow from the south far more difficult than it otherwise would have been. When Denikin made his major bid to capture Moscow in the fall, he had to fight his way through the Ukraine rather than simply have it handed over to him by the Allies or by German troops, as Churchill would have wanted.

But perhaps the single most serious Allied mistake pointed out by Churchill was the April decision to repatriate those Russian prisoners of war captured before the February Revolution and still held in Germany to Bolshevik-held Russia, instead of sending them to the Whites, as Churchill and Foch had advocated. In a war in which both sides had greatly difficulty finding high-quality manpower, this was surely an error of the first magnitude. Soon after he heard of this decision, Churchill wrote a memorandum to top British military officials in which he expressed his fears:

> Whereas we could have made out of these an army of loyal men who would have been available to sustain the defence of Archangel and Murmansk or to aid General Denikin and Kolchak, we are now I presume simply sending a reinforcement of 500,000 trained men to join the armies of Lenin and Trotsky. This appears to me to be one of the capital blunders in the history of the world.[190]

Unfortunately, no historian of the Russian Civil War has so far, to my knowledge, attempted to determine the impact which these troops might have had if transferred to the Whites or moulded by the Allies into a separate anti-Bolshevik army. Equally, no scholar has attempted to estimate how many of them were, upon their return home, utilized in Trotsky's continuing efforts to build up the Red Army.[191] Nonetheless, even given the fact that the Whites would probably not have been able to fully integrate so large a force into their armies, their potential significance was surely great. To give some idea of its possible magnitude, it is worth pointing out that, at the height of its strength in October 1919, Denikin's Armed Forces of Southern Russia[192] could commit just 111,000 troops to its penultimate effort to take Moscow, while the Bolsheviks opposed it with some 186,000.[193] On both sides, particularly that of the Reds, most of the troops were poorly trained. The Reds also suffered from a shortage of reliable, trained officers. In these circumstances, given that Denikin almost captured Moscow even without them, it is fair to suggest that the outcome of the Russian Civil War might well have been different if even one-tenth of the "500,000 trained men" Churchill referred to had been incorporated into Denikin's army, the White force to which they were geographically closest and the one with the best chance of dealing the Bolsheviks a decisive defeat.

In the spring of 1919, Britain and the other Allies rejected offers from several nations to send forces to help fight the Bolsheviks if the former were willing to equip the necessary troops. Prince Alexander of Serbia, a strong supporter of Denikin, had offered to send the latter a corps of 30,000 Serbian volunteers in March, on condition that the Allies supplied the necessary arms, supplies, and transportation. Although the Allied governments had large stocks of excess war supplies of their own and also controlled the immense reserves of Germany, Austria and Bulgaria, the defeated Central Powers, they spurned this proposal, apparently with little thought.[194] Later, they rejected a similar offer from Bulgaria, whose government had hoped to provide Denikin with both troops and supplies.[195] And, despite repeated requests from the White Russian representatives in Paris, they failed to put sufficient pressure on the Rumanian government to force the latter to release the vast quantities of Russian-owned supplies stored there—enough to equip as many as forty-three divisions, by some estimates.[196] Here was another example of the failure to heed Churchill's admonition to link all of the anti-Bolshevik powers into "one system of war."

Although the British thus failed to take advantage of a number of valuable opportunities, they did provide Kolchak and Denikin with large quantities of supplies and, for the time being, retained the troops stationed in North Russia, as well as the much smaller contingent in Siberia. Lloyd George's entire policy during this period was based on a willingness to provide supplies coupled with an almost total rejection of direct military intervention and diplomatic initiatives to persuade others to intervene in Britain's stead. He set forth this view in a February 19 letter to Philip Kerr:

> No foreign intervention in...Russia...but material assistance to be supplied to these [White] Governments to enable them to hold their own in the territories which are not anxious to submit to Bolshevik rule. If these territories are sincerely opposed to Bolshevism then with Allied aid they can maintain their position. If, on the other hand, they are either indifferent or very divided, or lean towards Bolshevism though they must collapse, I see no reason why, if this represents their attitude towards Bolshevism, the Powers should impose upon them a government they are not particularly interested in or attempt to save them from a government they are not particularly opposed to. Our principle ought to be 'Russia must save herself.'[197]

The belief that any White defeats would necessarily indicate that the people did not prefer them to Bolsheviks became one of the cornerstones of Lloyd George's position. Intervention in Russia, he claimed, could only be justified if "Russia wants it."[198] And it could only be said to "want" it if the Whites were, with limited military aid, able to defeat the Reds on their own. In addition, it is worth noting, as most other scholars have not, that he saw the purpose of assistance as helping the Whites to "maintain their position" rather than to defeat the Bolsheviks entirely. Although it would be wrong to conclude from this that the prime minister didn't want to see the Bolshevik regime overthrown, it certainly suggests that he did not see such an outcome as a vital interest of Britain.

From the beginning of 1919 until November, Lloyd George's major public statement on Russia was his April 16 address to the House of Commons. In this speech, he condemned Bolshevism vehemently, deploring "its horrible consequences, starvation, bloodshed, confusion, ruin and horror."[199] However, he argued, "that does not justify us in committing this country to a gigantic military enterprise in order to improve conditions in Russia."[200] He urged Parliament to remember "the fundamental principle of all foreign policy in this country—a very sound principle— that you should never interfere in the internal affairs of another country, however badly governed."[201] A cynic might find it difficult to understand how such noninterference could be considered the "fundamental principle of all foreign policy" in an empire which ruled over millions of people precisely—it was claimed—on the grounds that they would be "badly governed" otherwise, even though the oppressions practiced by the native rulers of India or Africa were minor compared to those which Lloyd George himself had just attributed to the Bolsheviks. But, for obvious reasons, few were prepared to dispute the point.

Lloyd George went on to justify limited assistance to the Whites strictly on the grounds of prior bonds of gratitude and obligation:

> They [the Whites] raised armies at our instigation and largely.... at our expense. That was an absolutely sound military policy.... Had it not been for those organisations that we improvised, the Germans would have secured all the [Russian] resources which would have enabled them to break the blockade.... Bolshevism threatened to impose, by force of arms, its domination on those populations which had revolted against it, and that were organised at our request. If we, as soon as they had served our purpose.... .had said, 'Thank you; we are exceedingly obliged to you. You have served our purpose. We need you no longer. Now let the Bolsheviks cut your throats,' we should have been mean—we should have been thoroughly unworthy of any great land.[202]

For this reason, Lloyd George concluded in something of a non sequitur, "I do not in the least regard it as a departure from the fundamental policy of Great Britain not to interfere in the internal affairs of any land that we should support General Denikin, Admiral Koltchak and General Kharkoff."[203]

What Lloyd George did not say in the speech was as significant as what he did. At no point did he suggest that there was any reason to support the Whites other than gratitude for their assistance during the World War. He did note that it was important to "prevent the forcible eruption of Bolshevism into Allied lands,"[204] but avowed that this could be done simply by "organising all the forces of the Allied countries bordering on Bolshevist territory from the Baltic to the Black sea."[205] He did not in any way make a connection between preventing the spread of Bolshevism abroad and combatting it in Russia itself. Nor did he consider the issue of how the weak Eastern European states could hope to hold out in the long run against a Russia unified under the Bolsheviks. Privately, he confided to Kerr that he did not see any reason to believe that "the Soviet Government have any intention or desire to invade these territories"[206]—a view which had already been falsified by the Soviet efforts to conquer Finland and Estonia in November and December 1918 and would again be refuted—on an even greater scale—by the Bolshevik attempt to destroy Poland's independence in 1920.

Simply put, Lloyd George had little understanding of totatalitarian states. At a July 17 meeting of the Council of Four, the Peace Conference forum which brought together the leaders of Britain, France, Italy, and the U.S., he endorsed the reports of unnamed "observers" in Russia, who claimed that "pure Bolshevik doctrine is being increasingly abandoned, and that what is being established over there is a state that doesn't differ noticeably from a bourgeois state."[207] Lloyd George even believed that, if peace were to come, "the Bolsheviks would not wish to maintain an army, as their creed was fundamentally anti-militarist."[208] By late 1919 and early 1920 he came to think that the Soviet Union could be liberalized merely through trade contacts with the West.[209] In light of such misconceptions, it is perhaps no accident that in 1940, Lloyd George would become the only major British political figure to refuse to join Churchill's coalition government and instead advocate a compromise peace with Nazi Germany.[210]

Despite the very limited nature of Lloyd George's commitment to the White cause, the aid that the British sent to them was not insubstantial. Between February 1919 and the end of the year, when deliveries largely stopped, Denikin received 558 guns, 30 tanks, almost 1.7 million artillery shells, 250,000 rifles, 160 million rounds of rifle ammunition, and numerous other supplies from the British.[211] Much smaller quantities of supplies were obtained from France and elsewhere.[212] From October 1918 to October 1919, Kolchak's forces received 600,000 rifles, 346 million rounds of small arms ammunition, 192 guns, and 200,000 military uniforms.[213] The British also equipped the much smaller forces of the northern Russian Whites. The total cost of this aid and the limited British military deployments in Russia was close to 100 million pounds, though, as Churchill pointed out, much of this consisted of "an unmarketable surplus of the Great War, to which no money value can be assigned."[214] Whatever the cost, it was small relative to overall British government expenditures of the time. The supplies certainly helped the White forces greatly, even though a large portion of the deliveries were wasted as a result of White inefficiency and corruption.[215] According to the best recent history of the Russian Civil War, since the Whites "occupied an area without major munitions factories...these supplies were tremendously important."[216] Allied aid was also "a great boost to White morale."[217]

Of particular importance were the small quantities of tanks and aircraft the British provided to Denikin. These were operated by British personnel, since there were no qualified Russians. In several important engagements during the summer and fall of 1919, the tanks allowed Denikin's troops to break through the Red lines and defeat superior enemy forces, most notably at the June 29 capture of the key city of Tsaritsyn by General Baron Peter Wrangel, who was to replace Denikin in early 1920.[218] As one military historian puts it, "[t]he Reds could do nothing against the tanks."[219] In 1918, attacks by British tanks had repeatedly broken through German positions on the Western Front, even though the Germans were generally considered the best infantry in the world; it was clear that the hastily thrown together Red Army could hardly hope to do better. And southern Russia, with its vast plains, was ideal tank country. On a more limited basis, the Whites were also able to make effective use of British aircraft, for both reconnaissance and bombing purposes.[220] The results of these special deployments confirmed the validity of Churchill's belief that the Whites could especially benefit from the services of "volunteers, technical experts, arms, munitions tanks, [and] aeroplanes."[221]

However, the British sent too few of these special weapons to make a decisive difference. Denikin only received some thirty tanks and two squadrons of planes,[222] and it is not clear that all of these saw action. Kolchak received virtually no tanks or planes. During the fall of 1919, six tanks and six planes were sent to assist the White General Yudenich in his efforts to capture Petrograd from Estonia. These performed well, but, once again, were too few too make a decisive difference.[223] Likewise, small numbers of planes were used by the British forces in northern Russia.[224]

Thanks to the enthusiastic support of Churchill, who in his earlier capacity as minister of munitions had been among the first to recognize the value of the new weapon, the British had built hundreds of tanks for operation on the Western Front.[225] There is no telling what might have happened had Denikin or Kolchak been provided with 100 or 200 of these now idle weapons instead of thirty. Such an effort would not have represented a major imposition on British manpower, nor would it have widened British involvement in the War much beyond what it was already. But it might well have made the difference between victory and defeat. To a lesser extent, the same analysis can be applied to aircraft.

Even as he acted to provide the White forces with increasing quantities of supplies, Lloyd George moved to withdraw British troops from Russia. On March 4, the War Cabinet decided to withdraw the British contingents in Murmansk and Archangel. The decision resulted from a combination of Lloyd George's general preference for removing British troops from Russia and the recommendation of General Sir Henry Wilson, the chief of the Imperial General Staff, who believed that the deployment in northern Russia was wasteful and militarily ineffective.[226] Against the advice of British officials on the spot, the White government of northern Russia was not informed of this decision until much later.[227]

Meanwhile, Churchill was authorized to make any arrangements he considered necessary to insure the safe evacuation of the British troops, which could not depart immediately because the Russian Arctic ports were still frozen.[228] Churchill made use of this authority to raise two brigades of volunteers totalling 8000 men and send them to northern Russia, ostensibly to insure that the safety of the troops already there[229]— although the Allied position seems to have been fairly secure at this time.[230] The necessary volunteers were quickly and easily obtained from the ranks of soldiers about to be demobilized, even though "[e]nlistment was open only to fully trained troops in excellent physical condition."[231] This fact challenges the standard view that it would have been impossible to obtain volunteers for more extensive operations in Russia against the Bolsheviks.

With the arrival of the volunteer brigades, the only first-class British ground troops to be deployed in Russia during the entire Civil War period if the small contingents in the Caucasus are excluded, Churchill hoped to effect a conjunction between the northern Russian Whites and the forces of Admiral Kolchak, then advancing from Siberia and about to reach the height of their power. He developed a number of ingenious, but unrealistic, schemes to advance this purpose, including one which planned to utilize the by then moribund Czech Legion.[232] In conjunction with the greatly strengthened northern Russian White forces led by General Eugene Miller, the British and Allied units launched a number of successful local operations, including one in August in which a combined British-Russian force of 4000 inflicted over 6000 casualties on the Bolsheviks for negligible losses of their own.[233] But the Allied and White forces in northern Russia were simply too weak to break through to Kolchak, particular after the Bolsheviks began to drive the latter back in late May.

The northern Russian area was, in any case, clearly a "strategic sideshow"[234] in the Russian Civil War. Its small population and lack of resources prevented the buildup of a large White army. Once the initial chance to capture Moscow with relatively small forces had been lost in the summer of 1918, only the deployment of quite large British units could have allowed the northern Russian expedition to play a decisive role in the outcome of the war, an option which Lloyd George and all his colleagues, other than Churchill, were unwilling to countenance. For these reasons, the concentration of British military effort in northern Russia represented a substantial maldistribution of resources, even though considerable Bolshevik forces were tied down by the British operations. The volunteer units sent to northern Russia might have had a much bigger impact if sent to assist Kolchak, Denikin, or Yudenich. But such a policy would have conflicted with Lloyd George's refusal to allow any new deployments to Russia other than those considered necessary to facilitate the withdrawal of British forces already there.

In October, the British expedition in northern Russia was finally withdrawn. The total British losses in northern Russia from July 1918 to October 1919—which represented virtually all their casualties in the entire Russian Civil War—were 983 killed, wounded and missing, including 327 dead.[235] The low casualties were symptomatic of the half-heartedness of the British commitment. Although the British offered to evacuate the White Russian soldiers and civilians in Murmansk and Archangel, most of them chose to stay.[236] Contrary to all expectations, General Miller's forces were able to successfully resist the Bolsheviks for almost six months after the departure of the Allies. Their final defeat in 1920 came about as a result of the collapse of White resistance in southern Russia and Siberia. Miller's army eventually contained as many as 50,000 troops, a remarkable total by Russian Civil War standards, given the small size of the population in northern Russia.[237]

During the spring of 1919, the most promising Russian Civil War front, from the British and White point of view, was that of Kolchak. After reforming their armies in the winter, the Siberian Whites began a major offensive which achieved significant successes. Aided by peasant and worker uprisings behind the Red lines and by the poor quality of the forces facing them, the Siberian Whites reconquered the Ural Mountain region, and almost reached the Volga River.[238] They were now only a little over 500 miles from Moscow.[239] At this point, Kolchak's troops actually outnumbered the Red forces opposing them, a rare advantage for the Whites, and, according to a secret Red Army report, they had better officers.[240]

The Bolsheviks were clearly worried by this development, especially since it coincided with a series of victories by Denikin in the south. Lenin expressed serious concern about "the extremely grave position on the Eastern Front."[241] In a secret April 23 memorandum on the military situation, the Red Army Commander-in-Chief, Colonel Vatsetis, warned that "[t]he further fate of the Revolution depends on the outcome of the battles on the Southern and Eastern Fronts."[242]

In the Allied camp, Churchill and the French constantly urged Lloyd George and Wilson to increase assistance to Kolchak. Even Lloyd George briefly seemed enthusiastic about the prospect of further Kolchak victories. He hoped that Kolchak might break through to the Allied forces in northern Russia and considered coming into closer relations with him.[243] Even at this point, however, the prime minister worried about Kolchak's possible reactionary tendencies and warned Nikolai Chaikovsky, the socialist leader of the northern Russian White government, that "[o]ur preoccupation is to do nothing which might help in the triumph of a militaristic or autocratic regime."[244] The Allies debated the issue of recognizing Kolchak and sending him more aid for weeks.

Finally, on May 26, Lloyd George and Wilson agreed to send Kolchak a communiqué jointly signed by the Big Four promising partial recognition and increased assistance in exchange for assurances that the new

Russian regime would be liberal and democratic, that it would pay Russia's foreign debts, that it would recognize the independence of Finland and Poland, and that it agree to submit other border and sovereignty issues to League of Nations arbitration.[245] On June 4, Kolchak sent a reply agreeing to all the Allied conditions, except that he was willing to grant only de facto recognition to the Finnish government until such time as the Constituent Assembly could be reestablished.[246] By June, Kolchak's status as the official leader of the White movement in Russia had been recognized by Denikin and all the other White governments in Russia.[247] On June 12, The Big Four endorsed Kolchak's response and pronounced themselves "willing to extend to Admiral Koltchak and his associates the support set forth in their original letter."[248]

Historians critical of the Whites and the intervention have correctly noted that the "liberal" sentiments expressed in Kolchak's telegram were the result of coaching by General Knox, the chief British military representative at Kolchak's headquarters in Omsk.[249] However, it is also the case that most of its promises merely reiterated goals which Kolchak had proclaimed long before. The reestablishment of a freely elected Constituent Assembly, for example, had been his constantly reiterated purpose since the beginning of the admiral's tenure as "Supreme Ruler." Few White leaders had ever really doubted that Poland and Finland would become independent states. In earlier statements intended for internal consumption, Kolchak had already endorsed most of the liberal positions that the Allied communiqué required him to accept. "The future Russia will be a democratic Russia," he said in a speech on April 19, "The Government, of which I have the honor to be the head, believes in universal suffrage, in the autonomous development of the nationalities comprising Russia, in a democratic solution of the main Russian problems: the land and labor problems."[250] In fact, some of General Denikin's more conservative supporters had urged him not to recognize Kolchak as supreme leader of the White movement precisely because they considered him and his government to be *too* liberal.[251]

While there is little doubt that Kolchak himself, who disliked the burden of supreme power, fully intended to carry out his promise to "transfer to the Constituent Assembly all the power which now belongs to the Government,"[252] it is, of course, possible that, in the event of a White victory, liberal policies would have been sabotaged by others in his regime. In any case, however, the assurances the Allied leaders gained from their communiqué gave them little more than what they had already. And even at this point, they refused to actually recognize Kolchak's newly unified White movement as the legitimate government of Russia, a move that might have increased its authority with the Russian population.[253]

The belated decision to grant Kolchak increased aid came too late to help him. While the Allies dithered in Paris, the Bolsheviks gathered additional forces on their Eastern Front and began a counteroffensive. This attack was highly successful and it rapidly drove back the White forces.[254] The Kolchak regime was too weak to recover from this sustained series of defeats, although the Admiral's troops launched several successful counterattacks before their final collapse.[255] In November, the Reds captured Kolchak's capital of Omsk. Kolchak himself was captured by the Bolsheviks in January 1920 and executed.[256]

"No sooner had the Correspondence between Koltchak and the Big Five terminated satisfactorily..." Churchill bitterly recalled , "than his collapse began."[257] He himself had urged that Kolchak be recognized earlier—and more fully—when the Siberian Whites still had a good shot at winning. "If this...decision was wise...in June," he argued,

> would it not have been wiser in January? No argument existed in June not obvious in January; and half the power available in January was gone by June. Six months of degeneration and uncertainty had chilled the Siberian Armies and wasted the slender authority of the Omsk Government. It had given the Bolsheviks the opportunity of raising armies, of consolidating their power and of identifying themselves with Russia. It had provided enough opposition to stimulate and not enough to overcome the sources of their strength. The moment chosen by the Supreme Council for their declaration was almost exactly the moment when that declaration was certainly too late.[258]

It is not clear that increased British aid to Kolchak earlier could have made a decisive difference. As we shall see in chapter 3, the United States had much greater opportunities to affect the outcome of the struggle in Siberia. Nonetheless, the Whites would surely have had at least a somewhat better chance of winning had Lloyd George been willing to act earlier.

Kolchak's defeats during the summer increased the prime minister's doubts about the value of intervention in Russia even further. By August, he and most of the rest of the Cabinet were ready to wind down Britain's commitment to the Whites. Even though Denikin's forces in southern Russia and Yudenich's near Petrograd were close to the peak of their success, he advocated limiting the aid to be sent to the Whites in the future. At an August 12 War Cabinet meeting on Russia, Churchill strongly advocated continued support of Denikin, "the one bright spot in Russia."[259] But Curzon reasserted his old fear that Denikin's real ambitions "lay not in the direction of Moscow but towards the Caucasus," and Lloyd George decided that Denikin should be given just one "last packet" of aid.[260] He and Curzon were both skeptical about the likelihood that Denikin would succeed and they expressed doubts about the value of such a success to Britain.[261] It was at this meeting that Lloyd George expressed the view that the Bolsheviks would disarm in the event of peace because "their creed was fundamentally anti-militarist."[262]

Meanwhile, Denikin's forces continued to advance, winning repeated victories over the Bolsheviks. On July 3, he had issued his famous "Moscow Directive" which envisioned the capture of the capital by means of a three-pronged offensive and the expulsion of the Bolsheviks from the "heart of Russia."[263] By October, the White army had advanced to within 250 miles of Moscow, having repeatedly defeated numerically stronger Red forces. All of South Russia, and most of the Ukraine was now under Denikin's control. "Never before," Denikin recalled, "had Soviet Power been in a more difficult position or experienced such fear."[264] The Bolshevik leaders fully shared this assessment. A secret October 15 Communist party Politburo acknowledged "the presence of a military threat of the utmost gravity" and urged "the conversion of Soviet Russia into an armed camp" in order to meet Denikin's challenge.[265] Even earlier, just before Denikin's final offensive began, Lenin had seen the importance of the southern front and issued a circular letter to Bolshevik party organizations entitled "All Out for the Fight Against Denikin!"[266]

Moscow was the center of Bolshevik authority and popular support, the locus of the Russian transportation network, and the largest industrial concentration in the country. It also had great psychological significance for the Whites. "In the minds of the troops..." Denikin wrote, "'Moscow' was, of course, a symbol. All dreamt of the 'March on Moscow,' and all succumbed to that hope."[267] For these reasons, Denikin's offensive against Moscow rapidly turned into the most decisive battle of the entire war.

Churchill had high hopes for Denikin, and urged the British Cabinet to step up assistance to him and persuade the anti-Bolshevik states bordering Russia on the West to join in the fight at this critical juncture. He was guardedly optimistic about Denikin's prospects, writing on September 9 that it was "anybody's victory at the present time."[268] By September

20, he was confident enough to predict that "[n]othing can preserve either the Bolshevik system or the B[olshevik] regime. By mistakes on our part the agony of the Russian people may be prolonged. But their relief is sure."[269] Churchill had begun to believe that victory was near and that his lonely advocacy of intervention was about to be vindicated.[270]

Even at this moment of excessive optimism, however, Churchill never ceased to press for measures that might make Denikin's victory more likely. In particular, he still hoped to persuade Lloyd George and the other Allied leaders to "use their whole influence to combine the operations of all the states at war with Soviet Russia."[271] Finland, Poland, Rumania, and the Baltic States had all had clashes with the Bolsheviks at different times in 1919, and all had offered to assist the Whites on condition that the Allies provide the necessary financial backing and guarantee their independence for the future. Churchill fervently wished to accept these offers, but he could not persuade Lloyd George and Curzon to go along with them.[272] Allied inaction led to the formation of a tacit Polish-Soviet agreement in which the former promised not to attack the Bolsheviks while Denikin's offensive was still on.[273] This assurance of a secure western border allowed the Reds to transfer numerous troops to Denikin's front and was a material factor in his eventual defeat.

Perhaps the most important single opportunity which was lost was the chance to cooperate with Finland in operations against Petrograd. The Finnish Whites, led by General Carl Gustaf Mannerheim, later to become famous for his role in the Russo-Finnish War of 1939–40, had defeated their own Bolsheviks in 1918, and had fought skirmishes against Russian Bolshevik forces since then. Mannerheim himself was a strong advocate of overthrowing the Russian Bolsheviks, believing—presciently, as it turned out—that "a lasting Bolshevik regime—assuming that it were not stamped out now—would constitute a danger for practically the whole of the world—not least for Finland."[274] But he and other Finnish leaders were not prepared to act unless the Whites were willing to recognize their independence and/or the British were prepared to guarantee Finland's security and provide needed military supplies.

During the summer and fall of 1919, Petrograd was seriously threatened by General Nikolai Yudenich's White northernwestern Army, operating from bases in Estonia. In July, Yudenich, supported by Kolchak, urged the Finns to help them attack Petrograd. But the Finns were put off by White unwillingness to recognize their de jure independence, even though Kolchak had already recognized it de facto. Finland might very well have entered the war in earnest anyway, however, if it had gotten suitable guarantees of its independence and military assistance from the Allies. On July 14, General Sir Hubert Gough, the British military representative in Finland reported to Foreign Minister Balfour that a deal could be obtained if the Allies were willing to offer assistance:

> It is absolutely certain that Finns will not march against Petrograd without any guarantee of definite support of Allies, trusting merely to the vague expression of approval so far offered by Allies.
> If Allied and Associated Powers desire to participate in Finland in the capture of Petrograd this summer a definite immediate offer of support is necessary.... With such support however it is probable that agreement could be reached.[275]

But no guarantees were ever offered. The British and the other Allies maintained their "vague" position. Privately, Curzon even warned Gough *not* to encourage the Finns to attack the Bolsheviks[276] and worried about Yudenich's possible "reactionary tendencies," a fear shared by Lloyd George.[277] Curzon particularly feared that Yudenich might seek to reconquer the border states of Russia.[278] Yudenich was indeed most likely a reactionary in his personal views. But he had agreed to subordinate himself to Kolchak, had made a number of liberal pronouncements,[279] and, in any case, his army was too small for him to have a major impact on the postwar development of Russia in the event of a White victory. In September, Yudenich himself made a personal appeal to Lloyd George, explaining that "[t]here is one condition... with which the success of the whole operation on Petrograd would be not only... probable, but certain: that is the active participation of Finland with her troops in this operation. In this matter only strong and continued pressure by England can play the deciding part.... Very soon it will be too late."[280]

But, despite the pleas of Churchill and the British representatives on the spot, Lloyd George remained opposed to any assistance to Yudenich, whom he denounced as a "notorious reactionary.... [and] not a man of any military distinction."[281] In the Prime Minister's view, "Yudenitch never had a chance of taking Petrograd."[282] Yudenich may well have been a "reactionary" but Lloyd George's statement that he was "not a man of any military distinction" was simply at variance with the facts. During World War I, Yudenich, while commanding the Russian forces in the Caucasus, had won numerous victories against superior Turkish forces; he was widely considered one of the best Russian generals.

In addition, there is every reason to believe that Yudenich could have captured Petrograd if he was provided with Finnish assistance. In fact, in October, he almost took the city with his own small, heavily outnumbered army.[283] The Finnish Army had some 100,000 high-quality troops led by competent commanders. There can be little doubt that, in combination with Yudenich's 14,000-man army, they would have easily overwhelmed the Bolshevik defenders of Petrograd, who, even after massive reinforcement in October, had less than 75,000 men of very mixed reliability.[284]

Petrograd was an important target for the Whites because of its military industries, its strategic location close to Moscow and the heart of Russia, and its psychological significance to the Bolsheviks as the city in which the Revolution began. The Bolsheviks greatly feared that the former capital would fall. Trotsky worried that "in Petrograd Yudenich will find huge industrial resources and manpower," and that "there are no serious obstacles between Petrograd and Moscow."[285] Lenin referred to "the tremendous threat hanging over Petrograd. A few days," he said in October, "will decide the fate of the city and that means half the fate of Soviet Power in Russia."[286] The area was also an ideal location for British operations because it was so close to the large British naval forces in the Baltic. For these reasons, Russian Civil War historian Evan Mawdsley suggests that "[h]ad the Allies intended a serious and general anti-Soviet campaign, Petrograd Province would have been an ideal theater."[287] Unfortunately, they didn't.

Compelled to operate alone, Yudenich nearly took Petrograd and forced the diversion of large numbers of Red troops from Denikin's front. But he could not prevail in the face of overwhelmingly superior numbers and, by the end of 1919, his army was driven back to Estonia where the authorities, having made peace with the Bolsheviks, forced it to disband. Both the Whites, with their refusal to formally recognize Finnish independence until it was too late,[288] and the British bore responsibility for the failure. Either could have saved the day, since the Finns were willing to act if their independence was guaranteed by *either* the Whites *or* the Allies, particularly if the latter were willing to provide military aid.

By November, Denikin's offensive had stalled before Moscow, as a result of large Bolshevik troop transfers from other fronts and a number of other difficulties. The Reds were now beginning to drive him back.

Lloyd George, who had not made a major public pronouncement on Russia since the April 16 speech at Parliament, chose this moment to make a public statement effectively dissociating Britain from the White cause. Without even consulting the Cabinet beforehand,[289] Lloyd George delivered his November 8 Guildhall address, in which he announced that Denikin's advance on Moscow had been "temporarily checked," military aid to the Whites had not been fully successful, and that, therefore, "other methods must finally be resorted to for restoring peace and good government in that distressed land [Russia]."[290] He warned that "[w]e cannot...afford to continue so costly an intervention in an interminable civil war."[291]

In a November 17 debate in Parliament, Lloyd George sounded a Curzonesque note, expressing doubts that a White victory would really be in the imperial interests of Britain. "[A] very great Statesman, a man of great imagination...Lord Beaconsfield [Disraeli]," he averred, "...regarded a great, gigantic, growing Russia rolling onwards like a glacier towards Persia and the borders of Afghanistan and India as the greatest menace the British Empire could be confronted with."[292] No one seemed to notice the irony of the Liberal Party leader and heir of Gladstone citing Disraeli to justify his policies. In a private discussion with the American ambassador to Britain, Lloyd George explained that he "favor[ed] encouraging the ultimate division of Russia into a number of independent states leaving none of sufficient size to threaten the genuine peace."[293] On November 30, he said, in another private discussion, that "*Russia should be broken up*. He was against the reconstitution of the old Russia whether under a Kolchak-Denikin rule or a Bolshevik rule."[294] It is probably too much to claim on the basis of these statements, as Richard Pipes does, that "behind" Lloyd George's decision to end British support of the Whites "lay fear not of White defeat but of White victory."[295] But his lack of enthusiasm for such a victory surely contributed to his willingness to give up the fight when the tide turned against the Whites.

Lord Curzon, as we have seen, shared these fears of a Russia united under White rule. Only Churchill argued relentlessly for the necessity of a united, anti-Bolshevik Russia as a necessary counterweight to Germany. He also believed that a Russia divided with Allied connivance would harbor dangerous grievances against the West.[296]

Lloyd George's November speeches caused great consternation among the Russian Whites. Denikin saw in them a "conclusive withdrawal from the fight and from aid to the anti-Bolshevik forces—at the most difficult possible time for us."[297] In his view, the British decision was a major material and psychological blow to the White army and an important cause of its final collapse. While self-serving,[298] his analysis was confirmed by the testimony of British observers in south Russia, one of whom wrote that

> [t]he effect of Mr. George's speeches was electrical.... In a couple of days the whole atmosphere in South Russia was changed. Whatever firmness of purpose there had previously been, was now so undermined that the worst became possible. Mr. George's opinion that the Volunteer cause was doomed helped to make that doom almost certain.[299]

Deprived of British supplies and perilously overextended, Denikin's forces were steadily driven back. In early 1920, Denikin was replaced as head of the Armed Forces of Southern Russia by General Wrangel. Wrangel's skilled generalship and political astuteness allowed him to hold out in the fortress-like Crimean peninsula until November 1920 and won him retrospective kudos from historians, even those highly critical of other White leaders.[300] But his position was too weak to allow him to change the outcome of the war. In November, 1920, he was forced to evacuate the Crimea with his troops and the White movement effectively came to an end.

British intervention in Russia had failed. While Lloyd George disliked the Bolsheviks and never considered their regime fully legitimate, he could not understand the necessity of defeating them or how this could be done. Lord Balfour largely shared his views, which were rooted in the foreign policy ideals of the British Liberal Party. For somewhat different reasons, the Conservative Curzon was only marginally more supportive of intervention.

Among the top British Cabinet members, only Churchill, also a Liberal at this time, truly understood the nature of the Bolshevik regime, and he came up with an impressive variety of schemes for overthrowing it without a full-scale commitment of British troops to all-out war. But he could not push his policies through in the face of opposition from all his most powerful colleagues. The imbalance of political leverage between Lloyd George and Churchill was so great that Ullman is surely right to conclude that "within...the Cabinet there was really no contest between Churchill and Lloyd George over Russian policy."[301] Many of Churchill's detailed memoranda on Russian policy in 1919 were never even answered.[302]

Churchill's arrogance and obstreperousness in pushing for his policies probably helped destroy whatever small chance he might have had of prevailing on his colleagues to change their minds. His dogged advocacy of the anti-Bolshevik cause offended his colleagues, stimulated fears that what he really wanted was a full-scale war against Russia, and led the intervention to be unfairly labeled "Mr. Churchill's private war," in the opposition press. After reading one Churchill memorandum on Russia, an exasperated Lloyd George replied by urging Churchill to "throw off this obsession which, if you will forgive me for saying so, is upsetting your balance."[303] Churchill's response, penned in anger on the very day he received the prime minister's epistle, was telling: "I may get rid of my 'obsession' or you may get rid of me; but you will not get rid of Russia; nor of the consequences of a policy wh[ich] for nearly a year it has been impossible to define."[304] But it was hardly likely to get the Prime Minister to change his mind.

Churchill was a great leader and a statesman of extraordinary insight, originality and erudition. He was one of the very few democratic politicians who truly understood the nature of totalitarian states. In the supreme crisis of World War II, these qualities would shine in their plenitude. But Churchill always had great difficulty persuading those less knowledgeable than himself of the correctness of his views. At four critical points in his career, this failing helped to change history for the worse in major ways: In the 1930s, when he failed to persuade his countrymen of the gravity of the German threat; in 1944–45, when he could not convince President Roosevelt to take a stronger line against Soviet ambitions in Europe; in 1945, when he was unable to adequately portray to the British electorate the dangers of the Labor Party's program of foreign policy retrenchment and massive welfare statism at home; and, as argued here, in 1919, when he was unable to carry through the cause of intervention in Russia. In the words of Henry Kissinger, "it was Churchill's fate to be rejected by his countrymen except for a brief time when their very survival was at stake."[305] To be sure, in each of these situations, there were major obstacles to success inherent in the very nature of the situation. Perhaps no one else in Churchill's place would have achieved greater results. But Churchill's defects of personality made it likely that he would be unable to fully exploit such opportunities as did exist.

Churchill's failure to convince Lloyd George led to a weak and indecisive Russian policy. Lloyd George opposed Churchill's schemes, but he could not bring himself to end intervention completely until the fall of 1919, when the British contingents in northern Russia and the Caucasus were finally withdrawn and aid to Denikin was cut off. As Churchill described it, "enough foreign troops entered Russia to incur all the objections which were patent against intervention, but not enough to break the then gimcrack structure of the Soviet power.... Half-hearted attempts to make peace [Prinkipo] were companioned by half-hearted attempts to make war."[306]

The White leaders likewise recognized the dual nature of British policy, and their morale suffered as a result. While expressing gratitude for British aid, General Denikin nonetheless concluded that they lacked the will to fight the Bolsheviks until victory. The British, he wrote, had "[t]wo principles, two policies, two 'hands'—one that gave and one that took away."[307]

Notes

1. David Lloyd George, *War Memoirs of David Lloyd George*, vol. 6, (Boston: Little Brown 1937), p. 150, hereafter cited as Lloyd George, *Memoirs*.
2. Churchill, Memorandum, December 15, 1919, reprinted in Churchill, *Aftermath*, p. 259.
3. Lloyd George, *Memoirs*, vol. 5, p. 7.
4. See ibid., ch. IX, esp. pp. 413–17.
5. Lenin, "Decree on Peace," November 8, 1917, in Tucker, ed., g. 540.
6. "Reply of the Soviet Government to the Statement of the British Embassy," November 30, 1917, in C.K. Cumming and Walter W. Pettit, eds., *Russian-American Relations, March 1917–March 1920: Documents and Papers*, (New York: Harcourt, Brace & Howe, 1920), p. 53.
7. Quoted in Adam Ulam, *Expansion and Coexistence: Soviet Foreign Policy 1917–73*, 2nd ed., (New York: Praeger, 1974), p. 54.
8. Arthur Balfour, "Notes on the Present Russian Situation," December 9, 1917, reprinted in Lloyd George, *Memoirs*, vol. 5, p. 113.
9. Ibid.
10. Ibid.
11. Some cabinet members, such as Lord Cecil, under-secretary for foreign affairs, opposed contacts with the Bolsheviks. Cecil believed that the Bolsheviks were mere German agents. See R.H. Bruce Lockhart, *British Agent*, (New York: G.P. Putnam's Sons, 1933), p. 198.
12. Lloyd George, *Memoirs*, vol. 5, p. 114.
13. Ullman, vol. 1, p. 59; Lockhart, pp. 197–98.
14. For a detailed account, see Ullman, vol. 1, ch. II
15. "Policy of the War Cabinet Relative to Revolutionary Governments at Petrograd," quoted in ibid., p. 52.
16. Ibid., p. 53.
17. Lloyd George, *Memoirs*, vol. 5, p. 110.
18. Ibid., p. 105.

19. Ibid., p. 125.
20. See Ullman, vol. 1, ch. V.
21. See Lockhart, book 4, chs. 3–4.
22. Quoted in Ullman, vol. 1, p. 131; The "must" in this sentence is used, in accordance with standard British usage, to mean "will." This interpretation is borne out by contextual considerations.
23. Quoted in Lockhart, p. 237.
24. Ibid., p. 226.
25. See ibid., esp. pp. 226–27.
26. Ibid., p. 236.
27. Ullman, vol. 1, pp. 136–37.
28. Kennan, *Decision,* p. 131.
29. Ibid. These two fears are explicitly stated by Lenin in his "Theses on the Present Political Situation," May 12–13, 1918, in Lenin, *Collected Works,* vol. 27, (Moscow: Progress Publishers, 1965), p. 360.
30. Lenin, "Report on Foreign Policy," May 14, 1918, in ibid., p. 379.
31. See, e.g., "Six Theses on the Immediate Tasks of the Soviet Government," April 30–May 3, 1918, in ibid., p. 314.
32. Lenin, "Theses on the Present Political Situation," op. cit., p. 361.
33. See, e.g., Williams, *American-Russian Relations,* ch. 6.
34. Sir William Wiseman to Colonel Edward M. House, May 1, 1918, in Charles Seymour, ed., *The Intimate Papers of Colonel House,* vol. 3, (Boston: Houghton Mifflin, 1928), p. 421.
35. Ibid.
36. Ibid.
37. General Alfred Knox, "The Delay in the East," paper circulated to the British Cabinet, March 18, 1918, quoted in Ullman, vol. 1, p. 132.
38. See excerpt in Ullman, vol. 1, p. 160.
39. Quoted in ibid., pp. 161–62.
40. Kennan, *Russia and the West Under Lenin and Stalin,* (New York: Mentor, 1961), p. 44; hereafter cited as Kennan, *Russia and the West*
41. Ullman, vol. 1, p. 128.
42. Ibid.
43. Ibid., p. 129.
44. Quoted in ibid.
45. Kennan, *Soviet-American Relations, 1917–20,* vol. 1, *Russia Leaves the War,* (Princeton: Princeton University Press, 1958), p. 183.
46. See Ullman, vol. 1, ch. V.
47. Kennan, *Russia and the West,* p. 92.
48. Ibid., p. 69.
49. Churchill, *Aftermath,* p. 88; figure calculated by subtracting 160,000 (the quantity at Archangel) from "More than 600,000 tons," (ibid.), Churchill's estimate for the total at Murmansk and Archangel combined.
50. Ibid.
51. Kennan, *Russia and the West,* p. 69.
52. Ibid. pp. 70–71, 92.
53. This issue is discussed in more detail in chapter 3.
54. Ullman, vol. 1, p. 118.
55. See Kennan, *Decision,* pp. 31–57, for a meticulous account of the special relationship between the Murmansk Soviet, the Allies, and the Moscow Bolshevik leader-

ship. Eventually, the former were condemned as traitors by Lenin and Trotsky. See also Vyacheslav I. Goldin, "Interventy ili Soyuzniki? Murmanskii 'Uzel' v Marte-Iiune 1918 Goda," ["Interventionists or Allies? The Murmansk 'Knot' in March-June 1918"], *Otechestvennaya Istoriya,* January-February 1994.

56. Lloyd George, *Memoirs,* vol. 6, p. 159.
57. Ullman, vol. 1, p. 182.
58. Ibid., pp. 143-44; Kennan, *Decision,* pp. 95-100.
59. These are outside the scope of this work. The best account of them is Kennan, *Decision,* esp. pp. 31-57, 95-100; see also discussion in Ullman, vol. 1.
60. See Ullman, vol. 1, p. 183.
61. Ibid., p. 184. Neither side suffered any casualties.
62. For details, see ibid., chs. V-VI.
63. Mawdsley, p. 46; Mawdsley himself—rightly in my view—dissents from this position.
64. Lloyd George, *Memoirs,* vol. 6, p. 159.
65. On the origins of the Legion, see Kennan, *Decision,* pp. 136-38.
66. Strangely, this latter reason for the Czechs' desperate desire to escape European Russia is generally ignored by most historians.
67. See Joseph Stalin, Commissar of Nationalities, to Czechoslovak National Council, March 26, 1918, in James Bunyan, *Intervention, Civil War and Communism in Russia, April-December 1918: Documents and Materials,* (Baltimore: Johns Hopkins Press, 1936), pp. 81-82, hereafter cited as Bunyan, *Intervention.*
68. Kennan, *Decision,* p. 150.
69. S.E. Aralov, telegram to Siberian Soviets, May 20, 1918, in Bunyan, *Intervention,* p. 88.
70. For details of these governments, see David Footman, *The Civil in Russia,* (London: Faber & Faber, 1961), ch. II; For an account more critical of the Komuch S-Rs, see Pipes, *Bolshevik Regime,* pp. 25-26.
71. Pipes, *Bolshevik Regime,* pp. 23-24.
72. Churchill, *Aftermath,* p. 93.
73. The issue of possible Allied instigation is examined in detail by Kennan (*Decision,* pp. 153-65), who persuasively argues that no such instigation occurred.
74. Churchill, *Aftermath,* p. 94.
75. Kennan, *Decision,* pp. 310-12.
76. FRUS, 1918, vol. 2, p. 243.
77. Lloyd George, *Memoirs,* vol. 6, p. 169.
78. Ibid., p. 159.
79. Ibid., p. 169.
80. Balfour, memorandum, July 16, 1918, reprinted in Ibid., pp. 177-78.
81. Excerpted in Ullman, vol. 1, p. 222.
82. Interestingly, the usually meticulous Ullman fails to notice this point.
83. Ullman, vol. 1, p. 221.
84. Ibid.
85. Ibid.
86. Balfour, memorandum, July 16, 1918, op. cit., p. 177; For Lloyd George's similar statement, see ibid.
87. Ibid.
88. Ibid.
89. Ullman, vol. 1, p. 235.
90. Ibid., pp. 235-36.

91. See Footman, pp. 172-74, 181-82.
92. Ibid., p. 188.
93. Ullman, vol. 1, p. 243.
94. Footman, p. 189.
95. This change of mind had come in late May, because of indications of continuing German-Bolshevik cooperation; see Ullman, vol. 1, pp. 187-88. In his memoirs (Lockhart, op. cit., pp. 285-87), Lockhart gives a misleading account of this shift which implies that it occurred later, less wholeheartedly, and more reluctantly than seems actually to have been the case. Ullman's account, stressing the importance of Lockhart's pro-interventionist telegram to Balfour on May 23, is a useful corrective. After the defeat of the Whites in the Russian Civil War, Lockhart retrospectively reverted to his original anti-interventionist stance, as his 1933 memoir demonstrates.
96. Lockhart, p. 308.
97. Ibid.; see also Ullman, vol. 1, pp. 186-88.
98. Ibid., p. 306.
99. Ibid.
100. Ibid.
101. Pipes, *Bolshevik Regime,* p. 27.
102. Pipes, *Russian Revolution,* pp. 638, 659.
103. During the elections to the Constituent Assembly in November 1917, the Bosheviks made their best showing in Russia's two largest cities, where they won a plurality of the vote. See ibid., p. 543.
104. Ullman, vol. 1, p. 333.
105. War Office to Poole, August 10, 1918, quoted in Ullman, vol. 1, p. 240.
106. Ibid.
107. Quoted in ibid., p. 286.
108. Lockhart, p. 309.
109. Ullman, vol. 1, p. 261.
110. Ibid., p. 263.
111. Ibid., p. 262.
112. Ibid.
113. Ibid.
114. Ibid.
115. Footman, p. 158.
116. Mawdsley, pp. 66-68.
117. See Peter Fleming, *The Fate of Admiral Kolchak,* (New York: Harcourt, Brace & World, 1963), pp. 108-11; Pipes, *Bolshevik Regime,* pp. 40-42; Kolchak's own account of the coup, which has been accepted as accurate by most historians, is in Elena Varneck and H.H. Fisher, eds., *The Testimony of Admiral Kolchak and other Siberian Materials,* (Stanford: Stanford University Press, 1935), pp. 168-77.
118. Quoted in Fleming, p. 111.
119. See Ullman, vol. 1, pp. 279-84.
120. Churchill, *Aftermath,* p. 164.
121. Peter Kenez, *Civil War in South Russia, 1918: The First Year of the Volunteer Army,* (Berkeley: University of California Press, 1971), p. 117; hereafter cited as Kenez, *Volunteer Army.*
122. For details, see ibid., pp. 96-117; General Anton Denikin, *Ocherki Russkoi Smuty* [Notes on the Russian Turmoil], (Paris and Berlin: Povolozky and Russkoye Slovo, 1921-26), vol. 2, chs. XIX-XXIV; hereafter cited as Denikin, *ORS.*

123. Kenez, *Volunteer Army,* p. 96.
124. Ibid., pp. 115–16.
125. Ibid., p. 177.
126. Churchill, *Aftermath,* p. 164.
127. Balfour, War Cabinet memorandum, November 29, 1918, reprinted in ibid., p. 165.
128. Ibid.
129. Ibid.
130. Ibid.
131. Ibid., pp. 166–67.
132. Quoted in Lloyd George, *Memoirs of the Peace Conference,* [British ed. title: *The Truth about the Peace Treaties*], vol. 1, (New Haven: Yale University Press, 1939), p. 211; hereafter cited as Lloyd George, *Peace Conference.*
133. Ibid., p. 209.
134. See, generally, Ullman, vol. 1; On Lockhart's new attitude, see Ullman, vol. 1, pp. 296–99.
135. This issue is addressed in chapter 4.
136. The politics of the White movement is discussed in some detail in chapter 4.
137. Quoted in Lloyd George, *Peace Conference,* p. 214.
138. Ibid.
139. Ibid.
140. Ibid., p. 215.
141. Ibid., p. 216.
142. See, e.g., Kennan, *Russia and the West,* p. 114, for an especially forceful assertion of this view.
143. For a more complete discussion of this issue, see Chapter 5.
144. See, e.g., Lloyd George, *Peace Conference,* pp. 240, 251.
145. Churchill, "The Bolshevik Menace," speech at the Aldwych Club, London, April 11, 1919, in James, ed., p. 2771.
146. Ibid., p. 2773.
147. Ibid.
148. Churchill, "Russia and Germany," speech at the English-Speaking Union, February 22, 1919, in ibid., p. 2672.
149. See, e.g., ibid.
150. Churchill, "Peace Policy," speech at Dundee, May 14, 1919, in ibid., p. 2783.
151. See Churchill to Lloyd George, February 21, 1919 [letter never sent], reprinted in Martin Gilbert, *Winston S. Churchill: The Stricken World, 1916–22,* (Boston: Houghton Mifflin, 1975), p. 260.
152. Churchill, *Aftermath,* p. 169.
153. Ibid.
154. Figure obtained from ibid., p. 166.
155. Ullman, vol. 2, p. 324.
156. Lloyd George, *Peace Conference,* p. 213.
157. Quoted in Gilbert, p. 264.
158. Ullman, vol. 2, pp. 359–60.
159. See ibid.
160. Curzon to Wardrop, October 2, 1919, in E.L. Woodward and Rohan Butler, eds., *Documents on British Foreign Policy, 1919–39,* Series 1, vol. III, (London: His Majesty's Stationery Office, 1949), pp. 574–75; hereafter cited as *DBFP.*
161. Curzon, statement at Cabinet meeting, December 31, 1918, quoted in Lloyd George, *Peace Conference,* p. 217.

162. Ullman, vol. 2, p. 296.
163. Denikin's ideas on autonomy are considered in chapter 4.
164. Churchill, statement at March 6, 1919 interdepartmental Foreign Office conference, quoted in Gilbert, p. 265.
165. Excerpted in Gilbert, p. 903.
166. Curzon had been involved with imperial issues related to India for almost thirty years before 1919. See Gilbert, p. 23.
167. Curzon to Lloyd George, June 8, 1917, reprinted in Gilbert, p. 25.
168. Lloyd George, *Peace Conference*, p. 218.
169. Foreign Relations of the United States, 1919, *Russia*, (Washington, D.C.: G.P.O., 1937),p.31; hereafter cited as FRUS, 1919.
170. Ibid.
171. See reports of White reactions to the proposal in ibid., e.g., pp. 35-36, 37-8, 53-54; see also Thompson, *Russia, Bolshevism, and the Versailles Peace*, pp. 119-26.
172. Georgi Chicherin, Soviet Commissar for Foreign Affairs, to the Principal Allied and Associated Governments, February 4, 1919, in ibid., p. 39.
173. Kennan, *Russia and the West*, p. 123.
174. Thompson, pp. 123-24.
175. Quoted above.
176. See Foreign Relations of the United States, *The Paris Peace Conference, 1919*, vol. III, (Washington, D.C., G.P.O., 1942-47), pp. 471-481, hereafter cited as FRUS, *Conference*; Thompson, pp. 98-99.
177. FRUS, *Conference*, vol. III, p. 1043.
178. Ibid.
179. Ibid., vol. IV, pp. 13-14.
180. Ibid., p. 14.
181. Ibid.
182. Ibid., p. 15.
183. Ibid., p. 17.
184. Lloyd George to Philip Kerr, February 16, 1919, reprinted in Lloyd George, *Peace Conference*, p. 243.
185. Ullman, vol. 2, pp. 127-28; Thompson, pp. 135-45.
186. Lloyd George, *Peace Conference*, p. 241.
187. Ullman, vol. 2, p. 120; This is not to suggest, however, that Lloyd George ever endorsed Churchill's proposals. Most likely, he simply did not anticipate the forcefulness of the war minister's presentation.
188. Churchill to Lloyd George, February 27, 1919, in Churchill, *Aftermath*, pp. 176-77.
189. Churchill to Lloyd George, March 14, 1919, in Ibid., p. 177
190. Quoted in Gilbert, p. 279.
191. This number, however, is not likely to be extremely large, since the prisoners were repatriated only gradually, and in small groups (ibid.).
192. This was the new name of the Volunteer Army.
193. Peter Kenez, *Civil War in South Russia: The Defeat of the Whites, 1919-20*, (Berkeley: University of California Press, 1977), p. 216, hereafter cited as Kenez, *Defeat of the Whites*; Kenez's figures are taken from Bolshevik sources. Denikin estimated his forces at 98,000 combat troops and those of the Reds facing him at 140,000 to 160,000; Denikin, *ORS*, vol. 5, p. 230.
194. Brinkley, *The Volunteer Army and Allied Intervention in South Russia*, pp. 212-13.
195. Ibid., p. 212.
196. Ibid., pp. 211-12.

197. Lloyd George to Philip Kerr, February 19, 1919, in Lloyd George, *Peace Confer-ence,* p. 246.
198. Lloyd George to Kerr, February 16, 1919, reprinted in Churchill, *Aftermath,* p. 175.
199. Lloyd George, speech before the House of Commons, April 16, 1919, in *DBFP,* p. 309.
200. Ibid.
201. Ibid.
202. Ibid., pp. 310-11.
203. Ibid., p. 311; The reference to the fictitious "General Kharkoff" represented a con-fusion on Lloyd George's part with the major Russian city of Kharkov. In itself meaningless, the guffaw nonetheless highlights his relative ignorance of Russia.
204. Ibid.
205. Ibid., p. 312.
206. Lloyd George to Kerr, February 19, 1919, op. cit., p. 247.
207. Arthur Link, ed., *The Deliberations of the Council of Four,* vol. 2, (Princeton: Princeton University Press, 1992), p. 483, hereafter cited as *Council of Four;* In actuality, few, if any, British representatives in Russia were prepared to go this far in their evaluations of the Bolsheviks. Most of them, in fact, were advocates of intervention.
208. Lloyd George, statement at War Cabinet meeting, August 12, 1919, quoted in Gil-bert, p. 318.
209. See, generally, Richard Ullman, *The Anglo-Soviet Accord,* (Princeton: Princeton University Press, 1973), hereafter cited as Ullman, vol. 3.
210. Gerhard Weinberg, *A World at Arms: A Global History of World War II,* (Cam-bridge: Cambridge University Press, 1994), p. 143; At the time, Churchill specu-lated, referring to the notorious French collaborator, that Lloyd George would have liked to become the British Petain (ibid.).
211. Denikin, *ORS,* vol. 4, p. 86; Churchill, *Aftermath,* p. 250; see also Mawdsley, p. 167.
212. Brinkley, p. 216.
213. Mawdsley, p. 144.
214. Churchill, *Aftermath,* p. 275; Churchill also pointed out (ibid.) that some money was actually saved on the "additional charges for storage, care, and maintenance," which this equipment would have incurred to the British had they kept it.
215. See, e.g., Pipes, *Bolshevik Regime,* p. 76.
216. Mawdsley, p. 167; Mawdsley has in mind only the south Russian theater of opera-tions, but the same reasoning applies equally well to Kolchak's forces in Siberia.
217. Ibid.
218. See Richard Luckett, *The White Generals: An Account of the White Movement and the Russian Civil War,* (New York: Viking, 1971), pp. 271-72, 280.
219. Ibid., p. 280.
220. See, e.g., ibid., pp. 275-76, 322-23.
221. Quoted above.
222. Luckett, p. 322.
223. Ibid., p. 316.
224. Ullman, vol. 2, p. 181.
225. See Gilbert, pp. 60-61, 72-74, 144-45.
226. Ullman, vol. 2, pp. 134-35.
227. Ibid., pp. 178-79.

228. Ibid., p. 135.
229. Churchill, *Aftermath*, p. 239.
230. Ullman, vol. 2, p. 180.
231. Ibid., p. 181.
232. Ibid., pp. 181-86, 188-90.
233. Ibid., pp. 196-97.
234. Mawdsley, p. 158.
235. Churchill, *Aftermath*, p. 244.
236. Ibid.
237. Mawdsley, p. 158.
238. Pipes, *Bolshevik Regime*, pp. 77-78; Mawdsley, ch. 10.
239. Mawdsley, p. 147.
240. Pipes, *Bolshevik Regime*, p. 77.
241. Lenin to E.M. Sklyansky, April 10, 1919, in Jan Meijer, ed., *The Trotsky Papers, 1917-22*, vol. 1, 1917-19, (London: Mouton, 1964), p. 344.
242. Vatsetis to Lenin, April 23, 1919, in Ibid., p. 354.
243. See *Council of Four*, vol. 2, p. 16.
244. Ibid., p. 28.
245. See text of dispatch in *DBFP*, pp. 331-32.
246. Ibid., pp. 362-64.
247. For details of the unification of the White command, see Thompson, pp. 268-77.
248. *DBFP* p. 377.
249. See e.g., Ullman, vol. 1, p. 216; Kennan, *Russia and the West*, p. 140.
250. Kolchak, speech at Ekaterinburg, April 19, 1919, in Rex A. Wade, ed., *Documents Of Soviet History*, vol. 1, *The Triumph of Bolshevism, 1917-19*, (Gulf Breeze: Academic International Press, 1991), p. 349.
251. Pipes, *Bolshevik Regime*, p. 79.
252. Kolchak, speech at Ekaterinburg, April 19, 1919, op. cit., p. 349.
253. This point is well-argued in Pipes, *Bolshevik Regime*, p. 78.
254. Mawdsley, pp. 148-55.
255. Ibid.
256. Fleming, pp. 215-16.
257. Churchill, *Aftermath*, p. 245; "Big Five" refers to the Big Four plus a Japanese representative who had signed the declaration on his country's behalf.
258. Ibid., p. 183.
259. Quoted in Gilbert, p. 316.
260. Ibid., pp. 317-18.
261. Ibid.
262. Quoted in ibid., p. 318.
263. The text of the directive is reprinted in Denikin, *ORS*, vol. 5, pp. 108-109.
264. Ibid., p. 109.
265. Minutes of the Politburo of Central Committee, October 15, 1919, in Meijer, ed., p. 686.
266. Lenin, "All Out for the Fight Against Denikin!" in Lenin, *Collected Works*, vol. 29.
267. Denikin, *ORS*, vol. 5, p. 109; On the central role of Moscow in the White strategic imagination, see also Luckett, op. cit.
268. Quoted in Gilbert, p. 327.
269. Ibid., p. 330.
270. Ibid., pp. 336-49.

271. Churchill, *Aftermath*, p. 254.
272. Ibid., pp. 254-59.
273. Pipes, *Bolshevik Regime*, pp. 91-92.
274. Marshal Carl Gustaf Mannerheim, *The Memoirs of Marshal Mannerheim*, trans. Count Eric Lewenhaupt, (London: Cassell and Co., Ltd., 1953), p. 233.
275. General Sir Hubert Gough to Balfour, July 14, 1919, in *DBFP*, p. 430; For Lloyd George's views, see below.
276. Pipes, *Bolshevik Regime*, p. 93.
277. Curzon to Mr. Bosanquet, July 16, 1919, in *DBFP*, p. 436.
278. Ullman, vol. 2, p. 260.
279. Pipes, *Bolshevik Regime*, p. 122.
280. Yudenich to Lloyd George, September 12, 1919, in *DBFP*, pp. 547-48.
281. Lloyd George, memorandum, August 24, 1919, reprinted in Gilbert, p. 324.
282. Ibid.
283. See Pipes, *Bolshevik Regime*, pp. 122-25; Luckett, pp. 314-22.
284. Figures and information on the quality of Bolshevik troops from Mawdsley, pp. 198-201.
285. Quoted in ibid., p. 202.
286. Lenin, "To the Workers and Red Army Men of Petrograd," October 17, 1919, in Lenin, *Collected Works*, vol. 30, p. 68.
287. Mawdsley, p. 198.
288. Yudenich, rebuffed by Kolchak, eventually recognized it on his own authority in October (Luckett, p. 319-20), but by then it was too late.
289. Ullman, vol. 2, p. 304.
290. Lloyd George, speech at Guildhall, November 8, 1917, excerpted in Ullman, vol. 2, p. 305.
291. Ibid., p. 306.
292. Quoted in ibid., p. 309.
293. Ambassador Davis to Secretary of State Lansing, December 3, 1919, in FRUS, 1919, p. 129.
294. C.P. Scott, recounting conversation with Lloyd George on November 30, 1919, quoted in Peter Rowland, *David Lloyd George: A Biography*, (New York: Macmillan, 1975), p. 505.
295. Pipes, *Bolshevik Regime*, p. 129.
296. See Ullman, vol. 2, p. 299.
297. Denikin, *ORS*, vol. 5, p. 172.
298. It is, perhaps, worth pointing out that Denikin's memoirs are remarkable for his willingness to admit his own mistakes, for example with respect to the internal government of the territories he occupied.
299. C.E. Bechofer, quoted in Pipes, *Bolshevik Regime*, p. 129.
300. See, e.g., Luckett, pp. 357-62; Kenez, *Defeat of the Whites*, ch. 9; Pipes, *Bolshevik Regime*, pp. 132-34.
301. Ullman, vol. 2, p. 302.
302. Ibid.
303. Lloyd George to Churchill, September 22, 1919, reprinted in Gilbert, p. 332.
304. Churchill to Lloyd George, September 22, 1919, reprinted in ibid., p. 334.
305. Henry Kissinger, *Diplomacy*, (New York: Simon & Schuster, 1994), p. 443.
306. Churchill, *Aftermath*, pp. 273-74.
307. Denikin, *ORS*, p. 173.

3

"Why Not Save Siberia?"[1]
The Development of U.S. Policy

*"The treatment accorded Russia by her sister
nations in the months to come will be the acid
test of their good will, of their comprehension
of her needs as distinguished from their own
interests, and of their intelligent and unselfish
sympathy."*[2]

—Woodrow Wilson, Fourteen Points Address,
January 8, 1918

The Bolshevik coup of November 1917 and the imminent withdrawal
of Russia from the war did not inspire the same desperation in the United
States as it did in Britain and France. While American leaders were certainly perturbed that Russia's power might no longer be available, they
were relatively confident about their own country's ability to offset the
loss to the Allies. America's resources were vast and mostly untapped.
Moreover, the American army, unlike the British and the French, was
mostly not yet deployed on the Western Front, and so was not immediately threatened with heavy losses and possible destruction in the German offensives of spring 1918. To be sure, the Americans certainly hoped
that Russia could somehow be persuaded to reestablish the Eastern Front
against Germany, but this was not as much of an overriding concern for
them as for the European Allies.

On the other hand, the fall of the Russian Provisional Government was
deeply disconcerting to President Wilson and his liberal advisers from an
ideological point of view. While the replacement of the tsarist autocracy
by the liberal-socialist Provisional Government had been welcomed by
public opinion throughout the Allied world, nowhere was the enthusi-

asm greater than in the United States. In fact, the February Revolution had been one of the events that influenced Wilson to finally make the decision to ask Congress for a declaration of war in April 1917. From the Wilsonian liberal point of view, the end of autocracy in Russia constituted "the removal of the blight that had burdened the Allied cause since the beginning of the war."[3] Now the war could legitimately be seen as a war of democracy against despotism. As Wilson famously put it in his April 2, 1917 declaration of war message to Congress, Russia was now "a fit partner for a league of honor."[4]

Few in the United States had understood the precarious position of the Provisional Government. The Root Commission, a delegation of American political and civic leaders that visited Russia during the Kerensky period had come back with generally favorable impressions.[5] President Wilson and his most influential adviser, Colonel Edward M. House, were also optimistic about Kerensky's prospects.

The one important member of the administration who had entertained doubts about Kerensky's viability was Secretary of State Robert Lansing, who on August 9 had written an insightful memorandum criticizing the Root Commission's report and arguing that Kerensky was likely doomed because "[h]e compromises too much with the radical element of the Revolution."[6] Alone among the leading American officials, Lansing understood that Kerensky's acceptance of the extralegal powers of the Petrograd Soviet and his refusal to crush the Bolsheviks when he had the chance to do so were likely to spell his doom.[7]

In the aftermath of the Bolshevik coup, it was Lansing who devoted more time to Russian affairs than any other high official and attempted to develop a new Russian policy for the United States. Lansing's December 2, 1917 memorandum embodied the views he presented to Wilson at this time. The secretary of state confessed that "[t]he Russian situation is to me an unanswered and unanswerable riddle."[8] Nonetheless, he attempted to answer it. The "one thing" of which Lansing was totally "convinced" was that "it would be unwise to give recognition to Lenin, Trotsky, and their crew of radicals."[9] In part, this was because "recognition of the Bolsheviks... would not be the slightest inducement for them to continue the war. If they should continue it," Lansing accurately predicted, "it will only be because their power is menaced."[10] However, Lansing's advocacy of nonrecognition was based on ideological considerations as well as expediency. Like Churchill in Britain, Lansing took the ideological pretension of the Bolsheviks seriously:

I cannot see how this element which is hostile to the very idea of nationality can claim that they are the government of a nation or expect to be recognized as such. They are avowedly opposed to every government on earth; they openly propose to excite revolutions in all countries against existing governments; they are as hostile to democracy as they are to autocracy. If we should recognize them in Russia, we would encourage them and their followers in other lands. That would be a serious error.... The correct policy for a government which believes in political institutions as they now exist and based on nationality and private property is to leave these dangerous idealists alone and have no direct dealings with them. To recognize them would give them an exalted idea of their own power, make them more insolent and impossible, and win their contempt, not their friendship.[11]

In any case, Lansing believed that "Russia as a nation will never come under the Petrograd Bolsheviki. They are far more likely to break up into separate units claiming independence. We are apt to see several distinct states each maintaining its own affairs."[12] Lansing also accurately predicted that Bolshevik policies would result in economic collapse, famine, and civil war, though he failed to predict the eventual victory of the Bolsheviks who, he thought, were likely to be defeated.[13] It was in this memorandum, also, that he foresaw that "the Russian 'Terror' will far surpass in brutality and destruction of life and property the Terror of the French Revolution."[14]

Although he fell prey to a few misconceptions, notably in his assertion that "[t]he Bolsheviki are anarchists rather than Socialists,"[15] Lansing's analysis of the Russian situation was remarkably accurate, particularly when we consider that Lansing had little specialized knowledge of Russia and that the information coming in from American representatives in that country was often fragmentary, outdated, and inaccurate.[16] Unlike many British officials, such as his counterpart Lord Balfour, Lansing recognized that there was little or nothing the Allies could do to convince the Bolsheviks to stay in the war. He accurately forecast the likely immediate consequences of Bolshevik domestic policies and grasped the essence of their revolutionary approach to international relations.

For these views, Lansing has been condemned by some historians as the bete noir of American interventionist policy.[17] However, his staunch opposition to Bolshevism did *not*, in fact, lead Lansing to advocate intervention calculated to overthrow the Bolshevik regime. In his December 2 memorandum, Lansing did state the view that "[t]he only possible remedy would be for a strong commanding personality who would be able to gather a disciplined military force sufficiently strong to restore order and maintain a government," and took note of the activities of the nascent anti-Bolshevik movement in Russia.[18] But he also stated that "I am opposed to giving these leaders any open support, as their enterprise seems to me too uncertain and the whole situation too chaotic to put faith in any one group or faction."[19] In conclusion, Lansing recommended a wait-and-see approach to Russia:

> 'Do nothing' should be our policy until the black period of terrorism comes to an end and the rising tide of blood has run its course. It cannot last forever, but Russia will sink lower before better days come.[20]

Thus, the single most anti-Bolshevik member of the administration recommended what was essentially a policy of noninvolvement until such time as the Bolshevik regime should collapse of its own accord. President Wilson endorsed Lansing's approach of combining nonrecognition with nonintervention.[21]

A few days later, on December 10, Lansing wrote a memorandum for the President in which he correctly concluded that "the Bolsheviki are determined to prevent Russia from taking further part in the war" and expressed the fear that "the elimination of Russia as a fighting force will prolong the war for two or three years, with corresponding demand on this country for men and money."[22] The Secretary of State realized that "the Russian armies might be reorganized and become an important factor in the war" only if "the Bolsheviki domination" were "broken," and expressed the hope that this could be achieved through the efforts of "the group of general officers with General Kaledin, the hetman of the Don Cossacks."[23] It will be recalled that Kaledin's force was the nascent anti-Bolshevik movement financed by the British in late 1917 and early 1918. However, the only measure of support Lansing recommended was a message of encouragement to be transmitted to Kaledin, a message which was never sent.[24] On December 12, Lansing did, however, prepare a telegram, approved by Wilson, in which he advocated the release of U.S. funds to the British and French so that the latter could use them to help finance Kaledin's efforts.[25]

This document is cited by William A. Williams, the dean of left-wing historiography of the intervention, as conclusive proof of an early U.S. decision to support efforts to overthrow the Bolshevik regime on grounds of ideological hostility.[26] However, Williams' position is based on a fairly crude misrepresentation of the telegram's text. Williams quotes Lansing as writing that "[a]ny movement [against the Bolsheviks]...should be encouraged even though its success is only a possibility [bracketed material inserted by Williams]."[27] What the telegram written by Lansing and approved by Wilson actually said is this:

> In view of the policy being pursued by Lenine and Trotsky which if continued will remove Russia as a factor in the war and may even make her resources available to the Central Powers, any movement tending to prevent such a calamity should be encouraged even though its success is only a possibility.[28]

As the real text of the message indicates, Lansing's reason for advocating support of Kaledin, despite his antipathy to the Bolsheviks, was the fear that Russia would withdraw from the war. Moreover, Lansing did not actually state that the goal of the assistance was the overthrow of the Bolshevik regime per se. Rather, it was to "strengthen a movement which seems to provide the best possibility of retaining a Russian army in the field."[29] If that goal could only be achieved by the overthrow of the Bolsheviks, the secretary of state implicitly concluded, then so be it. But he was far from recommending a course of intervention based solely, or even primarily, on ideological hostility.

In any, case, no U.S. funds ever actually made their way to Kaledin, as a result of technical difficulties involved in the plan to transfer them through the British and French.[30] Moreover, the fact that neither Wilson nor Lansing made any substantial effort to promote active intervention for some eight months after the December 12 telegram suggests that their interest in such a course was hardly strong.

It is also important to note that, though Wilson certainly disliked Bolshevism and saw its establishment of a one-party dictatorship as a gross perversion of the February Revolution, he did not necessarily take as hard a line against it as advocated by Lansing. In fact, Lansing had only very limited influence on foreign policy in an administration where the President's ear was often almost totally monopolized by Colonel House, Wilson's closest friend, unofficial adviser, and personal diplomatic representative.[31] Unfortunately, this crucial point, well known to Wilson scholars, has been neglected by virtually all the major studies of the intervention.[32] Throughout 1918–19, House was a consistent opponent of anti-Bolshevik intervention and his stance clearly had an impact on the president, though much more so in the first part of this period than later, when House largely turned his attention to other issues.[33]

In a personal letter to Representative Frank Clark (D-Florida), written on November 13, Wilson seemed to suggest that Bolshevism would probably collapse of its own accord, without the need for intervention. "I have not lost faith in the Russian outcome by any means," he averred, "Russia... will no doubt have to go through deep waters but she will come out upon firm land on the other side and her great people... will in my opinion take their proper place in the world."[34] On January 1, 1918, Wilson sent Lansing a copy of a message from the British Foreign Office which described the two-track British policy of wooing both the Bolsheviks and anti-Bolsheviks for the sake of mobilizing them against Germany to whatever extent might be possible.[35] Wilson informed Lansing that he considered the British approach "a sensible program" and asked the secretary of state for his "opinion as to the most feasible and least objectionable way (if there is any) in which we could establish similar unofficial relations with the Bolscheviki."[36] While this statement and others like it should not be taken as an indication of any benevolent sentiments towards the Bolsheviks on Wilson's part,[37] it certainly indicated at least a limited willingness to cooperate with them in some, as yet indeterminate, way.

Wilson's major statement on Russia policy in his January 8, 1918 Fourteen Points Address was highly ambiguous, a fact reflected in the numerous contradictory interpretations of it by historians. The address, like many of Wilson's actions during the war years, had been heavily influenced by Colonel House.[38] With respect to Russia, House believed that "literally nothing should be done further than an expression of sympathy.... for Russia's efforts to weld herself into a virile democracy, and to proffer our financial, industrial and moral support in every way possible."[39] House did not specify whether the "virile democracy" he had in mind was the Bolshevik regime and whether that regime should therefore be the intended recipient of the "support" he advocated.

The Fourteen Points speech itself was almost as ambiguous as House's position. Nonetheless, certain conclusions can be made. Point 6 of the fourteen reaffirmed Wilson's long-standing support for Russia's territorial integrity and "independent determination of her own political development."[40] Wilson also endorsed the Bolshevik calls for a statement of war aims and a peace based on "self-determination" that they had put forward in their negotiations with the Central Powers at Brest-Litovsk. However, in doing so, he carefully attributed these demands not to the Bolsheviks but to "the voice of the Russian people."[41]

Here, it must be recalled that the demand for a peace based on self-determination and no annexations had been the avowed peace program not only of the Bolsheviks but of most the non-Bolshevik Russian left, including the Provisional Government under Kerensky. Wilson himself had long advocated it. The difference between Wilson and Kerensky on the one hand and Lenin and Trotsky on the other was that the former believed that such a peace could only be achieved by defeating the Central Powers, not by compromising with them from a position of weakness. Nothing in the Fourteen Points speech suggests that Wilson was prepared to back down from this stance. Indeed, his reiteration of American determination to fight until victory and "stand together until the end" with the Allies constituted an implicit rebuke of the Bolshevik policy of seeking a separate peace.[42] Thus, when Wilson spoke of his sympathy for the peace program of the "Russian people," this did not imply any sympathy for the Bolsheviks per se.

Similarly, the offers of assistance to Russia he proffered were directed not to the Bolshevik regime, but also to the "people." "Whether their present leaders believe it or not," the president exclaimed, "it is our heartfelt desire...that some way may be opened whereby we may be privileged to assist the people of Russia to attain their utmost hope of liberty and ordered peace."[43] This passage clearly draws a distinction between the "present leaders" of Russia—the Bolsheviks—and those whom Wilson proposed to aid. Thus, it is wrong to suggest, as Betty Miller Unterberger does, that Wilson "seemed to hold out the hope of American assistance to Russia's present rulers."[44]

It is even more misleading for Williams to claim that "Wilson viewed the Bolsheviks as...legitimate 'Russian representatives'" and that the Fourteen Points represented "a rare occasion when Wilson's sympathy with the deep urge for economic and social reform actually influenced a policy statement."[45] In Williams' view, Wilson's supposed recognition that the Bolsheviks represented the legitimate aspirations of the Russian people make his later decision in favor of intervention all the more distasteful.[46] However, Wilson never conceded any such thing. Following the lead of Colonel House, he merely expressed sympathy for and offered assistance to the "Russian people," without taking an unambiguous stance on the Bolshevik regime, which, however, he clearly disliked. At most, as N. Gordon Levin puts it, he *may* have hoped for "an absorption of Leninism into a pro-war consensus of democratic-nationalism" which, Levin concludes, would have excluded the prospect of a continuation of the Bolshevik dictatorship as it then existed.[47] Levin's conjecture seems reasonable, but there is no unambiguous documentary evidence that Wilson went even this far. In any event, this hope, assuming it ever existed in Wilson's mind at all, began to dim as the Bolsheviks' desire to make a separate peace and the tyrannical nature of their regime became increasingly clear.[48]

In the meantime, however, Wilson and Lansing refused the earliest in a long series of British requests to participate in intervention in Siberia.[49] As we saw in chapter 2, these British efforts were motivated primarily by wartime military considerations. "[A]ny foreign intervention in Russian affairs would," said the State Department's official response to the British note, "be most inopportune" because it would not "be welcomed by the people of Russia" and, in any case, there was still "hope of a change for the better to be brought about without foreign intervention."[50] Wilson would reject a long series of Allied requests of this sort right up until the final decision to intervene in July 1918.[51] The president's military advisers did not share the British and French hope that the Eastern Front could be reestablished by means of intervention,[52] and Wilson and House also feared that Japanese involvement in Siberia might discredit the Allied cause in Russia. Moreover, in view of the longstanding Japanese-American rivalry in East Asia, they were suspicious of that country's motives.[53] Since everyone recognized that Japan would probably provide the bulk of any intervening force, this latter point became an increasingly important issue.

House firmly believed that "the proposed Japanese action in Siberia may be the greatest misfortune that has yet befallen the Allies."[54] He feared that Japanese intervention would "mean a serious lowering, if not actual loss, of our moral position in the eyes of our own peoples and of the whole world."[55] In addition, he doubted that Japanese intervention would be well received by the Russians, particularly since "[t]he race question...will be sharply emphasized and an attempt made to show that we are using a yellow race to destroy a white one."[56] President Wilson accepted most of House's reasoning and the note he issued in response to Allied requests for Japanese intervention on March 5 reflected his influence.[57] Wilson also rejected calls for the use of American troops.

Even as Wilson continued to pursue the dual policy of nonrecognition of the Bolshevik regime and nonintervention in Russian affairs, his earlier instructions to seek an unofficial channel of communications with the Bolsheviks was belatedly carried out in Moscow. During the winter and spring of 1918, Colonel Raymond Robins, head of the American Red Cross mission in Russia, conducted a series of unofficial negotiations with the Bolsheviks that closely paralleled R.H. Bruce Lockhart's similar efforts on the part of the British. The two men, in fact, knew each other and worked together to promote Allied recognition of the Bolshevik regime and cooperation with it against the Germans.[58]

Robins was even more deluded about Soviet intentions than Lockhart had been. He was also much more a Bolshevik sympathizer than the British diplomat. Upon returning to the United States, Robins so skillfully dissembled about his views that even the meticulous George F. Kennan concludes that "Robins' feelings with respect to the Soviet government did not rest on any partiality to socialism as a doctrine or on any lack of appreciation...for the values of the American social and economic system."[59] However, his activities while in Russia suggest a very different conclusion. In a personal letter to Lenin, for example, Robins expressed his admiration for the Bolshevik leader in no uncertain terms:

> Your prophetic insight and genius of leadership have enabled the Soviet Power to become consolidated throughout Russia and I am confident that this new creative organ of the democratic life of mankind will inspire and advance the cause of liberty throughout the world.[60]

Even the sympathetic Lockhart recalled that Robins was "an anti-capitalist" and "a worshipper of great men" whose "imagination" had been "captured" by Lenin.[61] Lockhart also pointed out that Robins "knew no Russian and little of Russia" and was dependent for all his information on Alexander Gumberg, a Russian-born American agent of the Bolsheviks.[62] Thus, Robins' ideological predisposition to favor the Bolsheviks was surely reinforced by the fact that nearly all of his information on conditions in Russia and Bolshevik foreign policy came from Bolshevik sources. These were surely among the reasons why he persisted in his illusions even after the Treaty of Brest-Litovsk, signed on March 3, made Bolshevik intentions brutally clear and lent additional urgency to Allied calls for intervention.

In later years, once the "Red Scare" of 1919–20 had cooled off, Robins repeatedly flaunted his pro-Soviet sympathies. In 1933, he was granted an honorary audience by Stalin, and he later eulogized the Soviet dictator.[63] Perhaps his primary historical significance is that he was among the first of a long line of Western intellectuals who, without actually joining any Communist party, became "fellow travelers" sympathetic to the Soviet regime and hostile to nearly all efforts to oppose it.[64]

Fundamentally, Robins' mission failed for the same reasons as Lockhart's did. While Lenin was more than happy to accept any American military and economic assistance that might be offered and even to grant concessions to American investors to further these ends,[65] he was not prepared to reenter the war against Germany or aid in any Allied efforts to reestablish an Eastern Front unless the Germans themselves broke their truce with the Bolsheviks.[66] Meanwhile, Lenin and Trotsky did their best to feed Robins' and Lockhart's hopes and thereby forestall Allied intervention.[67] In addition, Bolshevik ideological intransigence would likely have made any long-term cooperation impossible except on a very limited basis which would ultimately have benefited the Soviet regime at the expense of both the West and its own people.[68] Lenin was always willing to take something for nothing or for very little, but at no time was he prepared to make fundamental changes in the Soviet domestic or foreign policy agenda in exchange for improved relations with the West.[69]

However, it is also important to note that Wilson and Lansing, unlike their British counterparts, were not prepared to provide assistance to the Bolsheviks even if the latter *had* been willing to reenter the war against Germany. On February 19, they jointly rejected as "out of the question" a French proposal to "give the Bolsheviki help in money and material" if they were willing to "resist the German menace and defend Russia against German aggression."[70] Lansing and, to a lesser extent, Wilson, were deeply hostile to Bolshevism, but were not prepared to accept intervention.

Wilson did, however, begin to show an interest in the various small anti-Bolshevik movements springing up in Siberia. On April 18, he asked Lansing for a "memorandum containing all that we know about these several *nuclei* of self-governing authority that seem to be springing up in Siberia. It would afford me a great deal of satisfaction to get behind the most nearly representative of them, if it can indeed draw leadership and control to itself."[71] Later, in May, he asked the secretary of state to "follow very attentively what [General Grigori] Semenov," a minor anti-Bolshevik Cossack leader in eastern Siberia, "is accomplishing and whether there is any legitimate way in which we can assist."[72]

These two documents are often viewed as important evidence of Wilson's willingness to support the White movement by means of intervention.[73] They do indeed suggest that he hoped for the overthrow of the

Bolsheviks. However, Wilson made little effort to follow up these inquiries. Moreover, there is no evidence that he considered military intervention or even large-scale provision of supplies to be one of the "legitimate ways in which we can assist." In fact, the May 20 letter requesting information on Semenov notes, apparently with approval, the president's military advisers' conclusion that "there is no sufficient military force, in Japan, or elsewhere, to do anything effective in Siberia."[74] At most, it seems reasonable to believe that Wilson hoped that the Whites might be able to prevail of their own accord, after which the United States could aid them in setting up a government and fighting Germany. This may have been the import of his statement that he would only support a Siberian White movement that could "draw leadership and control to itself."

Fundamentally, the Wilson administration clearly wished to see the end of the Bolshevik regime. But it was unwilling to do very much to help bring about this happy outcome. This was to remain the tragic flaw in American policy throughout virtually the entire period of the Russian Civil War. Meanwhile, by rejecting Allied proposals for intervention throughout the winter and spring of 1918, Wilson lost the chance to strike at the Bolsheviks while the latter were at their weakest.

In addition to examining the motives of Wilson and Lansing, William A. Williams and other scholars intent on proving that the U.S. was irremediably hostile to the Bolsheviks have attempted to demonstrate that U.S. diplomats stationed in Russia in the winter and spring of 1918 were constantly plotting against the new would-be government of Russia. There is no doubt that such officials as Ambassador David Francis and Maddin Summers, the U.S. consul in Moscow, disliked the Bolsheviks and were more inclined to support Allied proposals for intervention than their superiors in Washington. Summers even supported intervention as early as February, and his goal was clearly the overthrow of the Bolsheviks rather than simply opposition to the Germans.[75] On February 24, Francis recommended the "immediate possession of Vladivostok, Murmansk, [and] Archangel."[76] But this was only because he believed that the terms of peace about to be signed at Brest-Litovsk "make Russia a German province with good prospect of becoming an Ally."[77] Earlier Francis presented evidence that the Bolsheviks had taken money from the Germans for the purpose of undermining the Russian war effort—the famous Sisson documents.[78] While Francis' belief that the Bolsheviks were acting in the German interest has often been derided as foolish,[79] recent evidence suggests that the documents he cited actually presented a fairly accurate, though over-drawn, picture of the German-Bolshevik relationship.[80] Moreover, as we saw in chapter 1, Francis did not believe that the Bolsheviks were totally pliable agents of the Germans; rather, he viewed them as cooperating with Germany to serve their own ideological purposes, a view of the situation which was essentially correct.[81]

In Williams' view, however, "[t]he primary objective of Ambassador Francis was the destruction of the Bolshevik Government, and his negotia-tions via Robins...were a blind to cover this goal."[82] However, once again, Williams' position is based on a highly dubious use of documents. The only evidence he cites to support his claim is a March 29 dispatch from Francis to Washington in which Francis authorized two of Robins' assistants to aid Trotsky in the formation of an army to oppose the Germans. According to Williams, "Francis authorized Ruggles and Riggs to work for the creation of an army, but only so that it could, 'by proper methods' of course, be 'taken from Bolshevik control'."[83] The parts of the sentence in question left out by Williams reveal Francis' "primary purpose" to be very different from that posited by the historian. Here it is in full:

> My (real) and strictly confidential reason [for promoting Robins' efforts] is that army so organized can by proper methods be taken from Bolshevik control and *used against the Germans,* and even against its creators *if prove to be German allies.* (Emphasis mine)[84]

Clearly, Francis, for all his dislike of the Bolsheviks, was thinking in terms of strictly military aims, a point obscured by Williams' selective quotation of his despatch.[85] Williams also makes much of Francis' re-fusal to reveal his reasoning to Robins and his aides.[86] However, this de-cision is quite understandable in view of Robins' close relationship with Gumberg, whose status as a Bolshevik agent was well known to the Ameri-can diplomatic community in Russia.[87] When Francis finally came out unequivocally in favor of overthrowing the Bolsheviks in May, it was only after the failure of efforts to obtain an intervention by Bolshevik in-vitation.[88] In any case, Francis' and Summers' recommendations for in-tervention were never acted upon by Lansing and Wilson, and there is little evidence that either was substantially influenced by them.

By late May, however, Wilson's anti-interventionist stance was begin-ning to soften. In a May 29 interview with Sir William Wiseman, the Brit-ish special representative in the United States, Wilson continued to insist that "the schemes for [intervention] put forward were...impracticable and would have the opposite effect to that desired."[89] However, Wilson also "remarked that he would go as far as intervention against the wishes of the Russian people—knowing that it was eventually for their good—providing he thought the scheme had any practical chance of success."[90] This shows, contrary to the views of Unterberger and Williams,[91] that Wilson did not suffer from any scruples about intervention based on any supposed right of self-determination embodied by the Bolshevik regime.[92] His main reason for rejecting the Allied proposal reiterated by Wiseman was the prominent role of the Japanese, who he felt, were likely to alienate the Russian population:

> If we could have put a large British-American force into Vladivostock and advanced along the [Trans]Siberian railroad, we might have rallied the Russian people to assist in the defence of their country. But if we relied mainly on Japanese military assistance, we should rally the Russians against us, excepting for a small reactionary body who would join anybody to destroy the Bolsheviki.... [T]he Germans [would then be] in a position where they could organize Russian in a national movement against Japan. If that was done he would not be surprised to see Russian soldiers with the Germans on the Western Front.[93]

Thus, Wilson's opposition to intervention had, by late May, softened into a mere matter of contingent circumstances which he feared would make it ineffective. His support of intervention with a "practicable chance of success," however, was based more on wartime imperatives than on a desire to destroy the Bolsheviks per se. Thus, he told Wiseman that the goal of a successful intervention would be to rally "the Russian people to assist in the defence of their country" against Germany, and his opposition to a dominant Japanese role was based not on fear of strengthening the Bolsheviks relative to the Whites but on the possibility that it would strengthen the Germans relative to the Allies. There is no doubt that anti-Bolshevism influenced his thinking, but it played a clearly secondary role.

Even as Wilson continued to oppose intervention in Siberia, the administration became somewhat more amenable to Allied proposals for intervention in Murmansk and Archangel. On May 11, Lansing told Lord Reading, the British ambassador, that "intervention at Murmansk and Archangel would receive far more favorable consideration on our part than intervention in Siberia, for the reason that we could understand the military advantage of the former but had been unable, thus far to find any advantage in sending troops into Siberia."[94] That the "military advantage"

Lansing had in mind was an advantage against the Germans rather than against the Bolsheviks is shown by the fact that one of the reasons he cited for making a distinction between the northern Russian and Siberian projects was that "the communications which had been received from Trotsky as to his favorable attitude towards intervention might apply only to the northern part and not to the Far East."[95] It was during this period that Lloyd George and Balfour, under the influence of Lockhart's reports, came to believe that it might be possible to secure an invitation for Allied intervention from the Bolsheviks.[96] Thus, even Lansing, the most anti-Bolshevik member of the administration, viewed the issue of intervention primarily through the prism of wartime military considerations. In making this distinction between the military value of the two areas, Lansing and other American officials were influenced by the fear that German forces might capture Murmansk and Archangel, along with the vast stores of Allied supplies located there.[97]

In his reply to Lansing's note on his meetings with Reading, Wilson agreed that a distinction should be made between the two parts of Russia, but worried that it might be "unwise" to divert any forces to Murmansk from the Western Front.[98] He, unlike the secretary of state, was not yet entirely sold on the decision to intervene in northern Russia, a point generally ignored in the historical literature.[99] After a conference with the president on June 1, Lansing did persuade him to agree to send troops to Murmansk, but only "provided that General Foch [the Allied commander in chief] approved the diversion of troops and the necessary shipping for that purpose from those now going to France."[100]

It will be recalled that Wilson's objections to intervention in Siberia related primarily to the fear that the preponderance of Japanese troops in the intervening force would tend to drive the Russian population into the arms of the Germans. By June this difficulty seemed to be removed by the victories of the Czech Legion.[101]

On June 13, Paul Reinsch, the American minister in China sent a message to Lansing suggesting that the Czech Legion be retained in Russia for the purpose of holding Siberia against German influence, which it was feared might be established through the activities of the many German and Austro-Hungarian prisoners of war kept there. "[I]t would be a serious mistake," Reinsch contended, "to remove the Czechoslovak troops from Siberia. With only slight countenance and support they could control all of Siberia against the Germans.... Their removal would greatly benefit Germany and further discourage Russia. If they were not in Siberia it would be worth while to bring them there from a distance."[102] The Czechs, he emphasized, "are sympathetic to the Russian population, [and] eager to be accessories to the Allied cause.[103] Here, therefore, was an intervention force which would not alienate the Russian population as Wilson and House believed the Japanese would if allowed to provide the bulk of the Allied forces.

Wilson immediately seized on this point. "There seems to emerge from this suggestion," he wrote in a commentary on Reinsch's report which he sent to Lansing, "the shadow of a plan that might be worked, with Japanese and other assistance. *These people are the cousins of the Russians"* (emphasis mine).[104] This note, written on June 17, 1918, represents the first moment when Wilson expressed support for an intervention in Siberia, a project he had previously steadfastly opposed. Two points are critical. First, it is clear that Wilson intended not just to rescue the Czechs, as Unterberger contends,[105] but to use them to hold Siberia on behalf of the Allies. On the other hand, the purpose of this action was primarily to hold Siberia against the Germans, not, contra Williams, to achieve the overthrow of the Bolshevik regime, at least not in the first instance.

The Czech revolt was therefore the decisive factor that tilted Wilson in favor of intervention. On July 6, a cabinet meeting held at the White house formally decided to send 7000 troops to Vladivostok, provided that the Japanese agreed to send a similar number.[106] The cabinet continued to reject the Allied arguments for the reestablishment of the Eastern Front as "physically impossible,"[107] despite the recent decision of the Allied Supreme War Council to pursue such an outcome.[108] The purpose of intervention was explained as follows:

.... [T]he present situation of the Czecho-Slovaks requires this Government and other governments to make an effort to aid those at Vladivostok in forming a junction with their compatriots in Western Siberia; and that this Government on sentimental grounds and because of the effect upon the friendly Slavs everywhere would be subject to criticism if it did not make this effort and would doubtless be held responsible if they were defeated by lack of such effort.[109]

The word "Bolshevik" is not even mentioned in Lansing's memorandum describing the cabinet's decision, and the secret nature of the memorandum suggests that this omission was not the result of any public relations maneuver, whether to influence American opinion or Russian. This is not to deny that most members of the administration disliked Bolshevism, hoped for its overthrow, and even believed that the intervention might indirectly serve this purpose. But it was not the reason why the intervention was decided upon and it never came to dominate Wilsonian policy towards Russia.

The best known and most authoritative statement of the reasons for intervention in Siberia was the July 17 aide-memoire to the Allied powers, drafted by Wilson himself. In this document, Wilson averred that "military intervention there would add to the present sad confusion in Russia rather than cure it, injure her rather than help her, and that it would be of no advantage in the prosecution of our main design, to win the war against Germany."[110] For these reasons, Wilson concluded, the U.S. government "cannot...take part in such intervention or sanction it in principle."[111] Why, then, the dispatch of U.S. troops to Siberia and northern Russia, where Wilson had finally agreed to send troops after the receipt of the necessary assurances from Foch?[112] "Military action is admissible in Russia," Wilson explained,

> ...only to help the Czecho-Slovaks consolidate their forces and get into successful cooperation with their Slavic kinsmen and to steady any efforts at self-government and self-defence in which the Russians themselves may be willing to accept assistance.[113]

This "assistance" was to include only very limited use of American troops:

> Whether from Vladivostock or from Murmansk and Archangel, the only legitimate object for which American or allied troops can be employed...is to guard military stores which may subsequently be needed by Russian forces and to render such aid as may be acceptable to the Russians in their own self-defence. For helping the Czecho-Slovaks there is immediate necessity and sufficient justification.... [T]he Government of the United States is glad to contribute the small force at its disposal for that purpose. It yields, also, to the judgment of the Supreme Command in the matter of establishing a small force at Murmansk to guard the military stores at Kola and to make it safe for Russian forces to come together in organized bodies in the north. But it...can go not further than these modest and experimental plans. It is not in a position, and has no expectation of being in a position, to take part in organized intervention in adequate force from either Vladivostock or Murmansk and Archangel.[114]

Thus, Wilson, seems to have hoped that intervention in Siberia and northern Russia would improve the position of the Czechs and lead to a rallying of Russian forces to the Allied cause, the latter circumstance possibly leading to the overthrow of the Bolsheviks. However, he had no desire to use U.S. troops to actively fight the Bolsheviks and the memorandum does not mention their overthrow as a goal of U.S. policy. In fact, as in the cabinet discussion of July 6, the Bolsheviks are not mentioned at all.

In sum, Wilson's goals appear to have been twofold: First, he wanted to "help the Czechs consolidate their forces" in order to control Siberia against the Germans. Second, and less clearly, he hoped that intervention would lead to a spontaneous rallying of the Russian population against Germany and to the at least partial reestablishment of the Eastern Front— not by the Allied intervention force, but by the Russians themselves. This explains his references to "mak[ing] it safe for Russian forces to come together in organized bodies in the north" and to guarding "military stores which may subsequently be needed by Russian forces."

In the final analysis, therefore, Wilson's key motive was to aid the Czechs and indirectly promote indigenous Russian efforts to combat Germany. It is true, as N. Gordon Levin persuasively argues, that the administration saw the Bolsheviks as so closely linked to the Germans that any action against the latter would necessarily work against the interests of the former.[115] In this sense, the intervention was surely anti-Bolshevik in nature. However, the reason for intervening in a way which might harm the Bolsheviks was not hostility to them per se—though such hostility was undeniably present—but the fact that the Bolshevik regime was serving the interests of the Germans and attempting to repress the Czechs.

The belief that the Bolsheviks were serving German interests was strengthened by repeated reports of their use of armed German and Austrian prisoners of war to fight the Czechs.[116] The Soviets did, in fact, provide arms to prisoners of war, though it is difficult to determine exactly how many.[117] In April, American and British officers associated with Lockhart and Robins' effort to promote recognition of the Bolsheviks were invited by the Bolsheviks to Siberia to investigate the prisoner issue. Not surprisingly, their report concluded that only a few prisoners had been armed and that they posed no threat to Allied interests.[118] This document, known as the Webster-Hicks report, after its two authors, is sometimes cited to "prove" that the Allies knew that there was no threat from German prisoners of war in Siberia. However, Webster and Hicks were only able to see what the Bolsheviks showed them; as a result, they probably seriously undercounted the number of armed prisoners.[119] In addition, their connection to Robins, with his strong pro-Bolshevik bias, led to questions about the report's objectivity.[120] Thus, there is reason to believe that the prisoner-of-war issue continued to stoke American suspicions of Bolshevik-German ties, and probably influenced the decision to intervene.[121] However, it is not true that U.S. officials believed that the armed prisoners "were the only opponents by whom the Czechs were confronted."[122] In a July 10 dispatch to the U.S. ambassador to Japan, for example, Lansing noted that Czech troops near Vladivostok "have now defeated several thousand Red Guards *and* war prisoners [emphasis mine]."[123]

U.S. officials, both those in Russia and those in Washington did *not*, contrary to the arguments of Christopher Lasch,[124] believe that the Bolsheviks were German agents in the narrow sense of the term.[125] However, they did recognize, as did Bolshevik leaders such as Lenin, that a confluence of interests existed between the Germans and Bolsheviks that led the two sides to cooperate. To borrow a phrase from Professor Levin, Bolshevik policies were seen as "objectively of benefit to the interests of German imperialism in Russia"—even though the Bolsheviks themselves may not have had any pro-German sympathies.[126] As Ambassador Francis put it, "Lenin, [and] Trotsky may possibly not have been Germany's agents continuously but if had been could not have played more successfully into Germany's hands."[127] Given the vast benefits which Germany derived from the Bolshevik decision to sign a separate peace, this view was surely close to the truth, much closer than many subsequent writers are willing to allow.[128]

In addition to anti-Bolshevism, helping the Czechs, and opposing the Germans, opposition to the growth of Japanese influence has sometimes been cited as a motive for the U.S. intervention. Betty Unterberger has even argued that it was the primary one.[129] However, while some members of the administration—particularly, as we have seen, Colonel House, were suspicious of Japanese motives, there is little evidence that the decision to send U.S. troops was taken in order to provide a restraint on the Japanese. Japanese ambitions are not mentioned as an important factor in any of the documents in which Wilson and Lansing laid out their positions on intervention in the crucial days of June and July. Indeed, in most of them, notably the memorandum of the secret July 6 cabinet meeting at which intervention was formally decided on, they are not mentioned at all. Later on, during the intervention itself, Japanese ambitions became more of a concern for the Americans, particularly after it became apparent that the Japanese had no intention of abiding by their agreement to send a contingent of only about 7000 troops, and their determination to seize de facto control of Eastern Siberia became more evident. However, concern about the Japanese was not a decisive factor in the original decision to intervene.

If Wilson therefore decided on an intervention that would be highly limited in scope and would not attempt to overthrow the Bolsheviks directly, this was not because the administration had not been presented with other alternatives. As we have seen, Maddin Summers, the U.S. consul in Moscow, had advocated anti-Bolshevik intervention as far back as February. He even went so far as to suggest that Bolshevik policies of world revolution and domestic repression "will bring about a situation the nature of which will overshadow the present international conflict and demand the intervention of all the powers now at war [presumably including Germany]. The damage done," Summers warned, "cannot be remedied except by intervention."[130] In implicitly suggesting that the challenge of Bolshevism required the Allies to break off their fight against the Central Powers and unite with them to crush this new and greater menace, Summers became the only American official to advocate the kind of alliance that, however unrealistic, was also the greatest nightmare of the Bolsheviks themselves.

Secretary of State Lansing likewise believed that Bolshevism was "in many ways more to be dreaded than autocracy."[131] But, unlike Summers, he never drew the conclusion that the issues of the World War should somehow be set aside in order to suppress the Bolshevik regime. Nor did he ever come to favor American intervention in Russia primarily intended to achieve such a end. While Bolshevism may have been more repugnant than German military imperialism as a doctrine, the much greater immediate threat posed by the latter prevented American officials, with the solitary exception of Summers, from even considering the possibility of altering their wartime priorities. Moreover, unlike Lansing, President Wilson never expressed any belief that Bolshevism was as great a threat to civilization as was reactionary German imperialism, even in theory.

A more realistic, and more influential, plan of anti-Bolshevik intervention was presented to Lansing and Wilson by George Kennan, then widely considered the leading American expert on Russia. On May 26, Kennan had written Lansing, with whom he was previously acquianted, a detailed letter on the Russian situation.[132] Kennan, who should not be confused with his distant relative, George Frost Kennan, the architect of containment and historian of U.S. intervention in the Russian Civil War, had a particular interest in Siberia, where he had lived for several years in the 1860s and 1880s and conducted a study of the tsarist government's harsh prison system there.[133] He recognized that Siberia, with its comparatively liberal and individualistic political culture, would be friendly territory for U.S. intervention.[134]

In his letter, Kennan urged rejection of any dealings with the Bolsheviks, whom he considered "almost as great enemies of the Allies as are the Germans."[135] He advocated an alliance between the Allies and the Russian liberal and moderate socialist forces, such as the Constitutional Democrats (Kadets) and Right S-Rs, whom he had long defended against tsarism and who were now "the real friends of the Allies."[136] For the time being, Kennan believed, "[t]he best part of European Russia is already lost, so far as we are concerned."[137] But, he asked, "[w]hy not save Siberia?"[138] He urged that "an Allied expeditionary force consisting of Americans, Japanese," and others, "be sent to eastern Siberia... to help the Russians of the trans-Baikal to throw off the Bolshevik yoke and to set up an independent, anti-Bolshevik, and anti-German government of their own."[139]

In Kennan's view, this project would serve the double purpose of forestalling the spread of German influence to Siberia and weakening the Bolsheviks.[140] "The revolt of all Siberia, or even eastern Siberia against the rule of Lenin and Trotzky" he speculated, "might bring about the overthrow of the Bolsheviki everywhere, and then the Germans would soon have to hustle troops back from the western front."[141] This latter hope, whose preconditions were about to be realized by the successes of the Czech Legion rather than by Allied intervention, proved to be overly optimistic. But it is interesting to note that Lenin had anticipated a similar result in a statement given to Lockhart on June 23. "If a bourgeois government, supported by assistance from the outside, should consolidate its authority in Siberia, and Eastern Russia is lost to Soviet Power," he feared, "then, even in Western Russia, the latter would be weakened to such an extent that it could hardly hold out for long; it would be succeeded by a bourgeois government."[142] Considering how close the Czech victories came to toppling the Bolshevik regime in any case, it is quite possible that Kennan's hope and Lenin's fear might have been realized had the Allied intervention in Siberia been as forceful as the former proposed.

Unlike Lansing and Wilson, Kennan clearly envisioned the direct use of U.S. troops to oppose the Bolsheviks. This is made clear in a May 22 article he wrote for *Outlook* magazine which he helpfully enclosed with his letter to Lansing. "It comes, then," he argued in this piece, "to a question of helping a majority of the Russian people against the Bolshevik minority, and that might compel us to take part in a civil war, with all the Bolsheviki, and probably all the Germans against us."[143] Such action, Kennan asserted, would not constitute unjustified intervention in Russian internal affairs because "[i]t is not a case of taking the side of one 'faction' against another faction, it is a case of taking the side of a majority of the Russian people against a minority of criminal usurpers who have almost ruined them and who are unwilling or not able to resist German encroachment."[144]

Kennan's analysis of the Russian situation was largely accurate. To be sure, he made a number of errors. He underestimated the strength of the Bolsheviks, who he thought "are bound to be overthrown eventually (I regard this as an absolute certainty.)"[145] He also gave credence to exaggerated estimates of the role of German agents in the Bolshevik movement,[146] though it must be emphasized that he did not consider the top Bolshevik leaders to be mere German puppets. Nonetheless, Kennan was right to believe that the Bolshevik regime was very vulnerable—a perception shared by its leaders themselves, right to believe that it was irredeemably hostile to the West, and also right in assuming that the Bolsheviks were unwilling to make any kind of anti-German pact with the Allies. Most importantly, he was probably right to argue that a determined anti-Bolshevik intervention by the Allies might well lead to the overthrow of Lenin's regime.

Lansing was impressed by Kennan's letter, which he passed along to Wilson as an analysis "well worth reading."[147] Given that Kennan's appraisal of the Bolsheviks largely dovetailed with his own, this is not surprising. In the response he wrote to Kennan, Lansing praised him as "the highest authority in America on Russia," and expressed satisfaction that "your reaction to the confusion of the situation [in Russia] is very similar to my own."[148] However, he specifically questioned Kennan's advocacy of anti-Bolshevik military intervention in Siberia.[149] Just a few days earlier, Lansing had recommended the rejection of a more modest proposal for military intervention in Siberia emanating from Paul Reinsch, the American ambassador to China.[150] When the secretary of state finally came to advocate intervention in late June, it was for the purpose of aiding the Czechs and protecting the Trans-Siberian railway rather than the overthrow of the Bolshevik regime.[151]

Despite the transmission of Kennan's letter to Wilson, there is no evidence that the President's decision-making on intervention in Siberia was influenced by Kennan's views. Eventually, after the intervention had begun, Wilson would look favorably on some of Kennan's proposals for American economic and humanitarian assistance to Siberia, but he never budged on the military issue.[152] Thus, even "the highest authority in America on Russia" could not open the administration's eyes to the importance of the opportunity it was missing. This was extremely unfortunate, for it is quite possible, given the weakness of the Bolsheviks at this time, that a major success could have been achieved—and without any substantial drain on the Western Front. "Any real effort by Japan or the United States," Winston Churchill was to conclude, "though made with troops which could never have reached the European battlefields, would have made success certain in 1918."[153] Though it is difficult to be "certain" about the success of any military operation, Churchill's argument is nonetheless extremely plausible.

In July and August, U.S. troops were finally deployed to Vladivostok, Archangel, and Murmansk. A small force of fifty American Marines from the cruiser *Olympia* participated in the British-led capture of Archangel on August 2.[154] Some 5500 troops, mostly belonging to the completely inexperienced and only partially trained 339th Infantry Regiment, were placed under British command and eventually sent to northern Russia, arriving at Archangel on September 4.[155] The largest American contingent—and the only one which operated under American command—was that sent to Vladivostok on the Pacific coast of Siberia. Beginning on August 16, the American force, which eventually numbered 8,763 men in all,[156] arrived at their destination, having made the long journey in troopships from the Phillipines.[157]

The U.S. troops in northern Russia served under British command during the entire period of their stay until most were withdrawn in June and July 1919.[158] President Wilson always insisted on their withdrawal at the earliest possible date and consistently refused Allied requests to extend their stay or to dispatch additional American troops.[159] Without authorization from Washington, some of the Americans were involved in a number of minor engagements with the Bolsheviks at the behest of General

Poole, the British commander in Archangel.[160] During their time in northern Russia, 139 of the American troops were killed, mostly as a result of non-combat-related injuries or accidents.[161] Their effect on the course of the Russian Civil War was minimal. The northern Russian expedition was largely a British project in both origins and execution, and it was the British who were responsible for its eventual failure, in a sequence of events already reviewed in chapter 2.

It was in Siberia where the United States made its most important effort, and it is on the results of that effort that any judgment of U.S. policy must be based. The commander appointed to lead the Siberian expedition was General William S. Graves, an officer with no prior knowledge of Russia. The only instructions he was given before leaving was a copy of Wilson's July 17 aide-memoire, discussed above. Upon handing Graves an envelope containing this document on August 3, Secretary of War Newton D. Baker confined himself to saying that "[t]his contains the policy of the United States in Russia which you are to follow. Watch your step; you will be walking on eggs loaded with dynamite. God bless you and good-bye."[162]

An unimaginative and politically unsophisticated officer, Graves took the aide-memoire's stricture against intervention in Russia to mean that he was to remain strictly neutral as between the Bolsheviks and their opponents.[163] After the original purpose of aiding the Czech Legion was quickly rendered irrelevant by the course of the fighting in eastern Siberia, which had ended in a Czech and White victory before most of the American troops arrived, Graves concentrated on the task of maintaining and protecting the Trans-Siberian railroad. In his mind, this was a purely technical and impartial enterprise. "We were," he writes in his memoirs, "guarding the railway, not against the actions of the Whites only; not against the actions of the Reds only; not against the Bolshevik or anti-Bolshevik depredations; but we were to see that no one interfered with the railroads."[164] This interpretation of the aide-memoire went beyond Wilson's own views. As we have seen, the president hoped that intervention would assist the Whites at least indirectly, though not through actual fighting against the Bolsheviks. But since Graves persisted in implementing *his* interpretation of administration policy throughout the entire period of American intervention in Siberia, his actions killed whatever chance there might still have been of American troops making a significant contribution to the White cause in the Russian Civil War.

In a July 31 telegram to Assistant Secretary of State Frank Polk, Lansing had expressed the fear that Graves "has not the tact and diplomacy...to deal with so delicate a situation where the Commanding Officer requires other than military ability."[165] However, this warning and others like it throughout the course of the intervention went unheeded,[166] and General Graves retained the post of commander of the American forces in Siberia right up until the time they were withdrawn in early 1920.

In fairness, it should be mentioned that General Graves' determination not to support the Whites was strengthened by what he observed of the incompetence and brutality of the White administration in eastern Siberia.[167] The S-R regime in Omsk and the Kolchak government that succeeded it were only nominally in control of this area, which was dominated by the Japanese-supported Cossack armies of Generals Grigori Semenov and I.M. Kalmykov. These forces, and several smaller ones like them, operated largely independently and their main interest was in looting, and occasionally massacring, the civilian population rather than in fighting the Bolshevik armies thousands of miles to the west.[168] The support of the Japanese rendered Kalmykov and Semenov immune to Kolchak's feeble efforts to master this situation. Faced with the reality of White rule in Eastern Siberia—and largely unaware of and uninterested in the much harsher despotism imposed on the Bolshevik-controlled areas—Graves became even more unwilling to support the Whites than he had been previously.

On the other hand, U.S. officials in Siberia were well aware that Kolchak was not really in control of Semenov and Kalmykov. Graves himself recognized that "Kalmikoff...did not recognize any superior Russian authority, but was a hireling and puppet of Japan."[169] He also knew of Semenov's similar status.[170] In fact, Kolchak even requested that the United States provide "protection" for his government against "Semenoff...Kalmikoff and Japanese intrigue."[171] For this reason, Graves' failure to cooperate with Kolchak even to the extent that his superiors would have allowed becomes less excusable.

General Graves' policies were severely criticized by both the Kolchak officials and by British and French representatives in Siberia, most of whom were committed to working for a White victory.[172] Kolchak indignantly complained that "[t]he American Command apparently treats the Bolsheviks as a political party of ordinary character."[173] At another point, Kolchak even went so far as to conclude that the presence of the American forces was doing his cause more harm than good and advocated "their removal from Russian territory."[174] Graves was also criticized by some U.S. State Department officials who were more sympathetic to the Whites.[175] Assistant Secretary of State Frank Polk, for example, called for Graves' replacement.[176] President Wilson, however, refused to replace the general and rejected all criticism of his conduct. "General Graves," he told Lloyd George in answer to British complaints in May 1919, "was a man of most unprovocative character, and wherever the fault may lie, he felt sure it was not with him."[177]

To a considerable extent, Wilson was right, for the primary "fault" was not so much Graves' as his own. Despite his obvious shortcomings, Graves was simply a traditional military officer with a narrow and rigid understanding of his duty. He was not a Bolshevik sympathizer like Raymond Robins, and he made a genuine effort to carry out his orders as he interpreted them. While Graves surely made mistakes in his dealings with the Whites, the more fundamental mistake was that of the President who appointed him and insisted on retaining him despite the urgings of both his own foreign policy advisers and the Allies.

As it was, the American forces in Siberia did very little fighting. On two occasions, they were involved in minor skirmishes with Bolshevik forces. Neither of them had any real impact on the outcome of the war; in one of these incidents, the U.S. troops may never have even actually fired a shot.[178] At all times after the defeat of the remaining major Bolshevik forces in eastern Siberia, which was completed soon after the initial U.S. landings took place, the American troops remained many hundreds of miles behind the front lines. They did render a valuable service to the Whites by guarding and maintaining the Trans-Siberian Railway, along which Allied supplies for Kolchak's army were transported, but it is quite a stretch to conclude from this that, "despite its denials, the United States became an active participant in the Russian Civil War."[179] In Wilson's view, the protection of the railway was not so much a part of the Russian Civil War as a continuation of the traditional Open Door economic policy in the Far East. "It is felt," said a February 1919 State Department communiqué approved by the president, "that this matter can be treated entirely apart from the general Russian problem, as, irrespective of further Russian developments it is essential that we maintain the policy of the open door with reference to the Siberian and particularly the Chinese Eastern Railway."[180]

The limited nature of American intervention in Siberia was underscored as early as August 1918, when Lansing, the most strongly anti-Bolshevik member of the administration, urged rejection of a French proposal to establish an Allied High Commission in order to insure "political direction...and connection between the two operations simultaneously set on foot at Archangel and Vladivostok."[181] The French even offered to let the Commission be chaired by an American.[182] Lansing believed that "in view of our policy it would be unwise to do this and that this is another move to impress our action in Siberia with the character of intervention rather than relief of the Czechs."[183] The President agreed, and instructed Lansing to "make it plain to the French Ambassador that we do not think cooperation in *political* action necessary or desirable in eastern Siberia because we contemplate no political action of any kind there, but only the action of friends who stand at hand and wait to see how they can help" (emphasis in the original).[184] Thus, Lansing and Wilson hesitated to be directly involved in open support for the Whites in the Russian Civil War.

This did not mean that the administration had no desire to see the Bolsheviks overthrown, or that they did not believe that intervention for the "relief of the Czechs" might indirectly contribute to this purpose. In a September 9 memorandum to the president, Lansing pointed out that "assistance to the Czechs amounts to assistance to the Russians," meaning, of course, the anti-Bolshevik Russians.[185] In this letter, Lansing also applauded the growth of White Russian forces under Czech protection.[186] However, he and Wilson did not want this assistance to be direct in nature, and, as their rejection of the French proposal indicates, they refused to openly commit themselves to the White cause. In any case, as argued above, anti-German and pro-Czech motives dominated anti-Bolshevik ones in the decision to intervene.

Another factor in administration calculations was the fear that a more decisive intervention might redound to the benefit of Russian and Allied reactionaries rather than Russian liberals. In the very same memorandum in which Lansing affirmed that "assistance to the Czechs amounts to assistance to the Russians," he also warned Wilson that "[r]eactionary influences in Russia and elsewhere are at work to shake off your leadership and to take advantage of any opportunity offered them to make use of Russia rather than to serve her."[187] In July, at the very time that the decision to intervene was taken, the British ambassador in Washington reported to Lloyd George that "ever since the question of intervention was first discussed Americans have feared that the interventionist movement would be controlled by friends of the old Imperial regime and...would eventually prove to be a reactionary weapon.... Further, the President is apprehensive lest any intervention should be converted into an anti-Soviet movement and an interference with the right of Russians to choose their own form of government."[188] "Anti-Soviet" in this context should not necessarily be meant to read "anti-Bolshevik," since the term "Soviet," as used in this period, referred to the workers' and soldiers' councils established during the Provisional Government period and mostly led by non-Bolshevik socialists. What Ambassador Lord Reading had in mind was that Wilson feared that Allied conservatives, in cooperation with reactionary Russians, would use intervention to crush the Russian left as a whole, not just the Bolsheviks. To avoid such an outcome, Wilson sought to strictly limit the extent of American intervention.

This picture is very different from William A. Williams' portrait of largely undifferentiated American support for "counter-revolution."[189] As N. Gordon Levin puts it, "the Administration sought to find a middle ground between its critics on the Left, who opposed intervention in Siberia as anti-Bolshevik, and its critics on the Right, who had long been insisting on firm anti-German and anti-Bolshevik action in Siberia."[190] In part, as Levin argues, this balancing act resulted in a policy of "aid[ing] 'Russia,' which is best read as Wilsonian shorthand for a liberal and pro-Allied Russia."[191] However, an even more important consequence was the drastic overall limitation of American involvement in Russia and a general reluctance to involve the United States with the White cause too closely.

Thus, in late August and September of 1918, the administration resisted Allied and Czech appeals to deploy U.S. forces far to the west in order to help the Czechs in the Volga region resist the Red counteroffensive that was now beginning to push them back.[192] Both Wilson and Secretary of State Lansing opposed the deployment of U.S. troops to the west. However, there is a distinct difference in their reasoning which has gone largely unnoticed in the existing scholarly literature.[193]

To Wilson, the Allied proposal was completely unacceptable. Instead of helping the Czechs drive the Bolsheviks back, he argued, "we should insist that the Czecho-Slovaks be brought out eastward to Vladivostok and conveyed to the Western front in Europe...according to our original agreement with them."[194] The only reason why the withdrawal of the

Czechs might be legitimately delayed for a few months is that "it may be...necessary to leave some portions of the Czecho-Slovak troops in Western Siberia, in the neighborhood of the Urals, to prevent the Germans taking agricultural and other supplies which might be accessible there."[195] In any case, the Czechs should withdraw completely from all territories in the Volga region to the west of the Urals. Wilson thus kept strictly to his original conception of limiting intervention to aiding the Czechs in protecting Siberia against German influence while aiding the Whites only indirectly.

To Lansing, on the other hand, "[t]he course which the Government of the United States is following is not the course of our free choice but that of stern necessity."[196] According to Lansing, "strongly as our sympathies constrain us to make every possible sacrifice to keep the country on the Volga front out of the hands of the merciless Red Guards, it is the unqualified judgment of our military authorities that to attempt military activities west of the Urals is to attempt the impossible."[197] Thus, for Lansing, the decision to refuse aid to the Czechs and Whites in the Volga region was purely a matter of practical impossibility. Even supplies, he believed, could not be sent there.[198]

These technical obstacles, while real, were not nearly as insuperable as Lansing was led to believe. The control of the Trans-Siberian Railroad, which had been one of the original purposes of the U.S. deployment in Siberia, gave the Allies the means to send substantial quantities of troops and supplies westwards, should they so choose. During the fighting in 1919, the Whites would use the railway to move bodies of troops much larger than the American contingent in Siberia; the railway also became the conduit for the British supplies sent to Kolchak.

American officials were well aware that the Czechs and Whites controlled the railway. The very letter in which Wilson rejected the Allied proposal for operations further to the west noted that "the railroad is open and under the control of our friends from Vladivostok all the way to Samara."[199] The latter city was close to Volga River and not far from the scene of the fighting. In fact, it was to be captured by the Bolsheviks on October 7, just three weeks after Wilson's letter.

To be sure, the American "military authorities" cited by Lansing believed that operations in the west were impractical. But most of these officers had opposed intervention in Russia to begin with, and their opinion was no more to be relied on than that of the Allied military officers, including the supreme commander, Marshal Foch, who supported the Volga project. Moreover, the American officials on the spot, including Roland Morris, the American ambassador to Japan then temporarily in Vladivostok, and even General Graves, urged that the American contingent at least be moved to Omsk, in western Siberia, from where they could provide the Czechs with greater logistical support.[200] Morris argued that "[t]he presence of an Allied force, and particularly of American troops in that part of Russia, would have a strong moral effect upon the entire population in a territory which so directly affects European Russia" and also noted that the forward deployment of U.S. troops would "render assistance to the Czech forces represented along the railway and concentrated at railway centers in the Volga region; and...open up the field for social and economic action" to help the Russians."[201]

The Volga campaign of the summer and fall of 1918 was a very close contest, and the Czechs and Whites nearly succeeded in retaining control of this vital region.[202] The forces involved on both sides were small and of lower quality than the American contingent in Siberia, which could therefore have had a significant impact on the fighting. Even deliveries of supplies alone could have made an important difference, since the White forces suffered from a shortage of arms.[203]

But Wilson's categorical refusal to countenance intervention in this region precluded any such assistance, even if Lansing had come to understand the military possibilities. As a result, the Whites lost control of the Volga area and were driven far back into Siberia. They did not return to the region until Kolchak's great offensive in the spring of 1919, by which time the Red Army was much stronger than it had been in the fall. Had the Whites, with Allied support, been able to retain control of the Volga region in September, it is likely that their next offensive could have been started much sooner and much closer to Moscow, the final goal, than it actually was. The chance of success would thereby have been much greater. It is by no means absolutely certain that a commitment of U.S. troops and/or supplies would have decisively altered the situation, but, given the extreme weakness of both Reds and Whites during this period, there is a good chance that it might have. As it was, Wilson and Lansing, for different reasons, allowed an important opportunity to go by the wayside.

To some extent, also, the "moral effect" that Morris had thought might be brought about by a wider intervention occurred in reverse as a result of Wilson and Lansing's determination to limit the scope of American involvement. The Russian Whites in Siberia came to resent the Allies, especially the Americans and Japanese, for not really having their victory at heart. "[T]he very purpose and character of the intervention," recalled Admiral Kolchak, who, in September 1918 was still serving as minister of war in the Omsk S-R government,

> were profoundly insulting. It was not help to Russia—it was all being advocated as assistance to the Czechs...to their safe return home, and in this connection everything assumed a character deeply humiliating and profoundly painful for the Russians. The whole intervention appeared to me as the establishment of foreign influence in the Far East.[204]

Kolchak probably exaggerated somewhat. Certainly, he could be in no doubt that the British, French, and even some of the U.S. representatives in Siberia ardently hoped for a White victory. However, it is likely true that the unwillingness of the Allies to make more than an extremely limited commitment had a negative impact on White Russian morale and on their perceptions of the Allies.

The Siberian intervention continued to drag on, even as World War I came to an end. Some American officials, notably Secretary of War Newton D. Baker, believed that the U.S. forces in Siberia should be withdrawn, now that the wartime military purposes they were intended to serve had ended.[205]

As the war came to a close, Wilson himself had doubts about the wisdom of further intervention in Russia. "My policy regarding Russia," he told Sir William Wiseman on October 16,

> is very similar to my Mexican policy. I believe in letting them work out their own salvation, even though they wallow in anarchy for a while. I visualize it like this: A lot of impossible folk, fighting among themselves. You cannot do business with them, so you shut them all up in a room and lock the door and tell them that when they have settled matters among themselves you will unlock the doors and do business.[206]

But, as in Mexico, "letting them work out their own salvation" did not mean that the U.S. would leave things entirely alone and Wilson did not accept Baker's proposal for withdrawing the U.S. contingent. In any case, he thought that "[t]he question of Russia...should be left to the Peace Conference."[207] He also admitted to Wiseman that "the whole question [of Russia] was causing him great anxiety."[208] Wiseman "gathered the impression that it was not impossible that he [Wilson] will modify his policy regarding Russia."[209] And, indeed, the President seemed undecided at this point, much as he was in the weeks preceding the initial decision to intervene. He clearly wished to defer any changes in policy until the Peace Conference.

Wilson, Lansing, and General Graves were also becoming suspicious of the Japanese presence in Siberia. From the agreed upon level of 12,000,[210] these forces rapidly grew to 72,000 by the end of the year.[211] As early as September 1918, Wilson was already complaining that "I can see no necessity for a large Japanese force in Siberia, and think the purpose of its continuance there needs to be defined."[212] Japanese efforts to prop up Kalmykov and Semenov against Kolchak and to seize control of the Trans-Siberian and Eastern Chinese railroads served to heighten U.S. suspicions. By March 1919, Lansing concluded that "reports received... from the American consuls at various places in Siberia seem...to confirm on the whole General Graves opinion of Japanese activities as intended to aid the reactionary party and as conducted with a view to the eventual domination of Eastern Siberia."[213]

U.S. suspicions of Japanese intentions were not wholly unreasonable, as later analyses of Japanese policy confirm.[214] But, while they served to prolong the presence of U.S. troops into Siberia, they also diverted the attention of U.S. officials, both there and in Washington, from the problem of opposing the Bolsheviks. General Graves, in particular, seems to have devoted far more effort to combating real and imagined Japanese intrigues than to assisting Kolchak in his battle against the Bolsheviks.[215] He was firmly convinced that the Japanese wanted to remove the U.S. contingent from Siberia so that they could then take over the region and annex it to their empire.[216]

U.S. officials were not irremediably hostile to the Japanese. Indeed, they were willing to recognize certain Japanese "special interests" in Siberia and elsewhere in the Far East.[217] Ultimately, they intended to coopt Japan into supporting the new liberal order of international relations which Wilsonians hoped would emerge in the postwar world.[218] In the near term, however, they were increasingly suspicious of Japanese activities in Siberia, and this concern made them at once more reluctant to withdraw from Siberia and more reluctant to use their resources in the area to aid the Whites rather than counterbalance the Japanese.

Somehow, it did not seem to occur to anyone in the U.S. camp that the best way to restrain Japanese ambitions might be to do everything possible to promote the fastest possible White victory in the Civil War so that the resulting unified Russian government could eventually defend Siberia against Japanese encroachment in its own right. Alternatively, of course, the same end could have been achieved by withdrawing all support from the Whites, allowing the Bolsheviks to win quickly, and then cooperating with them against the Japanese. But this policy was, of course, unthinkable for a wide range of reasons—and rightly so. As a result, the U.S. persisted in a very limited intervention providing marginal support for the Whites and insuring that Russia would remain divided for some time to come. These, of course, were the ideal conditions for stimulating Japanese expansion into the power vacuum of eastern Siberia, where Admiral Kolchak could hardly deploy troops to oppose them so long as he was engaged in a life and death struggle against the Bolsheviks. In this way, U.S. policy in Siberia tended to further the very Japanese expansion which it was, in part, designed to prevent.

As we have seen, President Wilson intended to defer a reconsideration of Russia policy until the Paris Peace Conference. When it finally began in January 1919, his first move was to oppose Marshal Foch's plans for intervention and support Lloyd George's Prinkipo proposal.[219] The reasons he gave for taking these steps reveal much about the President's thinking about the Russian situation and far-left revolutionary movements in general.

When Lloyd George first presented the Prinkipo proposal to the Council of Ten on January 16, 1919, Wilson immediately supported it, claiming that "in his mind there was no possible answer to the view expressed by Mr. Lloyd George."[220] In his view, Bolshevism could not and should not be opposed primarily by force because "[t]here was certainly a latent force behind Bolshevism which attracted as much sympathy as its more brutal aspects aroused general disgust."[221] Wilson pointed out that "[t]here were men in the United States of the finest temper, if not of the finest judgment, who were in sympathy with Bolshevism, because it appeared to them to offer that regime of opportunity to the individual which they desired to bring about."[222] To the president, Bolshevism was fundamentally a manifestation of a worldwide "feeling of revolt against the large vested interests which influenced the world both in the economic and the political sphere."[223] It could only be combatted by getting at what we might anachronistically refer to as its "root causes":

> Bolshevism was vital because of...genuine grievances. The seeds of Bolshevism could not flourish without a soil ready to receive them. If this soil did not exist Bolshevism could be neglected.[224]

In March, Wilson would flatly state that "[t]he sole means of counter-ing Bolshevism is to make its causes disappear."[225] Like Lloyd George, Wilson also believed that "[p]art of the strength of the Bolshevik leaders was doubtless the threat of foreign intervention," by which "they gath-ered the people round them."[226] Furthermore, Wilson reiterated his longstanding fear that reactionary forces would become the beneficiaries of intervention in Russia. "British and American troops were unwilling to fight in Russia," he argued, "because they feared their efforts might lead to the restoration of the old order, which was *even more disastrous than the present one*" (emphasis mine).[227] Unlike Churchill and Secre-tary of State Lansing, Wilson never really understood that Bolshevism represented a form of tyranny far more virulent and oppressive than the reactionary regimes which he had fought to destroy in the World War. To his mind, a "reactionary" Russia was, if anything, worse than a Bolshe-vik one.

In the president's mind, Bolshevism had a kind of legitimacy that right-wing ideological adversaries, such as the German military imperialists, lacked. It was a genuine, if misguided and brutal, effort to better the con-dition of mankind. It had at least some measure of real popular support based on valid "grievances." Moreover, it had the sympathy of "men of the finest temper," left-wing intellectuals whose opinions Wilson, the former academic and Princeton University president, felt bound to respect, even if he did not fully share them.

It would be wrong to suggest that Wilson somehow supported Bol-shevism, or even that he was "soft" on it, to dredge up another anachro-nism. He recognized that it was a "brutal" system and he thought that it—and other radical revolutionary movements—were misguided diver-sions from the more promising path of gradualistic liberal reform. He was opposed to both conservative reaction *and* radical revolution.[228] How-ever, by 1918-19 the former had become considerably more hateful to him than the latter. Thus, it never occurred to Wilson that the German Second Reich, which had far more genuine popular support than the Bol-sheviks and, for all its failings, had given its people far more in the way of real benefits, represented some sort of legitimate aspirations and should be treated gently until such time as its militant impulses could somehow be channeled into more beneficial directions by peaceful means. And Wilson certainly did not believe that the Allied war effort against Ger-many should somehow be moderated because its menacing nature might allow German reactionaries to "gather the people round them"—even though such a phenomenon certainly did occur in wartime Germany to some extent. To the contrary, the only answer to German imperialism, in the late Wilsonian mindset, was to destroy it by force.

Fundamentally, Wilson failed to properly understand the differences between the reactionary authoritarian regimes he had helped to defeat and the nascent totalitarianism of the Bolsheviks. He did not realize that the latter were both more brutal at home and more expansionist abroad than the former. In part, this was a result of the experience of World War I, in which the aggressive reactionary regime of Germany had come so close to dominating Europe and, by extension, the world.[229] Lansing and Churchill, however, had gone through the same experience, the latter, through his ordeal as First Lord of the Admiralty in 1914-15, in a much more harrowing way than Wilson. Thus, the impact of the World War cannot really account for Wilson's perspective on Russia. Fundamentally, his views were determined by his overarching left-liberal ideological vision, in which radicalism was seen as an at least partially legitimate form of liberalism gone astray, while reactionary conservatism was considered altogether irredeemable. In Wilson's mind, the Prinkipo proposal for a conference of the competing Russian factions was a means by which the reintegration of Bolshevism into the worldwide liberal movement might possibly be brought about.[230]

As we saw in chapter 2, the eventual failure of the Prinkipo proposal gave Winston Churchill an opportunity to present his case for a more vigorous and systematic intervention to the Peace Conference. On February 14, the first day that Churchill appeared at the Council of Ten, Wilson was still present, and a dramatic confrontation ensued. Churchill's presentation to the conference has been sufficiently described in chapter 2 above. In response to Churchill's arguments, Wilson firmly rejected all proposals for broader intervention. He flatly stated that "the troops of the Allied and Associated Powers were doing no sort of good in Russia" and concluded that "the...Powers ought to withdraw their troops from all parts of Russian territory."[231] He also opposed Churchill's idea of sending volunteers, technical experts, and special munitions on the grounds that, "[i]n some areas they would certainly be assisting reactionaries."[232]

Wilson's position did not, however, call for an immediate withdrawal. He admitted that he "felt guilty in that the United States had in Russia insufficient forces, but it was not possible to increase them."[233] However, this guilt arose not because he would have liked to crush the Bolsheviks militarily by means of intervention but merely because "if they [the Allied soldiers] were removed many Russians might lose their lives."[234] He believed, moreover, that "some day or other the Allied troops would have to be withdrawn; they could not be maintained there for ever and the consequences to the Russians would only be deferred."[235]

Wilson's response to Churchill is significant for two reasons. One, which has been pointed out by many scholars,[236] is that he was dead set against any significant armed intervention in the Russian Civil War. But the second, and less obvious, point, is that, even at this early date, he *already expected the Whites to lose.* That is the import of his comment that a Bolshevik massacre of those who opposed them would only be "deferred" if the Allies chose to stay a while longer. Wilson considered such an outcome inevitable. In February of 1919, the eventual outcome of the Russian Civil War was by no means cast in stone. Kolchak's forces in Siberia were recovering and preparing for their massive spring offensive, while Denikin was continuing to gain successes in the south; the Allied forces in northern Russia had beaten off a series of Bolshevik attacks in December and were in a relatively strong position. Thus, it is reasonable to assume that Wilson's expectation that the Whites would be defeated probably arose at least partially from his ideological belief that "reactionaries" could never have as much appeal to the population as could radicals.

At this time, another twist in the complicated plot of Allied-Bolshevik relations was introduced by the mission of William C. Bullitt to Russia. Bullitt was a young leftist member of the American delegation to the Peace Conference whom Colonel House had selected to lead an American delegation to the Bolshevik-controlled portion Russia for the purpose of obtaining accurate information about the state of affairs there.[237] As far as House and Wilson were concerned, fact-finding was the only reason for his mission.[238] For a number of reasons which need not concern us here, however, Bullitt himself was under the impression that he had a commission from Wilson and Lloyd George to negotiate a peace agreement with the Bolshevik leaders.[239]

If what House and Wilson wanted was unbiased information, Bullitt was hardly the ideal unbiased observer to provide it. As far back as March 1918, he was already a convinced supporter of the Bolshevik regime, which he saw as "the rudiments of a government of the people, by the people and for the people."[240] Abraham Lincoln must surely have turned in his grave!

Bullitt and his party, which included Lincoln Steffens, spent just one week in Russia in early March of 1919. During this time, as his biographer delicately puts it, "Bullitt did not distinguish himself in reporting the realities of Russia, 1919."[241] He concluded, for example, that "[t]he Red Terror is over"[242]—at the very time that it was actually near its height—and, even more amazingly, that "Lenin...stands well to the right of the existing political life of Russia."[243] Bullitt also believed that "the most striking fact in Russia today is the general support which is given the Government by the people in spite of their starvation. Indeed, the people lay the blame for their distress wholly on the [Allied] blockade and on the Governments which maintain it."[244] It did not occur to him that these statements of the Russians he met—who, in any case, hardly constituted a representative sample of public opinion—might have had something to do with fear of the very Red Terror which he, almost solely on the basis of Bolshevik assurances, had judged to be over. Bullitt even went so far as to say that, while the Bolshevik regime is "a form of Government which lends itself to gross abuse and tyranny ...it meets the demands of the moment in Russia and it has acquired so great a hold on the imagination of the common people that the women are ready to starve and the young men to die for it,"[245] a statement which might well have been disputed by the millions of people who were at that very time starving and dying *because* of the Bolshevik regime rather than for it.

Like the Bolsheviks, Bullitt tended to lay the blame for Russia's massive famine on the Allied blockade and on transportation difficulties allegedly caused by the Whites and the British,[246] forgetting that pre-Bolshevik Russia had been a major food exporter easily capable of feeding itself and ignoring the consequences of Bolshevik policies of confiscating grain from peasants, suppressing "kulaks," and imposing price controls on food sufficiently rigid to discourage supply.

In addition to his other distinctions, Bullitt, as John M. Thompson points out, was probably the first to declare that the trains "run on time" in a totalitarian society.[247] Bullitt's companion, Steffens, was even less openminded than his superior; it was upon his return from this trip that Steffens made his famous characterization of the Soviet regime: "I have seen the future and it works!"—a phrase Steffens apparently thought up before he even arrived in Russia to "see" what he was praising.[248] In general, Bullitt concluded that "the Soviet Government is the only constructive force in Russia to-day"[249] and strongly urged the Allies to end all intervention, cut off support from the Whites and make peace with it.[250]

More important than the onesided nature of Bullitt's reports, which ultimately served mostly to discredit him in the eyes of the American and Allied officials at the Peace Conference, were the peace terms he was offered by the Bolsheviks. In exchange for an end to the blockade, the withdrawal of the Allied troops in Russia, and a cessation of aid to the various White forces, the Bolsheviks promised to allow the White governments to retain control of the substantial territories they then occupied, to cease all military operations against both the White governments and the various non-Russian states carved out of the former tsarist empire, to grant assorted economic concessions to Western businesses, and to pay off the debts of the tsarist regime and the Provisional Government.[251]

Assuming that the Allies were willing to make vigorous efforts to enforce its terms against the inevitable Soviet attempts to circumvent them, this offer represented a much better deal than the one the Allies actually ended up with after the Whites were defeated. For this reason, numerous historians have retrospectively argued that the Allies would have been well advised to accept the proposal offered to Bullitt.[252] However, if—as seems to be the case—the Soviets were sincere about the offer,[253] it was only because of their fear of intervention. Only the possibility that they would lose even more territory than they had already could have possibly brought them to concede what amounted to the bulk of the Russian empire to the Whites and minority group nationalists.[254] Clearly, the Bolsheviks were driven to make sweeping concessions by the gravity of their predicament. "If we do not reach an understanding [with the Allies]," Bolshevik Commissar for Foreign Affairs Georgi Chicherin worriedly wrote on March 13, "the policy of blockade will be pressed with vigor. They will send tanks, etc., to Denikin, Kolchak, Petliura [Ukrainian nationalist leader], Paderewski [prime minister of Poland], etc."[255]

Under these circumstances, the optimal policy for the Allies was not to accept the Bullitt offer, as their retrospective critics suggest, but to exploit the Bolsheviks' manifest weaknesses by increasing the scale and improving the coordination of intervention as much as possible. After all, what the offer showed is that the Bolsheviks themselves were convinced that a stronger intervention might well lead to their own demise. Unlike Wilson, Lloyd George, and numerous historians, they were not under any delusion to the effect that intervention was somehow a net asset for their cause by virtue of the popular opposition it allegedly stimulated in Russia. As a second-best policy, the Allies might have accepted the offer and insisted on tight enforcement and verification measures.

In the end, they did neither. Through a perverse combination of circumstances, the Allied statesmen both rejected the Bullitt agreement *and* refused to up the ante of intervention to a significant degree. When Bullitt returned to Paris in late March, the only important figure at the Conference who was prepared to support his proposal was Colonel House.[256] Lloyd George may have been somewhat sympathetic to it, but he eventually refused to support the plan—in large part because of the opposition of Conservative members of the Coalition government and of British public opinion, then strongly anti-Bolshevik.[257]

President Wilson was implacably opposed to any deal with the Bolsheviks.[258] He rejected Bullitt's proposal out of hand, refusing even to let it be submitted to the Peace Conference.[259] However, it is not true, as William A. Williams claims, that "Wilson's failure to act on the [Bullitt] overture signified his final decision to attempt the forceful overthrow of the Soviet Government."[260] He made no effort to increase U.S. assistance to the Whites. In fact, with the exception of the minor indirect aid which Kolchak's forces derived from the presence of U.S. forces in Siberia and American participation in the Allied blockade of Russia, there was virtually no U.S. assistance to the Whites during this period at all. As late as May 23, Wilson could, with some credibility, tell Lloyd George and Clemenceau that "the United States...had not furnished supplies to Koltchak."[261] Even as Kolchak was winning his greatest victories in the spring of 1919 and even Lloyd George was beginning to incline towards a policy of support for the admiral, Wilson asserted at the Council of Four, on May 9, that "[o]ur government has no confidence in Admiral Kolchak, who is supported by France and England."[262]

Thus, Wilson was unwilling either to make a deal with the Bolsheviks or to provide any real support to the Whites. "[I]nsofar as Wilson had a policy on Russia at that moment," one leading historian concludes, "it was to do nothing."[263] And, indeed, Wilson himself admitted on May 20 that "I no longer regret as much as I did several months ago not having a policy in Russia; it seems to me impossible to define one in such circumstances."[264] What the President neglected to mention was that it was his own refusal to pursue either of the two promising alternatives before him which was the cause of the "circumstances" he so lamented.

Wilson's position on Russia in the spring of 1919 was not quite completely moribund. For a time, he was captivated by the idea of a food relief plan for Russia presented by Herbert Hoover, the head of American food relief operations in Europe and future president. In a memorandum to Wilson on March 28, Hoover outlined his idea for an arrangement for food relief to be arrived at with the Bolsheviks.[265]

Unlike Robins and Bullitt, Hoover was not a leftist Bolshevik sympathizer. He did not even believe, as Wilson and General Graves did, that Bolshevism was less to be feared than reaction. According to Hoover,

[T]he Bolsheviki most certainly represent a minority in every country[266] where they are in control, and as such they constitute a tyranny that is the negation of democracy.... As a tyranny, the Bolshevik has resorted to terror, bloodshed, and murder to a degree long since abandoned even amongst reactionary tyrannies. He has even to a greater degree relied upon criminal instinct to support his doctrines than ever autocracy did.[267]

In this way, Hoover's view of Bolshevism was very similar to that of Secretary of State Lansing. Both officials agreed that Bolshevism was, in important ways, worse than reactionary autocracy and both greatly feared its spread to unstable societies in Europe. Hoover also paralleled Lansing in that he opposed large-scale military intervention against Bolshevism. Like Wilson, he feared that anti-Bolshevik intervention would "make us a party to reestablishing the reactionary classes in their economic domination over the lower classes."[268] He also opposed intervention on the grounds that "[t]he American people cannot say that we are going to insist that any given population must work out its internal social problems according to our particular conception of democracy."[269] There was a further Wilsonian touch in Hoover's insistence that "this swinging of the social pendulum from the tyranny of the extreme right to the tyranny of the extreme left [Bolshevism] is based on a foundation of real social grievance."[270]

Food relief, Hoover believed, was the best way to escape the dilemma imposed on the United States by his and Wilson's unwillingness to either make a deal with the Bolsheviks or oppose them by force. He proposed that the Allies agree to provide "food and other necessities" to the population of the Bolshevik-controlled part of Russia on condition that the latter agreed to "cease all militant action across certain defined boundaries [agree to a cease-fire in the Russian Civil War] and cease their subsidizing of disturbances abroad."[271] The Bolsheviks would also have to accept "an agreement covering equitable distribution" of Western food to the Russian population, so that they could not use it for their political advantage.[272] By this plan, Hoover hoped, the United States could simultaneously "save an immensity of helpless human life" threatened by starvation,[273] end the Russian Civil War, and undermine the Russian population's support of Bolshevism by demonstrating the benevolence of the West and removing some of the "social grievances" which most Wilsonians were convinced had given rise to Bolshevism in the first place.[274]

Wilson, urged on by House, accepted Hoover's proposal with some enthusiasm. As far back as the July 17, 1918 aide-memoire which formally initiated American intervention in Russia, the president had hoped to provide economic and humanitarian aid to the Russian people.[275] Like numerous later twentieth-century American liberals, he was convinced that economic aid could often take the place of forcible coercion as an effective instrument of foreign policy.

In early April , Hoover enlisted Fridtjof Nansen, a widely respected Norwegian philanthropist and Arctic explorer, to help direct the relief plan and serve as an intermediary with the Bolsheviks. After some opposition from the reluctant French, the Hoover-Nansen plan, as it now came to be called, was adopted by the Peace Conference on April 16.[276] In late April, the offer was transmitted to the Soviets in the form of a letter signed by Nansen.[277]

The White Russian leaders in Paris protested the plan. A May 4 statement issued by the Russian Political Conference, the umbrella Russian anti-Bolshevik organization in Paris, warned that "this generous idea will end in a quite opposite result unless efficient precautions are taken to prevent the food supply of Russia from falling into the hands of the Bolshevist authorities; if it does, this act of humanity to the Russian nation will serve only to favor those who are profiting by the Bolshevist regime and to prolong their domination."[278] The Political Conference also hit on the greatest weakness of the plan when it pointed out that "[t]he feeding of the starving population is not a solution of the Russian question," which could only be truly resolved by the "liberation of Russia" from "those who have reduced her to the present state of impotence and to the necessity of seeking food from abroad."[279]

It was a sign of the diversity which constituted both a strength and a weakness of the White movement that the Political Conference declaration was signed by Prince Lvov, the first prime minister of the Provisional government, Sergei Sazonov, a former tsarist foreign minister, Nikolai

Chaikovsky, the socialist leader of the northern Russian Whites, and Vladimir Maklakoff, the Provisional Government's ambassador to France. Understandably, this coalition of liberals, socialists, and monarchists found it difficult to agree on much beyond the need to defeat the Bolsheviks and reestablish a Constituent Assembly.

The Whites need not have worried so much about the outcome of the Hoover-Nansen plan. For it was precisely those provisions of the plan intended to insure that the supplies would not "fall into the hands of the Bolshevist regime" which the latter could not accept, as Lenin made clear in his response to Nansen's letter. The Bolsheviks were quite willing to accept any food the Allies cared to give, but they refused either to relinquish control over its distribution or to submit to a unilateral cessation of offensive action in the war.[280] Given his generally correct understanding of the Bolshevik regime, Hoover should have been able to predict that such would be the outcome of his effort. However, his strong ideological belief in the efficacy of economic aid as a tool of foreign policy and, possibly, the confidence in his own abilities which he had developed in the course of his highly successful efforts elsewhere in Europe, blinded him to this likelihood.

In fairness, it should be said that Hoover's efforts to provide food relief for Russia eventually bore fruit in the American Relief Administration's efforts to alleviate the effects of the famine of 1921, which he directed. This operation, which the Soviets grudgingly permitted to operate free of political constraints, saved literally millions of lives and was one of the truly great humanitarian achievements of the twentieth century. Hoover, who is today remembered mostly for the failures of his presidency, arguably deserves greater credit for his humanitarian work than posterity has thus far accorded. But by the time the ARA began to operate, the Bolshevik regime was firmly in place, the Civil War was over, and there was little chance that much could be done to undermine Lenin and his colleagues.

In June, after Admiral Kolchak's favorable response to the Big Five's communiqué setting down terms for continued Allied assistance, Wilson finally agreed to partial recognition of the admiral's government. It was, in large part, Wilson's serious doubts about the White leader which prevented the partial recognition from occurring for so long, as the transcripts of the Council of Four discussions of the issue make clear.[281] Even as Kolchak's best chance for victory was about to slip away, Wilson delayed providing aid to the admiral until it was too late.

Even after the recognition, however, little in the way of American aid was actually sent to the Siberian Whites.[282] The assistance which was provided to Kolchak's forces was both very belated and much smaller than the British effort, much less was it commensurate with America's vast resources. As late as July 22, 1919, Wilson was to tell Congress that "the purpose of the continuance of American troops in Siberia is that we...may keep open a necessary artery of trade and extend to the vast population of Siberia the economic aid essential to it."[283] The goal of helping the Whites to overthrow the Bolsheviks was not even mentioned. In late June, a State Department official was forced to confess to Boris Bakhmetev, The Russian ambassador to the United States, that the Big Five communiqué of June 12 was not a step towards official U.S. recognition of the Whites and that there were as yet no plans for providing Kolchak with additional assistance.[284] Thus, after refusing any direct support to Kolchak at all until after his best chance for victory was past, the U.S. government procrastinated on giving aid even in the aftermath of its official decision to do so.

On June 30, Wilson dispatched Roland Morris, the American Ambassador in Japan, to Siberia. Morris' mission was to evaluate the status of Kolchak's regime and make recommendations for future U.S. policy towards it. The very fact that Morris was sent on such a mission suggests that Wilson was still undecided on the question of what, if any, assistance should be provided to the Admiral. Morris' instructions, drafted by the President himself, specifically stated that "the joint action taken...by the Supreme Council with reference to Kolchak still leaves open the question of his formal recognition and the extent and nature of support which should be given him."[285]

In a series of reports cabled to the State Department in July and August, Morris described his impressions of Kolchak and his government. The Ambassador was unsparing in his criticism of the Whites' many shortcomings. He noted the "[c]omplete demoralization of Kolchack's Siberian Army" under the impact of its recent defeats and attacked "Kolchak's failure to win any substantial popular support."[286] Morris also reported that "the army staff and supply departments were completely disorganized, inefficient, corrupt and unsettled."[287] In general, he concluded that Kolchak's government "has failed in administration; has failed in the organization of the army; has failed to retain the confidence of the moderate groups."[288] On the other hand, he rejected the view that the White regime in Siberia was reactionary:

The spirit and purposes of the Kolchak government are, I believe, moderately liberal and progressive. If one excepts the military officials of the old regime who compose a majority of the General Staff, the men around Kolchak could not be classed as reactionary in their aims. Some are monarchists, some republicans, and a few socialists. I am confident that Kolchak and his associates would, if retained in power, redeem their promise to call a constituent assembly.[289]

Morris emphasized that the Kolchak regime "still...has elements of strength," among which were the admiral's generally recognized "honesty of purpose" and "patriotic motives" and the recognition of the liberal elements in Siberia that the only alternative to the White government was Bolshevism.[290] He believed that "Kolchak and his colleagues have learned a great deal from the mistakes which they now recognize they have made during the last eight months. The [reactionary] military leaders," he pointed out, "have lost much of their influence because of their obvious failure in army organization and in civil administration."[291]

If the United States and the Allies were to act promptly and decisively, Morris argued, "I have confidence the Kolchak government might, with the exercise of tact and judgement and above all patience, be shaped into an instrument with which to combat Bolshevism."[292] Morris urged Lansing to "do everything possible to encourage Kolchak at this time."[293] He particularly emphasized "three absolutely essential requirements: the formal recognition of the Kolchak government, the grant of credits [for purchase of military supplies] and the despatch of at least 25,000 American troops to assist in guarding the railway."[294] The latter, he explained, were necessary to replace the Czech Legion, which was about to finally leave Siberia after spending the last few months guarding the railway and feuding with Kolchak's officials.[295]

By August 1919, when Morris submitted these recommendations, it was no longer likely that Kolchak could capture Moscow and defeat the Bolsheviks in the foreseeable future. But, had the measures recommended by the Ambassador been adopted, it is quite possible that the White position might have been stabilized and Kolchak enabled to retain control of Siberia. Such an outcome might well have prevented the large-scale transfer of troops from Siberia to the south which enabled the Bolsheviks to turn back Denikin's bid for Moscow in the fall. As it was, Kolchak's forces, led by the Czech General M.K. Dieterichs, was able to launch a temporarily successful counteroffensive in September even without significant additional Allied assistance.[296]

But, as Morris had foreseen, Kolchak could not survive without increased Allied assistance, and this was not forthcoming. In his reply to Morris' proposals, Secretary of State Lansing stressed that neither recognition, nor credits nor the dispatch of additional American troops would be provided. Aid to Kolchak was to be limited to a few additional shipments of rifles.[297] And, at the very time that Morris' proposals were rejected in Washington, the British were in the process of withdrawing most of their assistance from Kolchak as well.[298] Thus, it is clear that by late August 1919, both the Americans and the British were prepared to leave Kolchak, whom they had solemnly promised to support less than two months earlier, to his own devices. Despite a belated reform of his administration and the recognition of earlier errors, these were not enough to forestall the Admiral's imminent defeat.

Fundamentally, the American government had never been prepared to provide the Siberian Whites with military support on a scale sufficient to make a major impact on the course of the war. Even those members of the administration, notably Lansing and Hoover, who fully understood the nature of the Bolshevik regime and the threat it posed, were reluctant to sanction real intervention. Instead, they persisted in the hope that Bolshevism could somehow be countered by half-measures and unrealistic schemes for economic assistance, such as the Hoover-Nansen plan. At lower levels, officials such as Morris, Ambassador Francis, Consul Summers, and Ernest L. Harris, the U.S. consul in Irkutsk, recognized the necessity of forceful intervention and urged it on their superiors. The same conclusion was also reached by the elder George Kennan, then the leading American specialist on Russian affairs. But the advice of these men was rejected even by Lansing, the most strongly anti-Bolshevik high-ranking official in the administration. President Wilson and Colonel House, the figures who really counted, were still more unwilling to accept such views.

Unlike such American left-liberals as William C. Bullitt and Raymond Robins, President Wilson was not fundamentally sympathetic to Bolshevism. Nor, as is sometimes alleged, was he opposed to intervention because he saw the Bolshevik regime as some sort of embodiment of "the Russian [people's] right to self-determination."[299] In a September 1919 speech, he made clear his recognition that

The men who now are measurably in control of the affairs of Russia represent nobody but themselves. They have again and again been challenged to call a constitutional convention. They have again and again been challenged to prove that they had some kind of a mandate.... And they dare not attempt it; they have no mandate from anybody.... There is a closer monopoly of power in Petrograd and Moscow than there ever was in Berlin, and the thing that is intolerable is not that the Russian people are having their way but that another group of men more cruel than the czar himself is controlling the destinies of that great people.[300]

While Wilson's revulsion against Bolshevism was not as great as that of Lansing or Hoover, it was clearly substantial, as witness his consistent refusal to recognize the Soviet regime in any way and his belated decision to support Kolchak.[301] Wilson recognized Bolshevism and the broader revolutionary socialist tradition of which it was a part as a major ideological enemy of the liberal reformism he championed.[302] In the September 1919 speech quoted above, he even seems to have belatedly recognized that Bolshevism was, at least in some respects, worse than reaction.

Unlike Lloyd George and Curzon, Wilson, Lansing, and other American leaders had no desire to see Russia broken up in order to establish a better balance of power. They consistently advocated the cause of Russian unity throughout 1918–20, even to the point of refusing to recognize the Baltic States and other breakaway non-Russian elements of the former tsarist empire which sought to obtain their independence.[303] Thus, their failure to support the Whites cannot be explained on the grounds that they feared the reemergence of a strong Russian state. Like Winston Churchill, Lansing was convinced that breaking up Russia would be "a moral wrong and would pave the way for conflicts in the future."[304] A "dismembered" Russia, he thought, would lead to perpetual Russian grievances against the West and prevent Russia from serving as a necessary counterweight to German and Japanese imperialism.[305]

In the final analysis, Wilson could not bring himself to support a firm policy of intervention in Russia primarily because of his excessive fear that it would redound to the benefit of reactionaries and because of his refusal to recognize the efficacy of force in confronting socialist revolutionary movements. He simply could not bring himself to understand that a movement which had established its power almost entirely on the basis of coercion could only be effectively opposed by force, that even the best-intentioned schemes for economic and humanitarian assistance would not suffice. It is an important sign of his ideological biases that, at least after 1917, he had no such blind spots with respect to right-wing reactionary regimes, such as that of Germany under the Kaiser.

In the wake of Kolchak's collapse in late 1919, the position of the small American force in Siberia threatened to become untenable. In late December, the decision was made to withdraw it.[306] The Czech Legion, which had not taken part in serious fighting for months, was also withdrawn at this time. As the last American troop ship left Vladivostok on April 1, 1920, a Japanese military band stood on the dock and played "Hard Times, Come Again No More."[307] The "hard times" were indeed over for General Graves and his men. But for Russia and the many other lands affected by the triumph of the Bolsheviks, they had only begun.

Notes

1. Title taken from statement in letter from George Kennan to Robert Lansing, May 26, 1918, in Arthur S. Link, ed., *The Papers of Woodrow Wilson*, Vol. 48, (Princeton: Princeton University Press, 1966-94), p. 187, hereafter cited as *PWW.*
2. Wilson, "Fourteen Points Address," January 8, 1918, in Ibid., vol. 45, p. 537.
3. Ross Gregory, *The Origins of American Intervention in the First World War,* (New York: Norton, 1971), p. 126.
4. Wilson, "Declaration of War Message," April 2, 1917, reprinted in ibid., p. 145.
5. See FRUS, 1918, vol.1, pp. 107-53.
6. Lansing, memorandum, August 9, 1917; in Lansing, *War Memoirs*, p. 337.
7. See Pipes, *Russian Revolution,* chs.10-11, for a strong reassertion of the argument that these were indeed the mistakes which led to the Provisional Government's overthrow.
8. Lansing, memorandum, December 2, 1917, in Lansing, *War Memoirs,* p. 339.
9. Ibid., p. 341.
10. Ibid.
11. Ibid., p. 340.
12. Ibid., p. 341.
13. Ibid., pp. 341-42.
14. Ibid., p. 342.
15. Ibid., p. 340; Ironically, at this very time, the Bolsheviks were beginning to take ruthless measures aiming at the suppression of the *real* anarchists. In Lansing's defense, however, it should be noted that his description of the Bolsheviks as "anarchists" referred primarily to their tactics rather than to their final ends, which he recognized to be a "despotism of the proletariat in every country" (ibid.) rather than the absence of all government.
16. On the difficulty of obtaining information on Russia during this period, see, generally, Kennan, *Russia Leaves the War.*
17. See, esp., Williams, *American-Russian Relations,* ch.5.
18. Lansing, memorandum, December 2, 1917, op.cit., p. 342.
19. Ibid.
20. Ibid.
21. Ibid., p. 345.
22. Lansing to Wilson, December 10, 1917, in FRUS, *The Lansing Papers, 1914-20,* vol.2, (Washington, DC: Government Printing Office, 1940), p. 343, hereafter cited as *Lansing Papers.*

23. Ibid.
24. Ibid., p. 344.
25. Lansing, Draft Telegram to the Ambassador in Great Britain, December 12, 1917, in ibid., pp. 345-46; U.S. funds could not be provided to Kaledin directly because of statutes preventing the allocation of money to foreign movement not recognized as legitimate governments.
26. Williams, *American-Russian Relations,* pp. 117-18.
27. Ibid., pp. 105, 117.
28. Lansing, Draft Telegram to Ambassador in Great Britain, op.cit., p. 345.
29. Ibid., p. 346.
30. See Kennan, *Russia Leaves the War,* p. 178.
31. See Alexander George and Juliette George, *Woodrow Wilson and Colonel House,* corrected ed., (New York: Dover, 1964); while the Georges' psychological explanation of the Wilson-House relationship is dubious, the fact that such a relationship existed is relatively undisputed. See also Christopher C. Gabriel, "Colonel House and the Development of American Peace Policy, 1918," unpublished M.Phil. thesis, New College, Oxford University, 1993.
32. See, e.g., Williams, *American-Russian Relations;* Levin, *Woodrow Wilson and World Politics;* Kennan, *Decision;* Kennan, *Russia Leaves the War.*
33. See Thompson, *Russia, Bolshevism, and the Versailles Peace,* pp. 45, 97, 288-89.
34. Wilson to Rep. Frank Clark, November 13, 1917, in *PWW,* vol.45, p. 39.
35. See my analysis of the British policy in chapter 2 above.
36. Wilson to Lansing, January 1, 1918, in *PWW,* vol.45, p. 417.
37. As they are in Unterberger, "Woodrow Wilson and the Russian Revolution," pp. 55-56.
38. On House's influence on the speech, see Levin, pp. 60-61; Seymour ed., *Intimate Papers of Colonel House,* vol.3, pp. 316-49.
39. House, January 2, 1918, in Seymour ed., vol.3, p. 389.
40. Wilson, Fourteen Points Speech, op.cit., p. 537.
41. Ibid., p. 535.
42. Ibid., p. 538.
43. Ibid., p. 536.
44. Unterberger, "Wilson and the Russian Revolution," p. 53.
45. Williams, *American-Russian Relations,* p. 123.
46. See ibid., p. 159, and Williams, "American Intervention in Russia, 1917-20, Part II," *Studies on the Left,* Winter 1964.
47. Levin, pp. 63-64.
48. Ibid., pp. 71-73.
49. For the British proposal and U.S. rejection, see FRUS, 1918, vol.2, pp. 33-42.
50. State Department to Foreign Office, February 8, 1918, in ibid., p. 42.
51. For details, see Kennan, *Decision;* Unterberger, *Expedition,* chs.2-3.
52. Unterberger, "Wilson and the Russian Revolution," pp. 68-69.
53. See ibid. and Unterberger, *Expedition;* Unterberger probably overstates the extent of this fear, but there can be little doubt that it was present.
54. House to Arthur Balfour, March 4, 1918, in Seymour, ed., vol.3, p. 394.
55. Ibid., p. 395.
56. Ibid., pp. 394-95.
57. See Wilson to Allied Ambassadors, March 5, 1918, in ibid., pp. 419-20.
58. Lockhart, *British Agent,* pp. 220-23.

59. Kennan, *Decision,* p. 240; not surprisingly, Williams also holds to the view that Robins viewed the Soviet regime objectively. See Williams, *American-Russian Relations,* p. 124.

60. Raymond Robins to Lenin, April 25, 1918, quoted in Pipes, *Russian Revolution,* p. 590.

61. Lockhart, p. 220.

62. Ibid.; see also Kennan, *Decision,* pp. 170, 200–203, 226.

63. Pipes, *Russian Revolution,* p. 590.

64. For additional evidence of Robins' continuing support for the Bolsheviks, see Christopher Lasch, *American Liberals and the Russian Revolution,* (New York: Columbia University Press, 1962), pp. 165–66. On the general phenomenon of Western leftist intellectuals taking back distorted images from visits to communist states, see Paul Hollander, *Political Pilgrims,* (New York: Oxford University Press, 1981).

65. On Lenin's willingness to grant concessions to U.S. businesses, see Williams, *American-Russian Relations,* pp. 141–42.

66. See analysis in chapter 2.

67. This is also the conclusion of Pipes, *Russian Revolution,* p. 589.

68. This issue is analyzed in chapter 1 above. Recall that Lenin viewed limited cooperation with capitalist states as merely another way of continuing the struggle against them, "selling capitalists the rope to hang themselves."

69. A partial exception was the offer he made to the Bullitt Mission, discussed below. However, this offer was motivated by a desperate fear that his regime might be overthrown by Allied intervention—an outcome he wished to avoid at all costs— rather than any fundamental change in orientation.

70. FRUS, 1918, vol.1, p. 383 and n1. The importance of this document was first noted by Levin, op.cit., p. 72. However, as Levin himself recently pointed out to me, it is not clear whether Lansing and Wilson's resolve to have nothing to do with the Bolsheviks would have held if the latter were actually engaged in large-scale combat against the Germans.

71. Wilson to Lansing, April 18, 1918, in *PWW,* vol.47, p. 357.

72. Wilson to Lansing, May 20, 1918, in *Lansing Papers,* p. 362.

73. See, e.g., Levin, p. 95; Williams, *American-Russian Relations,* p. 147.

74. Wilson to Lansing, May 20, 1918, op.cit., p. 361.

75. See Summers to Lansing, February 22, 1918, in FRUS, 1918, vol.1, pp. 385–86.

76. Francis to Lansing, February 24, 1918, in ibid., p. 387.

77. Ibid.

78. Francis to Lansing, February 9–13, 1918, in Ibid., pp. 371–78.

79. See, e.g., Christopher Lasch, "American Intervention in Siberia: A Reinterpretation," *Political Science Quarterly,* June 1962.

80. See Volkogonov, *Lenin,* pp. 109–27.

81. See chapter 1 above, particularly the quote from Lenin confirming that this is exactly how *he* saw it.

82. Williams, *American-Russian Relations,* pp. 136–37.

83. Ibid., p. 137.

84. Francis to Lansing, March 26, 1918, in FRUS, 1918, vol.1, pp. 487–88.

85. Williams' highly dubious misrepresentation of documentary evidence in so many instances (see, e.g., his statements on the Fourteen Points speech and his misrepresentation of Lansing's December 12 draft telegram, analyzed above) raises serious questions about the ethical standards of his work. An earlier examination of his work on the origins of the Cold War shows numerous misrepresentations of evi-

dence in Williams' writings on this period as well; see Robert J. Maddox, *The New Left and the Origins of the Cold War,* (Princeton: Princeton University Press, 1973). Obviously, these gross errors could simply be honest mistakes. But it is difficult to believe that so intelligent and well-read a historian as Williams could be this incompetent in his use of evidence. In any case, what is truly disturbing is not the possibility that Williams might have distorted his evidence, whether intentionally or not, but that he is widely recognized as one of America's leading historians despite such massive flaws in his work. One wonders whether an equally dubious right-wing or moderate scholar could ever have received such acclaim. For a perceptive, but in my view insufficiently thoroughgoing, critique of Williams' broader theories of American diplomatic history, see N. Gordon Levin, Jr., "The Open Door Thesis Reconsidered," *Reviews in American History,* December 1974.

86. Williams, *American-Russian Relations,* p. 137.
87. See Kennan, *Decision,* p. 170.
88. See Francis to Lansing, May 2, 1918, in FRUS, 1918, vol.1, pp. 519–21; Francis writes (p. 519) that he "had been hoping for request.... [for intervention] by the Soviet and have been discreetly working for that end." He does, however, also state (p. 521) that "I greatly doubt whether Allies can any longer afford to overlook principles which Lenin is aggressively championing."
89. Wiseman to Sir Eric Drummond, May 30, 1918, in *PWW,* vol.48, p. 204.
90. Ibid.
91. See Unterberger, "Wilson and the Russian Revolution"; Williams, *American-Russian Relations,* chs.5–6.
92. The issue of self-determination is further discussed below.
93. Wiseman to Drummond, May 30, 1918, op.cit., p. 204.
94. Lansing to Wilson, May 11, 1918, in *PWW,* vol.47, p. 605.
95. Ibid.
96. See ch.2.
97. Kennan, *Russia and the West,* pp. 70–71.
98. Wilson to Lansing, May 20, 1918, in *Lansing Papers,* p. 361.
99. See, e.g., Kennan, *Decision,* pp. 266–67, which treats Lansing's statements to Reading as the official position of the administration.
100. Lansing, memorandum, June 3, 1918, in FRUS, 1918, vol.2, pp. 484–85.
101. See chapter 2, above, for a discussion of the Czech revolt.
102. Reinsch to Lansing, June 13, 1918, in FRUS, 1918, vol.2, pp. 206–207.
103. Ibid., p. 207.
104. Wilson to Lansing, June 17, 1918, in *PWW,* vol.48, p. 335.
105. Unterberger, *The United States, Revolutionary Russia, and the Rise of Czechoslovakia,* ch.14.
106. Lansing, "Memorandum of a Conference at the White House on the Siberian Situation," July 6, 1918, in FRUS, 1918, vol.2, pp. 262–63.
107. Ibid., p. 262.
108. For the text of the Council's July 2 decision, see ibid. pp. 241–46.
109. Lansing, "Memorandum of Conference," op.cit., p. 263.
110. Wilson, Aide-Memoire to Allied Ambassadors, in *PWW,* vol.48, p. 641.
111. Ibid.
112. See French Ambassador Jean Jusserand to Wilson, June 24, 1918, in ibid., p. 415; Wilson to Jusserand, June 25, 1918, in ibid., p. 421, asking for more details of Foch's views; Foch to Wilson, July 27, 1918, in ibid., pp. 445–46, where Foch definitely assures Wilson (p. 445) that "the sending by you of American troops to

Russia is justified, for no appreciable diminution of the number of troops to be sent to France will result therefrom."

113. Wilson, Aide-Memoire, July 17, 1918, op.cit., p. 641.
114. Ibid., pp. 641–42.
115. Levin, pp. 92–105.
116. See, e.g., Francis to Lansing, June 7, 1918, in FRUS, 1918, vol.2, p. 195; Admiral Knight (in Vladivostok) to secretary of the Navy, June 26, 1918, in ibid., pp. 230-31.
117. See Kennan, *Decision,* pp. 71–81.
118. W.L. Hicks and William Webster, report on prisoners of war in Siberia, April 26, 1918, in Cumming and Pettit, eds., pp. 177–84.
119. Kennan, *Decision,* p. 81.
120. Ibid.
121. This claim is well argued in Ibid., pp. 400–3.
122. Ibid., p. 400.
123. Lansing to Roland Morris, July 10, 1918, in FRUS, 1918, vol.3, p. 237; see also Lansing to Wilson, June 23, 1918, in *Lansing Papers,* p. 364, where the Czechs are described as "fighting the Red Guards along the Siberian line with more or less success."
124. See Lasch, op.cit.
125. See analysis of Francis' views above and in chapter 1; see also the excellent discussion of this issue in Levin, pp. 93–94.
126. Levin, p. 93.
127. Francis to Lansing, February 21, 1918, in FRUS, 1918, vol.1, p. 384.
128. See, e.g., Lasch, op.cit., and Kennan, *Decision*
129. Unterberger, *Expedition,* ch.5, esp. p. 88.
130. Summers to Lansing, February 22, 1918, in FRUS, 1918, vol.1, p. 385.
131. Lansing to Wilson, February 15, 1918, in *Lansing Papers,* p. 353.
132. George Kennan to Lansing, May 26, 1918, in *PWW,* vol.48, pp. 183–87.
133. For a brief description of Kennan's background, see Kennan, *Decision,* p. 329; unless the context obviously indicates otherwise, all mentions of "Kennan" in this study refer to George Frost Kennan.
134. Kennan to Lansing, May 26, 1918, op. cit., p. 186.
135. Ibid., p. 184.
136. Ibid.
137. Ibid., p. 187.
138. Ibid.
139. Ibid., p. 185.
140. Ibid., pp. 185–87.
141. Ibid., p. 187.
142. Lenin, statement given to Lockhart, June 23, 1918, reprinted in Lockhart, insert between pp. 268 and 269.
143. Kennan, "Can We Help Russia?," *Outlook,* May 22, 1918.
144. Kennan to Lansing, May 26, 1918, op.cit., p. 185.
145. Ibid. Although, the Bolshevik regime was, of course, eventually overthrown in 1991, Kennan clearly had a much shorter time scale in mind when he wrote his letter.
146. Ibid., p. 184.
147. Lansing to Wilson, May 28, 1918, in *PWW,* vol.48, p. 183.
148. Quoted in Kennan, *Decision,* p. 359.
149. Ibid.

150. See Reinsch to Lansing, May, 16, 1918, in *PWW,* vol.48, p. 72; Lansing to Wilson, May 21, 1918, in ibid., p. 104; Lansing's rejection was not total, however, since he only argued that "the time was not opportune" for intervention rather than that intervention was the wrong policy in principle. However, Reinsch's proposal, unlike Kennan's was primarily aimed at the Germans rather than the Bolsheviks.
151. Lansing to Wilson, June 23, 1918, in *Lansing Papers,* p. 364.
152. See Kennan to Lansing, August 18, 1918, in *PWW,* vol.49, pp. 320-23, transmitted to Wilson, August 22; Wilson to Lansing, August 24, 1918, in ibid., pp. 346-47.
153. Churchill, *Aftermath,* p. 273.
154. Ullman, vol.1, p. 235; Kennan, *Decision,* p. 425.
155. Kennan, *Decision,* p. 426.
156. Figure taken from Ullman, vol.1, p. 263
157. Kennan, *Decision,* p. 414.
158. Kennan, *Russia and the West,* p. 88.
159. See, e.g., Wilson to General Tasker Bliss, June 10, 1919, in *PWW,* vol.60, p. 359; see also Unterberger, "Wilson and the Russian Revolution," pp. 76-77.
160. Kennan, *Russian and the West,* pp. 78-79.
161. Ibid., p. 89.
162. William S. Graves, *America's Siberian Adventure, 1918-20,* (New York: Jonathan Cape, 1931), p. 4.
163. Ibid., pp. 10-11, 186-90.
164. Ibid., p. 186.
165. Quoted in Kennan, *Decision,* p. 414.
166. See, e.g., Frank Polk to Lansing, May 9, 1919, transmitted to Wilson on May 17, in *PWW,* vol.59, pp. 234-35.
167. See Graves, op.cit., esp.pp. 103-4, 107.
168. See Vladimir Brovkin, *Behind the Front Lines of the Civil War: Political Movements and Parties in Russia, 1918-22,* (Princeton: Princeton University Press, 1994), p. 196.
169. Graves, p. 131.
170. Ibid., p. 107.
171. Ernest Harris, U.S. consul at Irkutsk, to secretary of state, March 26, 1919, in FRUS, 1919, p. 201.
172. See Unterberger, *Expedition,* pp. 123-24; British Foreign Office to Lansing, May 19, 1919, in FRUS, 1919, pp. 499-500.
173. Omsk Government to Russian Ambassador to the United States, April 24, 1919, forwarded to Lansing, May 10, 1919, In FRUS, 1919, p. 496.
174. Quoted in W.H. Chamberlin, *The Russian Revolution,* vol.2, (New York: Macmillan, 1935), p. 163.
175. Unterberger, *Expedition,* p. 125.
176. Polk to Lansing, May 9, 1919, op.cit.
177. Notes of a Meeting held at President Wilson's House, Paris, May 14, 1919, in FRUS, 1919, p. 497.
178. See Kennan, *Russia and the West,* pp. 106-107 for a brief account of these two incidents.
179. Unterberger, "Wilson and the Russian Revolution," pp. 80-81.
180. Lansing and McCormick to Acting Secretary of State Polk, February 9, 1919, in FRUS, 1919, p. 251; this communiqué is cited by Unterberger, ibid., but she somehow contrives to sidestep its import.

181. French Ambassador Jean Jusserand to Lansing, August 12, 1918, in FRUS, 1918, vol.2, p. 340.
182. Ibid., p. 341.
183. Lansing to Wilson, August 22, 1918, in *Lansing Papers,* p. 378.
184. Wilson to Lansing, August 23, 1918, in ibid., pp. 378–79.
185. Lansing to Wilson, September 9, 1918, in ibid., p. 382.
186. Ibid., pp. 381–82.
187. Ibid., p. 382.
188. Lord Reading to Lloyd George, July 12, 1918, in *PWW,* vol.48, pp. 602–3.
189. Williams, *American-Russian Relations,* chs. 5–6.
190. Levin, p. 109.
191. Ibid.
192. See Unterberger, "Wilson and the Russian Revolution," p. 78; 193. Unterberger, *United States, Revolutionary Russia, and the Rise of Czechoslovakia,* pp. 293–97.
194. See, e.g., Unterberger, "Wilson and the Russian Revolution," Wilson to Lansing, September 17, 1918, in *PWW,* vol.51 p. 25
195. Ibid.
196. Lansing to Ambassador in Great Britain, September 26, 1918, in FRUS, 1918, vol.2, p. 395.
197. Lansing to Ambassador in Japan, September 26, 1918, in ibid., p. 393.
198. Ibid.
199. Wilson to Lansing, September 17, 1918, op.cit., p. 25.
200. See Roland Morris to Lansing, September 23, 1918, in ibid., pp. 387–90.
201. Ibid., p. 389.
202. For a good description of the fighting, see Mawdsley, *Russian Civil War,* ch.5.
203. Ibid., p. 65.
204. Varneck and Fisher, eds., *Testimony of Admiral Kolchak,* pp. 146–47.
205. Newton D. Baker to Wilson, November 27, 1918, in *PWW,* vol.53, pp. 227–29.
206. Wiseman, "Notes of an Interview with the President at the White House," October 16, 1918, in ibid., vol.51, p. 350.
207. Ibid., p. 351.
208. Ibid.
209. Ibid.
210. This had been negotiated in July 1918, as a modification of the original figure of 7000 for each country. See Kennan, *Decision,* pp. 411–12.
211. Ibid., p. 415.
212. Wilson to Lansing, September 17, 1918, in *PWW,* vol.51, p. 25.
213. Lansing to Wilson, March 22, 1919, in ibid., vol.56, p. 184.
214. See, generally, Morley, *Japanese Thrust into Siberia.*
215. See, generally, Graves, op.cit.
216. Ibid., p. 112.
217. For a general description of the Wilson Administration's position on Japanese expansion in the Far East, see Lansing, *War Memoirs,* chapter 20.
218. These points are well brought out in Levin, op.cit., esp. pp. 112–19.
219. These are analyzed more fully in chapter 2 above.
220. "Hankey's Notes of a Meeting of the Council of Ten," January 16, 1919 in *PWW,* vol.54, p. 102.
221. Ibid.
222. Ibid.

223. Ibid.
224. Ibid.
225. *Council of Four*, vol.1, p. 47
226. "Notes of a Meeting of the Council of Ten," January 16, 1919, op.cit. p. 103.
227. Ibid., p. 102.
228. This aspect of Wilson's thought is well brought in Levin, op.cit., esp. pp. 1-9.
229. That such was indeed the goal of German policymakers is well demonstrated in Fritz Fischer, *Germany's War Aims in the First World War,* (New York: Norton, 1967).
230. See Levin, pp. 210-11. Levin also argues (p. 208) that Wilson hoped to "use the Prinkipo Conference as a means to weaken Bolshevism in Russia by removing fear of Allied sponsored reaction as a lever which Lenin could continue to use to win Russian popular support." However, this "anti-Bolshevik" strategy only underlines the extent to which the president considered Bolshevism a different and more legitimate kind of enemy than reaction. For Wilson's argument that Prinkipo might undermine Bolshevism in this way, see, FRUS, *Peace Conference,* vol.3, pp. 663-64.
231. FRUS, *Peace Conference,* vol.3, p. 1042.
232. Ibid., p. 1043.
233. Ibid.
234. Ibid.
235. Ibid.
236. See, e.g., Unterberger, "Wilson and the Russian Revolution"; Thompson, *Russia, Bolshevism, and the Versailles Peace,* pp. 135-36.
237. Patricia Farnsworth, *William C. Bullitt and the Soviet Union,* (Bloomington: Indiana University Press, 1967), pp. 36-37.
238. Ibid.; See also FRUS, *Peace Conference,* vol.3, p. 1043, where Wilson asserts that he was "seeking not a rapprochement with the Bolsheviks, but clear information."
239. Farnsworth, p. 37.
240. William C. Bullitt, memorandum, March 2, 1918, in *PWW,* vol.46, p. 513.
241. Farnsworth, p. 47.
242. Bullitt to Committee to Negotiate Peace, March 25, 1919, in FRUS, 1919, p. 91.
243. Ibid., p. 87.
244. Ibid., p. 86.
245. Ibid., p. 86.
246. Ibid., p. 85; Bullitt to Committee to Negotiate Peace, March 18, 1919, in ibid., pp. 82-83.
247. Quoted in Thompson, p. 174; see also Bullitt to Committee to Negotiate Peace, March 18, 1919, p. 90.
248. Ibid., pp. 175-76.
249. Bullitt to Committee to Negotiate Peace, March 18, 1919, op.cit., p. 82.
250. In 1933, Bullitt became the first U.S. ambassador to the Soviet Union. His experience in Stalin's Russia eventually led him to become much more conservative and staunchly anti-Soviet. During World War II, he repeatedly warned an unmoved President Franklin D. Roosevelt to obtain definite guarantees against Soviet expansionism in Europe and the Far East in exchange for the massive Lend-Lease aid then being provided to Russia; see Farnsworth, pp. 3, 173. However, as late as 1953, Bullitt continued to believe that the terms he obtained from the Bolsheviks in 1919 would have been a good deal for the Allies at the time (Thompson, p. 173).
251. The exact text of the Soviet offer is in Bullitt to Commission to Negotiate Peace, March 16, 1919, in FRUS, 1919, pp. 78-80.

252. See, e.g., Thompson, esp.p. 167; Kennan, *Russia and the West,* p. 127.
253. A strong argument that they were is presented in Thompson, pp. 164-65.
254. See map in ibid., p. 168, showing territories controlled by the parties to the Rus-
     sian Civil War on March 15, 1919. Bolshevik Russia had been effectively reduced
     to the size of the original Muscovite state of the sixteenth century. Siberia, the
     Caucasus, the Baltic States, the Murmansk-Archangel area, and much of southern
     Russia and the Ukraine were in the hands of their enemies.
255. Quoted in ibid., p. 164.
256. Levin, p. 216.
257. Thompson, pp. 242-45.
258. See ibid., pp. 249-50; Levin, pp. 216-17.
259. Thompson, p. 249.
260. Williams, *American-Russian Relations,* p. 169.
261. "Notes of a Meeting held at President Wilson's House," May 23 , 1919, in FRUS,
     1919, p. 357.
262. *Council of Four*, vol.2, p. 14.
263. Thompson, p. 240.
264. *Council of Four*, vol.2, p. 123.
265. Herbert C. Hoover to Wilson, March 28, 1919, in *PWW,* vol.56, pp. 375-78; see
     also Hoover, *The Ordeal of Woodrow Wilson,* (New York: McGraw-Hill, 1958),
     pp. 117-23, for his account of the relief plan's genesis and evolution.
266. The country he had in mind, other than Russia of course, was Hungary, then under
     the dominion of the short-lived Bolshevik regime of Bela Kun.
267. Hoover to Wilson, March 28, 1919, op.cit., p. 376.
268. Ibid., p. 377.
269. Ibid., pp. 376-77; Hoover did grant, however, that intervention might be justified
     if the Bolsheviks "undertake large military crusades in an attempt to impose their
     doctrines on other defenseless peoples" (p. 376). Evidently, the Bolshevik efforts
     to conquer the Baltic states, Finland, the Ukraine, parts of Poland, and the nascent
     Caucasian and Central Asian republics—all of which had already occurred by the
     time he wrote—were insufficiently large "crusades" to justify intervention by his
     standards.
270. Ibid., p. 375.
271. Ibid., p. 378.
272. Ibid.
273. Ibid. It is worth pointing out that, unlike Bullitt, Hoover correctly realized that the
     famine in Russia was not caused by the Allied blockade but was "a result of Bol-
     shevik economic conceptions" (ibid., p. 375).
274. On the implicit anti-Bolshevik elements of Hoover's plan see Levin, pp. 217-18.
275. See Wilson, Aide-Memoire to Allied Ambassadors, July 17, 1918, in *PWW,* vol.48,
     p. 643.
276. For details of this process, see Thompson, pp. 254-57.
277. Ibid,. pp. 259-60.
278. Statement by the Russian Political Conference, May 4, 1919, in FRUS, 1919, p. 110.
279. Ibid.
280. Kennan, *Russia and the West,* pp. 136-37.
281. See, e.g., *Council of Four,* vol.2, pp. 14-16, 26-29; Even Lloyd George was be-
     ginning to support Kolchak at this time (see, e.g., pp. 16, 123-24).
282. I have been unable to find any accurate estimates as to the exact amount of U.S.
     aid sent to Kolchak. However, it seems clear that almost all of it arrived when

Kolchak's forces were already being driven back after their successes in the spring of 1919, and that much of what was ultimately allotted was held back because of bureaucratic snafus.

283. Wilson, Message to the Senate, July 22, 1919, in FRUS, 1919, p. 394.

284. Joseph Grew to acting secretary of state, June 25, 1919, in ibid., pp. 384-85.

285. FRUS, 1919, p. 388.

286. Morris to acting secretary of state, July 22, 1919, ibid., pp. 394, 396.

287. Morris to Lansing, July 31, 1919, in ibid., p. 401.

288. Morris to Lansing, August 4, 1919, in ibid., pp. 404-5.

289. Ibid., p. 404.

290. Ibid., p. 405.

291. Ibid.

292. Morris to Lansing, August 8, 1919, in ibid., p. 408.

293. Morris to Lansing, August 12, 1919, in ibid., p. 411.

294. Morris to Lansing, August 11, 1919, in ibid., p. 410.

295. Ibid., p. 409.

296. Luckett, p. 308; Churchill, Aftermath, p. 245.

297. Lansing to Morris, August 25, 1919, in FRUS, 1919, p. 421.

298. Churchill, p. 246; Luckett, p. 298.

299. Unterberger, "Wilson and the Russian Revolution," p. 88.

300. Wilson, speech at Kansas City, September 9, 1919, in FRUS, 1919, p. 119.

301. Betty Unterberger's attempt to demonstrate that Wilson's decision to support the admiral was merely a concession to the European Allies (Unterberger, "Wilson and the Russian Revolution," p. 87), is unconvincing. Wilson had defied the Allies on this point for a long time and he obtained no reciprocal advantages in exchange for changing his mind.

302. See generally, Levin, op.cit., esp. pp. 2-7.

303. Robert Lansing, The Peace Negotiations: A Personal Narrative, (Boston: Houghton Mifflin, 1921), pp. 99-100; Lloyd C. Gardner, Safe for Democracy: The Anglo-American Response to Revolution, 1913-23, (New York: Oxford University Press, 1984), pp. 268-69

304. Lansing to ambassador in Great Britain, December 4, 1919, in FRUS, 1919, p. 130.

305. Ibid.

306. Unterberger, Expedition, pp. 177-78.

307. Unterberger, The United States, Revolutionary Russia, and the Birth of Czechoslovakia, p. 336.

4

The Whites Reconsidered

*"If at that tragic moment in our history the
Russian people had not produced any men
prepared to rise against the madness and
criminality of Bolshevik power and give their
lifeblood for their country threatened by
destruction—they would not have been a people
but dung...Fortunately, we belong to the
martyred, but great, Russian nation."*[1]

—General Anton I. Denikin

*"[T]he Russians had been accustomed to the
rule of the strong hand; and for good or evil the
strongest hand on the board was that of Lenin.
But no one could at that time say whether a
stronger than he would arise."*[2]

—David Lloyd George

No analysis of the opportunities for intervention in Russia available to
the Allies in 1918–19 can be complete without an appraisal of the Russian forces they sought to support. Two questions are critical: were the
Whites really capable of defeating the Bolsheviks, and would it have been
better for Russia and the world if they had done so? Could they win and
did they deserve to?

History—and historians—have not been kind to the Whites since their
defeat. "The salient point about the White movement," writes one leading analyst, "is that it failed."[3] The Whites are routinely denounced as
hopeless reactionaries who hoped to roll back the clock to the time of
tsarism. Their alleged opposition to land reform, their unwillingness to
grant independence to the non-Russian nationalities, and their corrupt and
parasitic governments, are all seen as evidence of both their inability to

135

mount a serious challenge to the Bolsheviks and their moral bankruptcy.[4] In particular, the inability of the Whites to attract popular support is traced to these factors, and that inability is often seen as the main cause of the White defeat.[5] Further, it is argued that the Whites were primarily responsible for the massive anti-Jewish pogroms which occurred in the Ukraine and southern Russia in 1919-20.[6] According to one authority, "anti-Semitism was neither a peripheral nor an accidental aspect of White ideology; it was a focal point of their world view."[7]

The general tone of most Russian Civil War historiography in the West is to posit a kind of moral equivalency between the two sides. "The basic reality of those years," writes the leading "revisionist" historian Moshe Lewin, "was that the battle was being waged not between democracy and authoritarianism but between two different authoritarian political camps that could field big armies and fight it out. Supporters of the Constituent Assembly could not do the same—and they were eliminated from the historical arena."[8]

Lewin's portrait of a war between reactionary and radical authoritarians with moderate "supporters of the Constituent Assembly" squeezed between them ignores a number of important issues, most notably the fact that the reestablishment, in one form or another, of a Constituent Assembly based on universal suffrage was the primary announced war aim of all of the different White governments. It also crudely downplays the totalitarian elements of Bolshevik rule that, even in 1918-20, went far beyond anything that had been done by earlier advocates of despotism, whether among the Whites or elsewhere. On the other hand, his position was clearly shared by the Bolsheviks, who consistently argued that the only alternative to their rule was the reestablishment of tsarism. "At the present time," Colonel Vatsetis, commander in chief of the Red Army, wrote in April 1919, "the civil war has crystallized and taken on a decisive character; only the extreme tendencies have remained on the field of battle: the Communists and the monarchists."[9]

In the more narrowly military field, it is often claimed that the Whites faced almost insuperable disadvantages because of the numerical superiority of the Red Army, the ability of the Reds—who occupied the center of the country—to operate on interior lines, and their own disunity of command.[10] Richard Pipes even goes so far as to claim that "[f]rom a strategic point of view, nearly all the advantages lay on the side of the Red Army."[11]

Historians have been heavily critical of the political strategy of the Whites, which left all major outstanding issues to be settled by the Constituent Assembly after victory. "The Whites," it is said, "had no vision of a future Russia" and this failure led to their inability to offer an alternative to the Bolshevik program that the population could rally around.[12] One retrospective critic has even suggested that the Whites would have done better to openly declare themselves in favor of a restoration of monarchy.[13] Ironically, this criticism is often made by the very same scholars who also attack the Whites as hidebound reactionaries, a characterization that would lead us to believe that they *did* have a clear "vision" of the political order they wished to see after the war, even if not a pretty one![14]

Most of these criticisms of the Whites have at least some validity, but they are, in many cases, grossly overstated. Also, the critics have often chosen to ignore numerous countervailing influences and mitigating circumstances. The argument that the Whites were authoritarian reactionaries ignores the presence of numerous liberal, and even socialist, elements in their ranks, and also fails to come to grips with the fact that the crimes of the Bolsheviks were on an entirely different, incomparably greater order of magnitude. The claim that the Whites were doomed to failure downplays the numerous disadvantages faced by the Reds and sidesteps the reality that the anti-Bolshevik movement came extremely close to victory, as their enemies fully recognized at the time.[15]

Perhaps the strongest argument to be made in favor of the Whites is a negative one: their rule and their agenda for the future were not nearly as horrendous as that of the Bolsheviks. To be sure, many White officials were corrupt and repressive and they often tended to persecute even those leftists who were not Bolsheviks. Arbitrary imprisonment and execution were commonplace in the territories they controlled.[16] However, the White Terror was primarily a decentralized, irregular activity carried on by local commanders and officials, generally without the sanction of their superiors. Its victims nonetheless probably numbered in the thousands,[17] and the White leaders certainly deserve censure for failing to curb it more decisively. But it is highly unlikely that it even began to approach the figures for the Red Terror, which included some 140,000 political executions carried out by the Cheka alone.[18]

Moreover, the Red Terror was a highly organized program of repression approved at the highest levels of the Bolshevik power structure.[19] It was not just a temporary war measure but a policy aimed at the complete "extermination" of the Bolsheviks' "class enemies," whether they supported the Whites or not.[20] The Bolsheviks persecuted even those opposition parties, such as the Mensheviks, which actually supported them against the Whites. By contrast, non-Bolshevik socialist parties, including the Mensheviks and the S-Rs, operated more or less openly in White-controlled territories. Although individual members of these factions were often persecuted for dubious reasons, the parties themselves were never banned.[21] Indeed, under Kolchak, the S-Rs controlled most local governments in Siberia.[22] The White regime set up under British auspices in northern Russia was actually headed by Nikolai Chaikovsky, a longstanding S-R leader.

If the Red Terror had at least a partial equivalent in the repression carried out by the Whites, there was no real White counterpart to the Bolshevik agricultural policies which led to massive famines that claimed the lives of at least 5 million people during the Civil War and its immediate aftermath. Bolshevik efforts to forcibly requisition food for the Red Army, impose rigid price controls on agricultural products, and repress "rich" peasants ("kulaks") destroyed all incentive for the production and delivery of agricultural goods. Beginning in early 1918, and continuing throughout the Civil War period, the Bolsheviks waged an ever more intensive struggle against kulaks and other "bourgeois" elements in the countryside.[23]

As in the case of the Red Terror, Bolshevik agricultural policies were not the product of wartime necessity or of purely local initiative. They were undertaken for primarily ideological reasons at the behest of Lenin himself, and continued even after it became obvious that they were rapidly leading to the greatest famine in modern European history.[24] In fact, the Bolsheviks to some extent welcomed the famine, since it could be used to deny food to politically unreliable portions of the population and to weaken the peasantry.[25] A secret 1918 Bolshevik report on agricultural policy clearly stated that "the true purpose" of the regime's anti-kulak policies and agricultural supply requisitions "was *purely political*" (emphasis in original).[26]

The Bolshevik price controls, which required all surplus grain to be sold to the state at absurdly low prices twenty or thirty times less than free market value, were likewise instituted primarily for the purpose of combating "capitalist speculation." "Freedom to trade in grain," wrote Lenin in 1919, "is connected with the universal power of the landowners and capitalists."[27] State control of agriculture, he believed, "guarantees proper socialist production and distribution, guarantees the complete victory of the socialist system."[28] It was not a wartime necessity but an ideological imperative. While it would be wrong to say that the war had *no* impact on Bolshevik agricultural policy, it is clear that ideological factors were far more important. Indeed, it was ideology that shaped the Bolshevik perception of the war itself, for they saw themselves as fighting against not only the White armies and governments but all elements in Russian society that might in any way be opposed to their program, including the peasants.

In this connection, it is important to recall that the Bolsheviks had, long before the revolution, come to see themselves as defenders of the classic Marxist view of the peasantry as an essentially reactionary force, a view they vehemently asserted against the S-Rs and other Russian socialists who considered the peasantry to be potentially progressive. The Bolsheviks hoped to break the peasants as a political force and ultimately bring them under state control through the imposition of collective farming. In fact, far from helping them against the Whites, Bolshevik agricultural policies surely harmed their cause significantly by alienating the peasantry and stimulating massive peasant uprisings behind Bolshevik lines, uprisings which led to the diversion of scarce troops to the rear.[29] This outcome was not the result of ignorance, for Bolshevik leaders were well aware that peasant opposition to their economic policies was hurting their cause.[30]

Despite the many defects of their administration in other respects, it is clear that White agricultural policies actually served to alleviate the famine in the areas they occupied. Upon entering a territory, the Whites would immediately abolish the Bolshevik price controls and restrictions on the sale of grain and end the policy of repressing kulaks. As a result, "the entrance of the White troops in a city was immediately followed by a great drop in the price of bread."[31] In southern Russia, the Volunteer Army "supported the principle of free trade" in foodstuffs, which "was a popular principle, since the people...associated the trade restrictions prevailing in Bolshevik territories with shortages."[32] The result of this radical difference in policy between the two sides in the Russian Civil War was that the population of those territories controlled by the Bolsheviks declined by many millions of people as a consequence of the famine and the epidemics of disease it engendered. By contrast, the territories controlled by the Whites during most of the war actually experienced population increases.[33] Perhaps no other single fact more clearly demonstrates the relative merits of the two competing regimes.

Another particularly damaging Bolshevik policy which the Whites did not imitate was the program of deliberate inflation. The abolition of money had long been the dream of some utopian socialists and, in 1918-19, the new regime's monetary policy was in the hands of party functionaries strongly committed to this goal.[34] These officials deliberately set out to make money worthless by printing as much of it as possible. As a result, between January 1917 and January 1923, the price level increased a mindboggling 100 million-fold.[35] Hyperinflation harmed all portions of the Russian populace, but it was particularly damaging to the poorer workers and peasants whose savings were wiped out and who had little in the way of tangible wealth. Thus did the Bolsheviks treat those classes in whose name they had seized power. To be sure, there was inflation in the White areas as well, particularly under Denikin.[36] But it was nowhere near as high; nor was it deliberately stimulated by the White governments, which, on the contrary, made desperate efforts to curb it by backing their currency with gold.[37]

What was true of inflation was also the case for the entire complex of Bolshevik economic policies misleadingly known as "war communism"—misleadingly because it had only a tangential connection with the war and was adopted primarily for ideological reasons.[38] The Bolshevik economic program included the nationalization of industry and banks, the suppression of private economic transactions—denounced as "speculation," the widespread use of forced labor drafted from among the "bourgeois" classes,[39] and the imposition of strict discipline in the factories, which eventually reduced the allegedly dominant proletariat to the status of forced laborers themselves.[40]

In no sense was this policy a product of wartime need and crisis conditions, as has sometimes been argued by "revisionist" historians.[41] As early as March 1918, when the Whites had barely even begun to organize their forces and the Bolsheviks did not expect them to pose a serious threat to their power, Lenin proclaimed the goal of immediately introducing "socialist organization of production on the scale of the whole state."[42] He also urged that steps be taken towards "the full realization of universal compulsory labor service."[43] All private trade was to be replaced, "at first [by] state monopoly of 'trade' [and] subsequently [by the] replacement, complete and final, of 'trade' by planned, organized *distribution* through associations of trading and industrial office workers, under the leadership of Soviet power."[44]

Even when the Civil War was practically over, Soviet leaders would continue to speak of these policies as ideologically essential. In November 1920, at a time when the Whites were as good as finished, Leon Trotsky clearly explained that "War Communist" policies were not a temporary aberration but an integral element of the construction of socialism:

> The socialist organization of the economy begins with the liquidation of the market, and that means the liquidation of its regulator—namely, the "free" play of the laws of supply and demand. The inevitable result...the subordination of production to the needs of society—must be achieved by *the unity of the economic plan*, which in principle covers all branches of production.[45] (Emphasis in original)

The policies of war communism were not reversed until 1921, when the almost complete collapse of industrial production which it engendered necessitated a departure from Marxist-Leninist orthodoxy in the form of the New Economic Policy; even then, the loosening of restrictions on private enterprise was understood by Lenin and most other top Bolshevik leaders to be strictly temporary.[46]

By the time of the NEP, war communism had resulted in a catastrophic decline in production and living standards, on a scale virtually unequalled in modern history up to that time. The destruction of production incentives and price signals of consumer preferences which was the inevitable consequence of attempts to suppress the market had taken a fearsome toll. Russian GNP and living standards in 1920 were a mere one-third of the already low levels of 1913, with almost all of the decline coming in the period of Bolshevik rule.[47] This constituted a massive impoverishment of what was already one of the poorest populations in Europe. While wartime dislocation surely contributed to the disruption of industry, it cannot explain its extraordinary scale. In fact, the best argument against the view that wartime conditions were the cause of early Bolshevik economic policies is that no war before or since has ever caused a government to adopt such measures, in part for the very good reason that they tend to reduce the production available for wartime needs rather than increase it. Certainly, the Whites, who were just as influenced by wartime imperatives as their opponents, did not adopt them.

This list of Bolshevik abuses that massively outweighed those of the Whites could easily be extended. The ruthless campaign against religion,[48] the introduction of the Gulag system of concentration camps, the imposition of comprehensive censorship, and the attempt to control all aspects of cultural life are only a few of the oppressive elements of Bolshevik rule that had no real counterparts among their enemies. Of particular importance from the standpoint of the West was the determination of the Bolsheviks to further the establishment of communist regimes in as many other nations as possible, a foreign policy agenda which dwarfed the traditional imperialist expansionism of some of the Whites in its menacing implications, and should have persuaded British conservatives like Lord Curzon to rethink their position that a Bolshevik Russia would be no more dangerous to British imperial interests than a White one. The underlying point is that the Bolshevik regime of the Civil War era was a tyranny of unprecedented scope and brutality. None of the authoritarian tendencies of the Whites—or any previous European political movement, for that matter—could compare with it.

Thus, a strong negative moral case can be made for the Whites, in that they were far preferable to their enemies. But is it possible to go further than this? Can anything favorable be said about them in their own right?

To begin with, the Whites simply were not the monolithic reactionary clique they are often made out to be. In this connection, the standard practice of referring to a single, undifferentiated White movement is somewhat misleading, despite its use in nearly all historical studies—including this one. In fact, there were differences between the various White governments and even changes in the political orientation of the same government over time. Throughout most of 1918, the anti-Bolshevik governments in Siberia and the Volga region were dominated by the S-Rs, a party that can hardly be considered reactionary. The S-Rs also led the government of northern Russia, set up under British auspices.

The Volunteer Army, then in its formative stage, was established by former tsarist military officers. But it would be a mistake to conclude from this that it was a uniformly monarchist organization. General Mikhail Alekseev, the army's co-founder, had played a key role in persuading Tsar Nicholas II to abdicate in March 1917.[49] While his main motive in doing so seems to have been to insure the preservation of order and the continuation of the war against Germany, his action at least shows that he had no special sympathy for the monarchy. Later, Alekseev readily accepted the liberal-socialist Provisional Government and announced a generally liberal political program for the Volunteer Army.

General Lavr Kornilov, Alekseev's colleague, was certainly no liberal. But it is not clear that he was a reactionary either; at bottom, he considered himself an apolitical military officer. Kornilov's attempt to move troops into the capital in September 1917 may well have actually been an effort to save the Provisional Government from the Bolsheviks, rather than launch a military coup against it, though the issue remains controversial among historians.[50] General Denikin, who became the Volunteer Army's commander-in-chief in April 1918 upon the death of Kornilov, had, in the words of his biographer, "an undeniable leftist orientation... for an officer of that period."[51] During the prerevolutionary era, he had sympathized with the political agenda of the liberal Constitutional Democratic (Kadet) Party,[52] which, as its name suggests, had advocated the replacement of absolutism with a constitutional monarchy and the implementation of an assortment of social and economic reforms. In his memoirs, Denikin speaks of reactionary monarchists with contempt.[53] He condemned their tendency to blame the Jews for Russia's problems and lamented their influence "among the unbalanced and politically naive elements of the [White] officer corps."[54] Even Peter Kenez, a historian harshly critical of most aspects of the White movement, concludes that "Denikin...was and always remained a liberal."[55]

In September 1918, the task of drafting the Constitution of the Volunteer Army, a document intended to state the war aims of the Volunteers and define the legal basis of their authority, was entrusted to two Kadet lawyers, K.N. Sokolov and V.A. Stepanov.[56] The resulting document guaranteed "equal rights" to all citizens "irrespective of nationality, social class, and religious affiliation."[57] It also provided for freedom of the press and assembly, guarantees against arrest without due process of law, and protection for the right of private property.[58] Perhaps most important of all, the constitution recognized the validity of laws promulgated by the Provisional Government, thereby accepting the legitimacy of the overthrow of tsarism.[59]

A clause specially inserted by Denikin provided that "[t]he provisional government [of the Volunteer Army] must be unlimited, taking the form of a personal dictatorship."[60] But it is clear that this provision was inserted because the Volunteer leaders, including the liberal Kadet politicians, "all considered dictatorial authority the only possible option under the conditions of the struggle against...the concentrated dictatorial power of the Soviet."[61] Denikin's personal dictatorship, whether it was a good idea or not, was clearly intended as a temporary measure. There is no evidence that Denikin, any more than Kolchak, ever wanted to become the permanent dictator of Russia, although some of the more reactionary officers in his entourage clearly believed that a permanent authoritarian regime would be a good idea. Throughout his time as commander in chief of the Volunteers, Denikin remained committed to the reestablishment of the Constituent Assembly, which he considered to be the only body with the right to determine the future political structure of Russia.

Undoubtedly, the reactionary influences within Denikin's regime grew during late 1918 and 1919, particularly once the original Volunteer Army was diluted by alliances with the more conservative Don and Kuban Cossacks.[62] In Siberia, the Kolchak coup of November 1918 also increased the influence of reactionaries, though Kolchak himself probably had not intended such an outcome.

Even in the Murmansk-Archangel area, the January 1919 departure of Chaikovsky to take up a position with the Russian Political Conference in Paris led to a relative conservative ascendancy within the northern Russian Provisional Government, now effectively headed by General Eugene K. Miller.[63] Miller was not a reactionary and he maintained cordial relations with the socialists in northern Russia.[64] But he was hardly a committed liberal either. When, at one point, Alexander Kerensky, the former head of the Provisional Government, intimated that he might come to northern Russia, Miller threatened to have him shot if he dared to do so.[65] To be sure, Kerensky's failures in leading the Provisional Government were bitterly resented by anti-Bolshevik Russians of all political persuasions; the former prime minister would hardly have been an asset to any White government. Nonetheless, Miller's threat bespeaks a latent illiberalism which boded ill for the future of any post-Bolshevik regime in which he had a role. On the other hand, Miller, like Kolchak and Denikin, was unequivocal in asserting that the future of Russia must be decided by a Constituent Assembly based on universal suffrage. "The Tsar," he told General Ironside, the new commander of the British contingent in northern Russia, "had been his master and he would remain faithful to his memory. But it was for the people of Russia to decide whether there would be a Tsar once more."[66]

Thus, reactionary influence in the White governments tended to grow over time, particularly as the ongoing escalation of the war and the obvious ineptitude of many of the liberal and socialist politicians led to an increasing concentration of power in the hands of the generals. Even in the late stages of the conflict, however, the White leaders continued to adhere to the goal of establishing a democratic Constituent Assembly, and the White regimes remained far less repressive than that of the Bolsheviks. Admiral Kolchak, who became the recognized leader of all the White armies, was no monarchist, even if his regime was clearly more conservative than that of the S-Rs who preceded him. "Kolchak's politics," as Evan Mawdsley points out, "did not fit the stereotype of a black reactionary."[67] His political advisers were mostly young Kadet liberals.[68]

The only White government with a clearly reactionary leader was that in northernwest Russia led by General Nikolai Yudenich. But even he was forced to accept the goal of establishing a Constituent Assembly and subordinate himself to Kolchak. In any case, the importance of his small army was very much secondary compared to those of Kolchak and Denikin. The fact that both sides in the Russian Civil War were far from ideal should not blind us to the immense differences in degree, differences so great that they actually amounted to differences in kind.

But there is another, still more important, point to be made: *The moment of greatest liberal ascendancy in the White movement coincided almost precisely with the West's best opportunity for a successful intervention.* During the summer and early fall of 1918, the Siberian, Volga, and northern Russian White governments were still firmly in the hands of the S-Rs, supported, in the former two cases, by the liberally inclined Czech Legion. In southern Russia, Denikin, Alekseev, and the Kadet politicians were still able to impose a substantial measure of restraint on their reactionary colleagues. And, as we saw in chapters 2 and 3, it was at this time that even a modest intervention mounted by two or three divisions could probably have overthrown the Bolshevik regime with little difficulty, a point backed up by the testimony of the Bolsheviks themselves. There can be little doubt that a three-division strong British contingent landing in northern Russia and marching on Moscow, combined with a serious U.S. effort to intervene in the Volga region through Siberia, would have had a strong chance of overthrowing the Bolsheviks in the late summer of 1918. In fact, any one of these moves, particularly the former, might have led to victory all by itself.

One cannot be certain that a White-Allied victory at this time would have led to a liberal democratic regime. However, the chances would have been good, particularly if the first elections and the development of a new constitution took place under Allied observation and supervision. In the fall of 1918, reactionary forces had still had little chance to organize, and it was only the chaotic conditions of the Civil War, combined with the desperate need of the Whites for trained military officers and administrative officials, which allowed them regain some of their influence later. Ironically, it was precisely during this promising period, however, that President Wilson was especially worried about the possibility of aiding reaction. Later, he would provide considerably greater aid and recognition to Admiral Kolchak's regime, at a time when that government was much more dubious in its liberal credentials than were the White regimes in place in July-September 1918. The dithering of the Allies during this period lost them a golden opportunity to both end the Bolshevik menace and advance the cause of liberalism in Russia.

Among the charges levelled against the Whites, that of complicity in anti-Semitic pogroms was perhaps the most damaging, both in the eyes of contemporary Western public opinion and in those of later historians. During the Russian Civil War, at least 100,000 Jews were slaughtered in pogroms, almost all of them in the Ukraine and southern Russia.[69] The prominent role of Jewish Bolsheviks in the Red administration—particularly in the Cheka, the traditional antipathy of the Russian and Ukrainian peasants towards the Jews, the desire for loot, and the general lawlessness of the Russian Civil War period all contributed to these outbreaks.[70] The standard position of most Western—and, of course, all Soviet—historiography, has been to place primary blame for the pogroms on the Whites. "The officers of the Volunteer Army," Peter Kenez writes, "were obsessed with anti-Semitism.... In thousands of reports and documents in the Volunteer archives, one cannot find a single denunciation of pogroms. The agents sending reports to their headquarters simply assumed that Jews were responsible for all miseries, Bolshevism, inflation and lost battles."[71]

While it is undeniable that there were numerous anti-Semitic White officers and that many of them sanctioned—or even took part in—pogroms, it is simply not true that the White leadership supported pogroms or made no effort to stop them. Nor is it the case that anti-Semitism played a central role in its ideology.

The original Volunteer Army of 1918 was, in fact, remarkably free of anti-Semitism, especially by the standards of early twentieth-century Russia. Jewish officers served in it on an equal basis and took part in the Ice March.[72] In September 1918, General Alekseev had issued a stern warning that anti-Semitism was not acceptable in the White ranks.[73] The Jewish Kadet leader Mikhail Vinnaver, who had spent much of 1918 with the Volunteers, reported in November that he had not encountered any anti-Semitism among them.[74] The Kadet-led liberal government which ruled the Crimea under Volunteer auspices from November 1918 until the peninsula was recaptured by the Bolsheviks in April 1919 was in fact headed by a Jewish politician, the appropriately named Solomon S. Krym ("Krym" is Russian for "Crimea").[75] Other Jewish Kadets, including Vinnaver, had prominent roles in its administration.

As the Volunteers entered the Jewish Pale of Settlement territories to their northern in the spring and summer of 1919, the situation changed. Denikin bowed to pressure from anti-Semites and agreed to exclude Jewish officers from the Army, although he refused requests to discharge Jewish common soldiers.[76] The White propaganda agency, Osvag, began to spread vicious anti-Semitic rumors.[77] The arrival of the Volunteer Army in the Pale also was the beginning of its troops' participation in the pogroms.

It is true, as Denikin, noted in his memoirs that "[t]he wave of anti-Semitism had gripped the Southern long before the arrival of the army in the Pale of Settlement."[78] There had already been numerous anti-Semitic outbreaks on the part of various Ukrainian nationalist forces, particularly the army of Semyon Petlura, as well as spontaneous outbursts by the population at large. The forces of independent warlords and anarchist leaders such as Nestor Makhno, also committed numerous atrocities. In fact, a 1951 study conducted by an American Jewish organization found that some 65 percent of the outbreaks of anti-Jewish violence during the Russian Civil War can be attributed to the troops of the Ukrainian nationalists, the anarchists, or independent warlords.[79] Petlura, Makhno, and their ilk were enemies of both the Reds and the Whites, and Denikin can hardly be held responsible for them. Another 8.5 percent of the outbreaks were attributed to the troops of the Red Army; interestingly, this particular set of pogroms has received very little attention from historians.

Nonetheless, some 17 percent of the anti-Semitic incidents *were* the responsibility of the White troops. In Denikin's words, "the troops of the Armed Forces of Southern Russia did not escape the general affliction and besmirched themselves with anti-Jewish pogroms."[80] Most of the White pogroms were committed by Cossack units attached to the Volunteers, troops over which Denikin had only very limited control.[81] The core units of the original Volunteer Army were largely innocent of wrongdoing. Even so, Denikin and his subordinates could and should have done more to curb the violence.

This is not to suggest, however, that they did nothing. Kenez' claim that the Volunteer leaders never condemned anti-Semitism or tried to stop the pogroms is inaccurate. Denikin and other high-ranking general issued numerous orders attempting to prevent anti-Semitic outbreaks.[82] In a number of instances, they insisted on inflicting harsh punishments on those who flouted these commands, sometimes including execution of the offenders.[83] General Wrangel even had looters from his command hanged publicly.[84] Denikin also issued a general proclamation stating that "all citizens, regardless of their race or religion, will be guaranteed immunity and the inviolability of the individual, home, and private property."[85]

In his memoirs, Denikin rejected the view that the Jews were responsible for Russia's problems and expressed shame and remorse for the actions of his troops.[86] He believed that the pogroms were largely the result of "animal instincts unleashed by war and revolution.... How was it possible" he wrote, "to expect the seething masses to show particular kindness and humanity towards 'outsiders' when, over the course of several years, they had, with exceptional cruelty and sadism, been cracking the skulls of 'their own.'"[87] There is no evidence to support the claim that Denikin "held all of Jewry responsible for the 'crimes' of those who fought on the Bolshevik side" or that "he believed and proclaimed that Bolshevism and Judaism were almost the same."[88]

For a long time, Denikin refused the pleas of Jewish organizations and foreign supporters, notably those of Churchill,[89] to issue a general proclamation condemning pogroms.[90] However, he refrained from doing so only because he believed that such a step would backfire. He feared that a proclamation would only lead to accusations that he had "sold out to the kikes" without leading to any improvement in the condition of the Jews.[91] Instead, he argued that the Jews could only be protected effectively through an effort to "condemn and severely punish *any* crime, *any* violence against people—be they Orthodox, Moslems or Jews."[92] In October 1919, Denikin finally relented and made a speech denouncing pogroms explicitly.[93] It had virtually no effect.

If it is not correct to say that Denikin and the other Volunteer leaders sanctioned pogroms, it is still legitimate to criticize their failure to make a more thoroughgoing and systematic effort to stop them. For that matter, Denikin did not even succeed in suppressing the widespread looting

and violence which his troops perpetrated against the non-Jewish population. As Denikin's biographer notes, "the [Volunteer] army meted out
its punishments unskillfully, sporadically and secretively."[94] While
Denikin was well-intentioned, he lacked the will to force his men to abide
by his own principles. The general may have been right to believe that it
was impossible to stop the pogroms altogether, but a more forceful approach might have at least limited their scope. On the other hand, Denikin
was probably right to argue that the fate of the Jews would have been
"incomparably more tragic" if he had actually supported the pogroms, as
his Western critics charged.[95]

White commanders in areas with smaller Jewish populations were more
successful than Denikin in curbing anti-Jewish outbreaks. In Siberia,
Kolchak's regime, despite its incompetence in so many other areas, was
able to prevent them almost entirely,[96] although some massacres did occur in the areas controlled by Kalmykov and Semenov, which the Omsk
government's power could not effectively reach.[97] Ironically, in view of
this success, Kolchak, unlike Denikin, *was* personally anti-Semitic. He
is said to have been an avid reader of the *Protocols of the Elders of Zion*[98]
and he thought that the inadequacy of the support offered to his government by the American forces in Siberia was partially due to the presence
of Jewish soldiers in the U.S. contingent.[99] The White government in northern Russia also did not experience any major anti-Jewish outbreaks.

Inadequate as they often were, the efforts of the White generals to prevent pogroms stand in favorable contrast to the attitude of the Bolshevik
leaders. Lenin repeatedly refused to act on the numerous reports he received of pogroms committed by the Red Army.[100] "The reports he received on this subject," writes Dmitri Volkogonov, the first independent
historian to gain access to Lenin's private files, "invariably bear his usual
laconic scrawl: 'For the archives.'"[101]

Other Bolshevik leaders were no better. Ironically, the Jewish Bolsheviks who were the main targets of reactionary anti-Semitic propaganda were
particularly careful not to appear to make any effort to help pogrom victims. When a Jewish delegation asked Leon Trotsky, the most prominent
Jewish Bolshevik, to intercede on behalf of his people, the war commissar
angrily replied: "I am not a Jew but an internationalist."[102] Needless, to say,
Trotsky, like Lenin, ignored the numerous reports of Red Army pogroms
he received,[103] even though, as war commissar, he was directly responsible
for the conduct of Soviet troops. Karl Radek, a high-ranking Bolshevik of

Polish Jewish background even went so far as to say that he considered Judaism a "disease" and wanted to "exterminate" the Jewish people.[104]

Like the Whites, the Bolsheviks generally shied away from condemning pogroms openly, a policy that they considered counterproductive for propaganda reasons.[105] In March 1919, Lenin did bring himself to make a recorded radio message condemning the pogroms. Anti-Semitism, he announced was fomented by capitalists, "in order to blind the workers, to divert their attention from the real enemy of the working people, capital."[106] Only the "kulaks, exploiters, and capitalists," among the Jews, should be treated as enemies.[107]

Unfortunately, as Lenin well knew, the Jews were disproportionately represented in each of these groups, a disproportion greatly magnified in the eyes of the Russian peasants. Thus, Lenin's message, to the extent that it had any impact at all, likely served to stimulate anti-Jewish violence as much as to curb it. It was, after all, Lenin who once remarked that anti-Semitism is the socialism of the ignorant. Thus, it was not entirely accidental, to use a Marxian turn of phrase, that a wave of pogroms coincided with the massive Bolshevik propaganda campaign trumpeting the evils of "speculation" and "capitalist exploitation"—not to mention the Cheka's attempts to "exterminate the bourgeoisie as a class."[108] However surprisingly, the "reactionary" White leaders, including the anti-Semitic Kolchak, actually made more of an effort to curb pogroms than the "progressive" Bolsheviks.

Next to the accusation of complicity in pogroms, the most influential charge against the Whites, both at the time and later, was that they lacked popular support. As we saw earlier, Wilson and Lloyd George believed that this lack of support imperilled both the moral legitimacy of the White cause and their ability to prevail over the Bolsheviks.

With a number of important exceptions,[109] most Russian Civil War historians agree that "[i]n deciding the outcome of the struggle, political failures were more decisive than military ones."[110] One recent major study of the Russian Civil War even goes so far as to attribute nearly all changes in the strategic balance during the course of the war to fluctuations in popular support.[111] The Whites' inability to formulate a coherent and appealing ideological platform, it is argued, fatally compromised their chances of winning. In addition, their shortsighted refusal to support land reform for the peasants and promise independence to the non-Russian nationalities of the former empire alienated important potential allies. Even

Martin Malia, a scholar highly unsympathetic to the Bolshevik regime, concludes that the peasants had "a marginal preference for the Reds" and that this had an important impact on the outcome of the conflict.[112]

These arguments are not without their merit, but they ignore the decisive role of military power in determining the outcome of wars. Neglected is the wisdom of Clausewitz:

> [N]o matter what the central feature of the enemy's power may be—the point on which your efforts must converge—the defeat and destruction of his fighting force remains the best way to begin, and in every case will be a very significant feature of the campaign.[113]

In his analysis of British intervention in the war, Richard Ullman rightly criticizes the "fundamentally fallacious analogy" made by Lloyd George and Wilson in their conviction that "a civil war was like an especially violent election from which the party that can attract the most popular support will emerge victorious."[114] History knows many examples of civil wars won by a faction lacking in popular support but possessing a more powerful, better-led army than its opponents. In many cases, such an army can compel support, or at least quiescence, from even an unwilling population.

If only because of their own countries' history, American and British observers should have been especially suspicious of the analogy between wars and elections. After all, the Union was able to reconquer the Southern in the American Civil War despite the almost unanimous opposition of the southernern white population and the substantial doubts about the war harbored by large minorities in the North;[115] the application of superior military power, when finally placed in the hands of capable generals such as Grant and Sherman, allowed the cause of Union to prevail anyway.[116] Similarly, in the English Civil War, the comparatively unpopular royalists repeatedly defeated the parliamentary army until the latter was reinvigorated by the superior generalship of Cromwell. Obviously, it would be wrong to say that the Russian Civil War was directly analogous to the British and American conflicts; however, these precedents—and others like them, such as the Spanish Civil War—cast doubt on the notion that popular support is necessarily the decisive factor in civil conflicts.

In the Russian Civil War, popular support was particularly unlikely to be an overwhelmingly decisive factor because of the ignorance, isolation, and demoralization of much of the populace. It must not be forgotten that the Russian Civil War came directly on the heels of a massive

World War in which millions of Russians were killed. It also coincided with enormous famines and epidemics of disease, brought on primarily by Bolshevik policies. Throughout much of the conflict, the peasants who formed the bulk of the Russian population were primarily interested in simply surviving and trying to rebuild their shattered lives. They had little time and ability to provide meaningful support to any of the combatants, even had they wanted to. In addition, the parochial outlook of most of the peasants made it extraordinarily difficult to mobilize them for the sake of causes which reached beyond the confines of their native villages.[117] That is why the only armed forces that the peasants joined with some enthusiasm were not the Red or White armies but an assortment of "Green" detachments that sprang up on an ad hoc basis all over the country in order to revolt against specific local abuses of the Red or White governments in the area; some Green detachments were formed simply for the purpose of looting.[118]

The Greens "were the only true volunteer popular army in Russia," and their combined numbers probably exceeded the strength of the Red and White forces combined.[119] By contrast, both the Red and the White armies, suffered from massive desertion, to the point where there were usually more deserters at any given time than troops actually fighting in the field.[120] There is considerable evidence that many of these deserters joined the Greens.[121] But their disorganized and sporadic nature, combined with their almost total lack of a national agenda or perspective, prevented the Greens from playing a decisive role in the war. They could only launch revolts behind the lines of both sides, with effects on the outcome of the conflict that largely cancelled each other out. If anything, there is reason to believe that they caused more harm to the Bolsheviks than to the Whites, since the territories occupied by the former contained a higher percentage of poor peasants. The peasants of Siberia and southern Russia, where the Whites were based, were more likely to be marginally better-off freeholders with more to lose from participation in partisan bands than their cousins in Bolshevik-occupied central Russia.

Once the Whites were defeated, the Bolsheviks were able to crush the numerous Green rebels in a series of ruthless campaigns that should have demonstrated once and for all to doubting Western intellectuals that a government lacking in popular support is not necessarily incapable of prevailing against even an extremely large insurgency.[122] The successful Bolshevik tactics include massive hostage-taking, extensive executions, and the deportation of entire villages.[123] In a secret 1921 report, Vladimir Antonov-Ovseenko, the Bolshevik official in charge of suppressing one of the largest of the Green uprisings, frankly confessed that the Soviet regime was extremely unpopular in the countryside, noting that "the peasant uprisings develop because of widespread *dissatisfaction, on the part of small property owners in the villages with the dictatorship of the proletariat, which directs at them the cutting edge of merciless compulsion, cares little for the economic needs of the peasantry,* and does the countryside no perceptible service at all on either the economic or the educational side" (emphasis in the original).[124] Fortunately, he concluded, ruthless measures of repression had succeeded in breaking the resistance of the peasants by instilling "*an awareness of the hopelessness of fighting the Red Army* " (emphasis in the original).[125]

Historians who attempt to explain the outcome of the Civil War in terms of greater popular support for the Reds thus ignore the very limited nature of the extent to which public opinion could have any impact at all. It was very difficult for an impoverished, starving population to resist an organized and disciplined army, even if that army was as weak and ill-trained as those of the Reds and Whites tended to be. In addition, these explanations fail to come to grips with the fact that the peasantry, which constituted some 80 to 90 percent of the population, tended to oppose *both* sides in roughly equal proportion, albeit on the basis of local grievances rather than out of any strong preferences about the structure of national government. Furthermore, by focusing on the unpopularity of the Whites, the advocates of the popular support explanation of the Civil War's outcome ignore the very real extent to which the Bolsheviks had also managed to alienate most of the population, perhaps to an even greater degree than their enemies.

Unlike many Western observers, both contemporary and in later years, the Bolshevik leaders, as Antonov-Ovseenko's report suggests, were not under any delusion that they were popular in the countryside, even in comparison to the Whites. In July 1919 Lenin openly admitted that the Siberian peasants had supported Kolchak against the Reds during the latter's advance in the spring of 1919.[126] Though the White unwillingness to implement land reform and their tendency to return lands seized by the peasants to their former owners certainly tended to antagonize the rural population, Bolshevik policies were resented still more. While the White armies often brought back former landlords in their wake, they had no equivalent to the rigid price controls of the Bolsheviks, which effectively prevented the peasants from selling even such produce as remained after the Red Army's food requisitions. Moreover, it must never be forgotten that White rule held no horrors comparable in scale to the massive famines that resulted from Bolshevik policies. This factor alone surely led to a substantial "marginal preference" that was the opposite of that usually postulated.[127]

It is sometimes argued, nonetheless, that the peasants' fierce traditional resentment against the landlords associated with the Whites must have necessarily outweighed any grievances they had against the Bolsheviks.[128] This argument overlooks the fact that the peasants came to regard the Bolshevik regime *itself* as a kind of landlord, even referring to Communist officials as *pomeshchiki*—literally, "landowners."[129] One peasant petition even implored the Bolshevik authorities to "put an end to...serfdom," implying that at least these particular villagers saw communist policies not just as a new form of landlordism but as a return to the conditions of near-slavery that existed before the Great Emancipation of the serfs in 1861.[130] This latter perception must surely have been strengthened by the Bolshevik efforts to establish collective farms, which struck at the heart of peasant sensibilities by completely depriving them of their treasured individual plots and compelling them to work directly for the state, as opposed to merely paying a fraction of what they produced to the landlords, as was the practice in pre-1917 Russia and under White rule. And, indeed, attempts to establish state-run farms were among the principal causes of anti-Bolshevik peasant revolts, especially in the Ukraine.[131] While the peasants surely were not active supporters of the Whites, "[t]here exists no evidence," in the words of Richard Pipes, "that the Russian or Ukrainian peasants, given a free choice between Reds and Whites, would have opted for the former."[132]

Although it is rarely argued that the peasants were more than relative supporters of the Bolsheviks, it is still often assumed that the Bolsheviks had the "active support of the urban working class."[133] This, after all, was the class in whose name the Bolsheviks had taken power. In the elections for the Constituent Assembly in November 1917, the Bolsheviks had done relatively well among urban workers, particularly those in better-paying industries.[134] However, the imposition of harsh labor discipline in the first months of Bolshevik rule combined with the new government's heavy-handed attempts to bring independent unions under the control of the state quickly eroded this reservoir of good will.[135] In the spring of 1918, a wave of large-scale anti-Bolshevik strikes broke out in numerous cities throughout Russia, including Petrograd and Moscow, where Bolshevik strength was greatest.[136] These outbreaks were eventually suppressed, but they clearly indicated that the Soviet regime did not have the "active support" of the workers. In the Urals, many workers actually joined first the S-Rs and Czechs, and later even Kolchak, in fighting the Bolsheviks.[137] Likewise, in southern Russia and the Ukraine, numerous workers were prepared to support Denikin against the Reds because "the Volunteer army seemed most likely to bring stability."[138] A new pro-White union in Kiev supported by Denikin's officials grew rapidly in the fall of 1919.[139] Eventually, the arbitrariness, incompetence, and occasional repressiveness of White rule alienated most southern Russian unionists from the Volunteer Army. But even then, they refused to support the Bolsheviks and instead "denounced both sides in the civil war."[140]

Indeed, it is difficult to argue that the Bolsheviks ever had any substantial support for their real agenda, except among members of the Communist party and those who benefited from the privileges granted to the personnel of the Red Army, the Cheka, and other institutions which the new regime considered essential to retaining its hold on power. In the 1917 elections to the Constituent Assembly, the only relatively free nation-wide elections held during the entire history of Russia until 1991, the Bolsheviks had been soundly defeated by the S-Rs, who, capitalizing on their support among the peasants, won a large plurality of over 40 percent of the vote, 48 percent if one includes those votes won by the separate Ukrainian branch of the party.[141]

The Bolsheviks, it is true, came in a strong second, with about 24 percent.[142] However, this vote is highly misleading because the Bolsheviks cynically ran on a platform which was almost the exact opposite of what they actually intended to do.[143] Those who voted for the Bolsheviks thought they were supporting worker management of factories, redistribution of state- and landlord-owned lands to private peasant plots, self-determination for the non-Russian minorities, the continuation of a multiparty democratic system, and peace. In reality, of course, the Bolsheviks believed in economic central planning, the use of forced labor, the collectivization of agriculture, the forcible reestablishment of the tsarist empire under the aegis of socialist "internationalism," one-party dictatorship, and the unleashing of "the most intense, the most acute class struggle," which, Lenin wrote as early as December 1917, must necessarily "reach...heights of frenzy and desperation—and civil war."[144] It is highly doubtful that this real agenda would have received the support of even 2 or 3 percent of the population, much less 24 percent—it did not even have the unanimous allegiance of Bolshevik party members.[145] Thus, the Bolsheviks had to resort to blatant deception in order to assure themselves of even a modicum of support from the population. In some areas, the Bolsheviks were also able to pad their vote totals by intimidating opposition candidates.[146]

As the real Bolshevik agenda became increasingly clear, particularly after the forcible dispersal of the Constituent Assembly, their initial support quickly eroded, never really to return. By the time it did so however, the Bolsheviks had managed to build up a substantial party apparatus and the nucleus of the Red Army. It was these two institutions which formed the real bulwark of Communist rule. Bound to the regime by the privileges granted to them, by fear of retribution for their crimes in the event of a White victory, and, in many cases, by ideological commitment, the party cadres, some 600,000 to 700,000-strong by 1920, "represented an awesome force" in a nation "in which virtually no organized life above the village level had survived."[147]

Against such opponents, could the Whites really have derived much benefit from having a well-developed ideological agenda? The question is much more difficult to answer than is usually thought.

One line of evidence suggests that the benefits would have been negligible: the S-R governments which formed in Siberia and the Volga region in the summer of 1918 did, in fact, proclaim a moderate socialist ideological agenda of the sort which had won the S-Rs the largest share of the vote in the Constituent Assembly elections. The Committee of the Constituent Assembly (Komuch) government in Samara confirmed the peasant land seizures which the Bolsheviks and the Provisional Government had allowed to take place in 1917 and also promoted pro-union labor legislation.[148] Despite such efforts, it failed to generate any great wave of popular enthusiasm and was soon defeated by the Bolsheviks once the latter had gathered sufficient military forces to counter the Czechs.

According to Richard Pipes, the outstanding recent analyst of the early Bolshevik regime, "nothing demonstrates better the irrelevance of political and social programs during the Civil War than the fate of Komuch."[149] But it is hard to justify so categorical a conclusion. For, as Pipes himself describes, the S-R governments were, for the most part, administratively and militarily inept.[150] Had they been more competent, it is possible that they would have derived greater benefit from their ideological appeal. Even so, Pipes is surely right to suggest that a popular political platform could not have been the overwhelmingly decisive factor postulated by Wilson, Lloyd George, and numerous historians. Certainly, the case of the S-Rs suggests that it could not by itself overcome superior military strength.

With the exception of the S-Rs, none of the anti-Bolshevik governments formed in 1918–20 were willing to enunciate a detailed political program beyond the reestablishment of a Constituent Assembly. They adhered to a doctrine of "nonpredetermination" of Russia's future. Kolchak, Denikin, and the other White generals tended to see the Civil War as a primarily military struggle, in which ideological issues were secondary. This stance was not simply a cover for covert "reactionary" aims, for the White leaders adhered to this doctrine even in private. As Kolchak wrote in a secret December 1918 letter to Denikin:

> I accepted the functions of ruler and commander without any predetermined views on the future form of the Russian government, for I consider it impossible to discuss the future in the course of a harrowing civil war and before Bolshevism is liquidated. The extermination of Bolshevism and the establishment in the nation of conditions under which the solution of this problem can be approached—is the only practical aim at this moment.[151]

Many White leaders considered nonpredetermination to be essential to preserving the unity of the disparate elements which made up their movement. Unlike the Bolsheviks, the Whites were not an ideologically homogenous group which could readily agree on a single program. "If I raise the republican flag," Denikin wrote in 1918, " I will lose one half [of the Volunteers] and if I raise the monarchist flag—the other half will leave me."[152] This point was often ignored by those who urged the Whites to carve out a definite platform, both at the time and in retrospect.

Denikin and some others on the White side also believed that the deferral of political issues to the Constituent Assembly was actually a moral duty. "'[N]on-predetermination','" he writes in his memoirs, "was as much the result of my convictions as of clear necessity."[153] He really believed that only the Constituent Assembly had the proper authority to make binding commitments about the nation's future. "What right," he asked an assembly of Volunteer officers in response to pleas for a declaration in favor of monarchy, "have we, a small group of people, to decide the fate of the country without its consent, without the consent of the Russian people?"[154] Apparently, the Whites lacked the kind of ideological sophistication that allowed the Bolsheviks to consider themselves a "vanguard" empowered to make decisions in the name of the people whether the latter agreed to it or not.

Here, it is worth pointing out that the Whites were not entirely without a program, for the idea of leaving the fate of the nation up to the deliberations of a popularly elected assembly was itself a radical and ambitious agenda for a society which had known nothing but despotism throughout nearly all of its history. In this sense, the Whites were actually more radical than the Bolsheviks, who planned to run a government even more centralized and unaccountable to the popular will than that of the czars.

Nonetheless, it is likely that the Whites could have benefited from enunciating a platform more concrete than nonpredetermination, even though it might have lost them a measure of support in some quarters. Most likely, a platform based on a constitutional monarchy, land reform with compensation, a federal structure for the Russian state, and some sort of at least limited independence for non-Russian nationalities would have been the best bet. Such a stance would have won the support of liberals and moderate socialists, while simultaneously attracting many monarchists and avoiding the total alienation of the old upper classes; the latter two groups had little alternative to supporting the Whites in any case. To avoid infringing on the rights of the Constituent Assembly, the Whites might have announced that their agenda would be subject to its eventual ratification. A platform roughly similar to this one was urged on Denikin and Kolchak by some of the Kadets, notably Georgi Gins in Siberia and Nikolai Astrov in southern Russia. But the generals lacked the imagination and political insight to see the virtues of such a plan.

Ultimately, popular support was not *essential* to victory in the Civil War, as can be seen from the simple fact that the Bolsheviks won without it. Other factors, particularly military strength, were clearly more important. But it would be wrong to conclude from this, as Richard Pipes does, that popular support was almost wholly irrelevant. Had the Whites been able to win the support of the people, they would have found it at least somewhat easier to recruit new troops, always a major problem for both sides in the Civil War. In addition, they would have had less difficulty in mobilizing the resources of the territories they occupied for use against the enemy. Lacking any organizational equivalent to Bolshevik totalitarianism or to the at least comparatively disciplined Communist party cadres, the Whites often had difficulty obtaining supplies, information, and other necessary infrastructural support from the populace by force. They would have done well to get at least some of what they needed by consent. As it was, the absence of popular backing did not destroy the Whites' chances for victory, but it did reduce them to an appreciable extent.

In this respect, three failings in particular were especially damaging to the White cause. The first, already mentioned, was their refusal to sanction land reform, which was the single most important issue from the standpoint of the peasants who constituted the vast majority of the Russian population. The second, and perhaps most important, was the failure of the Whites to establish anything approaching orderly civilian government in the territories they controlled. Finally, the Whites significantly hurt their cause by their shortsighted policy of rejecting the national aspirations of non-Russian minorities within the Russian empire. While a complete analysis of these three highly complex issues cannot possibly be attempted within the confines of the present work, it is important to give each of them at least some consideration.

On the problem of land reform, the Whites were considerably less dogmatic than the "reactionary" stereotype would lead us to believe. Both Kolchak and Denikin expressed support for some type of land reform program.[155] Although Kolchak is often, not without reason, accused of political obtuseness, he clearly recognized that land reform was an essential concession to the peasantry. "I consider intolerable," he wrote to Denikin, "a land policy which leads the peasantry to believe that land will be in the hands of the *pomeshchiki*. On the contrary, in order to remove the most serious cause of the Russian revolution—the land-poverty of the peasants... it is essential to take measures strengthening the public's trust and good will towards the new authorities... [by] confirming the de facto transfer of land to the peasants which has already occurred."[156]

Denikin held a similar view. In April 1919, he issued a declaration, drafted by the Kadet liberal Nikolai Astrov, which announced a policy of limited land reform with compensation.[157] The plan was a reasonable compromise between the different constituencies that the Whites thought to woo. Though it did not satisfy peasant demands to the full, its implementation might have led to at least somewhat greater popular acceptance of the White regime, if not to enthusiastic support. But little was done to implement the proposal, even though it clearly had Denikin's genuine support. In fact, many local White officials and Volunteer commanders cooperated with landowners attempting to forcibly reclaim lands seized by the peasants in 1917–18. In June 1919, Denikin issued an order banning such practices,[158] but, like most other Volunteer Army civil regulations, it was poorly enforced.

Meanwhile, Kolchak had, in April, issued a land policy which went even further than Denikin's, in that it explicitly allowed peasants to retain all the land they had seized to date.[159] However, the absence of large estates in Siberia made his land policy far less important than Denikin's to the fortunes of the Whites. When his armies briefly reached the Volga region, where large estates were more common, in the spring of 1919, he was even less successful in enforcing his policy than Denikin had been. Not until Wrangel's last stand in the Crimea in 1920 did any White leader actually implement, as opposed to merely announce, a land reform program.[160] And, by that time, it was too late.

The failure of Kolchak and Denikin in the area of land reform was due not to the fact that they were "reactionaries"—they were not—or to lack of vision—they both recognized the importance of the issue—but to their inability to force adherence to the policies they themselves had announced. In addition, it is possible that the peasants' confidence in their good intentions was undermined by the fact that both White leaders always stressed that their land reform proposals were subject to review by the Constituent Assembly, when the latter should meet. While, for reasons analyzed above, the lack of a strong policy on land reform did not lead the peasants to support the Reds, it certainly insured that they would not be active supporters of the Whites. For this reason, the failure to address the issue properly surely hurt the White cause. But the damage was not necessarily irremediable, particularly since the Bolsheviks also lacked peasant support.

As a corollary to the discussion of land reform, it is worth noting that it is not at all clear that the redistribution of land into small peasant plots would have been to the benefit of the Russian population as a whole in the long run. While those peasants who seized landlord-owned fields certainly derived considerable short-term advantages, the destruction of the largest and most efficient farms may well have hurt the bulk of the people. Before 1917, large farms able to exploit economies of scale had produced a disproportionate percentage of the Russian countryside's saleable agricultural surplus and their disappearance surely contributed to the food shortages of the Civil War period, shortages that fell most heavily on the poorest segments of the population, the very people whom the liberal and socialist advocates of land reform had sought to help. While none of this justifies the singleminded efforts of the Russian landowners to regain lands taken by the peasants in 1918–19, it certainly calls into question the wisdom of a policy based on the wholesale transfer of landowner-controlled lands to the peasants.

The failure of the Whites to implement a land reform plan was part and parcel of the broader—and much more damaging—failure to establish functioning civil governments in the territories they occupied. It is difficult to believe that a movement which put so much emphasis on the imposition of law and order in principle could tolerate so much anarchy in practice. Nonetheless, White rule was characterized by almost universal corruption, arbitrary exactions and arrests by officials, and widespread ordinary crime.[161] The anti-Semitic pogroms in the Ukraine were only the most virulent manifestation of the anarchic conditions which prevailed. As Ambassador Morris reported to Lansing during his tour of Siberia in the summer of 1919,

> Much of the discontent with the present Government, the demoralization and panic, is in my judgment due to the utter insecurity of person and property. All over Siberia there is an orgy of arrest without charges; of execution without even the pretense of trial; and of confiscation without color of authority. Fear—panic fear—has seized everyone.[162]

Conditions under Denikin's rule were only marginally better. Both Denikin and Kolchak were aware of the problem and both made efforts to deal with it. But neither was prepared to make the kind of systematic policy changes that were necessary to curb the abuses of their officials. Denikin himself identified the main cause of his failure better than anyone else:

> We wrote harsh laws, under which the death penalty was the usual punishment. We sent generals invested with emergency powers, and accompanied by commissions of inquiry to examine...crimes committed by the troops. We...issued orders to combat violence, looting, the pillaging of prisoners, and so on. But these laws and orders often met with determined resistance from elements which refused to recognize their moral spirit and crying necessity. *We should have started at the top, but instead we went after the rank and file.* (Emphasis mine)[163]

Another contributing factor was the failure of the Whites to separate military and civilian authority in the territories they controlled. In addition to all the obvious shortcomings of such an arrangement, this left responsibility for the establishment of order in the rear to military commanders already overburdened with duties at the front.

The chaos that prevailed in the rear of the White armies alienated the population and prevented the Kolchak and Denikin regimes from effectively mobilizing the resources of the territories they controlled. It also served to discredit the White cause in the eyes of some segments of Western public opinion. This latter factor was somewhat limited in scope because of the well-known tendency of observers to believe atrocity stories only in so far as they confirmed their general view of which side is right in a given war. As George Orwell said of the Spanish Civil War, "atrocities are believed in or disbelieved in solely on grounds of political predilection." "Everyone," he complained bitterly, "believes in the atrocities of the enemy and disbelieves in those of his own side, without ever bothering to examine the evidence."[164] This tendency was certainly at work in Britain and the U.S. during the Russian conflict as well, with each side in the intervention debate highlighting the atrocities of the Russian faction it supported and ignoring those of the one it opposed.[165] Winston Churchill was a rare exception in his efforts to both assist the Whites and find ways to curb the atrocities in committed by their troops. As we shall see in chapter 5, the bulk of public opinion in Britain and the United States was sympathetic to intervention, a state of affairs that persisted throughout most of 1918-19. With the important exception of members of the Jewish community shocked by the pogroms, few changed their minds because of White atrocities. Even so, such outrages surely had at least some impact on Western public opinion; they certainly didn't help the White cause.

For a whole range of reasons, therefore, White misgovernment diminished their chances of victory. While a true reestablishment of order was probably impossible under wartime conditions, it is likely that the Whites could have done considerably better than they did, as evidenced by the examples of Wrangel in the Crimea and the Provisional Government of northern Russia, both of which managed to suppress the more flagrant abuses of White rule. For a short time, a similar feat was achieved by the liberal Kadet government which ruled the Crimea in early 1919.

Although Baron Wrangel is often considered one of the more conservative White generals, his view of the role of popular support in Civil War was hardly less sweeping than that of the Western liberals who came to see it as *the* decisive factor in the conflict. "Russia," he said in implicit criticism of his predecessor Denikin, "cannot be freed by a triumphant march on Moscow, but by the creation even on a small bit of Russian soil of such order and such living conditions as would attract the people, who are suffering under the Red yoke."[166] While Wrangel was right to believe that popular support was important, he erred in hoping that it might overcome the vast military disadvantage under which the Whites labored by the time he took command in 1920. His administrative reforms came too late to turn the tide of the war, while those of the northern Russian government under Chaikovsky and Miller were in a theater of operations too minor to have a decisive impact.

The role of maladministration in the White defeat should not be overstated. Red areas were also rife with crime, corruption, and arbitrariness, and the oppression of the Red Army and Cheka was much more severe than the sporadic abuses of Denikin's and Kolchak's officials. "An unstable rear," Evan Mawdsley reminds us, "was not a problem unique to the Whites."[167] Nonetheless, the totalitarian organization of the Bolshevik party and the systematic intimidation of the populace by means of the Red Terror allowed the Bolsheviks to impose their will in the areas under their control to a greater extent than the Whites were able to do. The relatively well-organized party cadres also provided the nucleus of a civil administration which was able to mobilize the nation's resources for war to at least some substantial extent. Neither Whites nor Reds really had firm control of much territory beyond the immediate reach of their armies and police, at least not by contemporary Western standards. But the rule of the latter was marginally less *in*firm than that of their enemies.

The final important political factor which hurt the Whites was their unwillingness to recognize the independence of the non-Russian minorities. The Whites fought under the slogan of "A Russia Great, United, and Indivisible." Their actual stance was somewhat less dogmatic than the slogan implied, since they did not claim that independence for the non-Russian areas was illegitimate in principle, merely that it could not be allowed without the consent of the Constituent Assembly—a politically naive but sincerely held position. Even on this point, the White leaders were willing to make exceptions. They recognized the independence of Poland and the de facto secession of Finland. Moreover, the fact that the Whites were not prepared to grant immediate independence to the other areas does not mean that they wanted to impose a policy of rigid Russification, of the sort which eventually became the dominant approach of the Soviet government in the

Stalin years. Kolchak advocated a government structure based on "the autonomous development of the nationalities comprising Russia."[168] Denikin
also believed that the defense of Russian unity had to be combined with a
respect for the autonomy of minority groups:

> The basis of the temporary government of the territories under the Armed Forces of
> Southernern Russia was *the preservation of the unity of the Russian state,* while of-
> fering autonomy to separate nationalities and self-governing entities (the Cossacks),
> as well as the broad decentralization of all government functions.[169]

Unfortunately, such a policy was not enough to secure the cooperation
of most of the non-Russian groups with the Whites. Armenia, Georgia,
Azerbaidjan, the Ukraine, Finland, the Baltic States, and a number of minor states had declared their independence, and most of them were unwilling to settle for anything less than the complete recognition of this
status. As a result of this disagreement between the Whites and non-Russian minorities, there was little military cooperation between the two
groups and even occasional armed clashes, notably the battles between
Denikin's forces and Ukrainian nationalist partisans that diverted a substantial portion of Denikin's troops away from the decisive drive on Moscow in the fall of 1919.

This is not to say that the non-Russian states supported the Bolsheviks, who had publicly recognized their independence. The repeated armed
clashes between the Bolsheviks and Ukrainian, Finnish, Baltic, and other
nationalist forces throughout most of 1918 and 1919 testify to the fact
that Lenin's promises were viewed with justifiable skepticism. However,
the non-Russian states did not commit anything approaching their full
power to the struggle against the Bolsheviks. Usually, they did not go
beyond defending their home territories against Bolshevik encroachment,
as the Finns did in late 1918. The repeated Bolshevik efforts to conquer
any non-Russian territories that came within their grasp exposed the hol-
lowness of their assurances. It was well understood that Lenin, Trotsky,
and their colleagues, were ideological universalists who saw national
borders primarily as obstacles to the worldwide spread of socialism. However, the refusal of the Whites to recognize their independence meant that,
from the non-Russian point of view, their was no more reason to cooperate with them than with the Bolsheviks.

For Kolchak, operating in Siberia and the Urals, non-Russian nation-
alism was not much of a problem. The native peoples of Siberia were

heavily outnumbered by Russian settlers and were in no position to assert their independence. However, the obtuseness of White nationality policy was a serious hindrance to Denikin in southern Russia, as well as to Yudenich operating near Petrograd. The latter was unable to secure the support of Finland and Estonia in his efforts to capture Petrograd because of Kolchak's obstinate refusal to recognize their independence, which the two states had already achieved on a de facto basis in any case.[170] Many of the non-Russian states disposed of substantial armed forces and considerable quantities of useful military supplies; most of them feared the Bolsheviks and would have been prepared to cooperate with the Whites and the Allies if their independence were guaranteed. Thus, the Whites paid a high price for their obstinacy, as was recognized at the time by Churchill and other British observers.[171]

To some extent, to be sure, Denikin was able to achieve his goals by means of his "autonomy" policy. He was, for example, able to establish a cordial relationship with the Armenian government.[172] Much more importantly, his willingness to grant autonomy and local self-rule to the Don and Kuban Cossacks led to an alliance that eventually provided Denikin with more than half of his troops and a decided advantage over the Bolsheviks in cavalry.[173] However, Denikin's success with the Cossacks served to underscore the cause of his failure with the others. For the Cossacks, after all, were not a minority nationality but a Russian special interest group. They did not *want* anything more than autonomy and the maintenance of their traditional privileges, which they—quite rightly— suspected the Bolsheviks of wanting to take away.[174] The situation was very different with the Armenians, Georgians and others. And even with the Cossacks, their parochial outlook made it difficult to persuade them to take part in operations far away from their homelands.

While the Whites deserve blame for the failure to cooperate with the non-Russian nationalities, it would be wrong to blame them exclusively, as most analysts have tended to do. In his memoirs, Denikin bitterly pointed out that the autonomy he offered to the minorities represented a far better deal from their own point of view than the status they would eventually get under Soviet rule. "What is better," he asked, "to become an integral self-governing part of the new, free Russian state, or...to be poured into the general melting pot of Soviet centralism...For," he warned, "there was no third choice."[175] By refusing to cooperate with the Volunteer Army, the Georgians, Denikin argued, had "destroyed their own people."[176]

Denikin's case is not without merit. The non-Russians *should* have realized that they faced a much worse fate in the event of a Bolshevik victory than a White one. They really did, however unintentionally, help insure the loss of their own independence. But, on the other hand, the absence of a "third choice" was Denikin's own fault. At the very least, he could have recognized the de facto independence of the non-Russian states subject to the later consent of the Constituent Assembly. Himself half-Polish, he should have been the first to realize that the decentralized, multinational Russia he hoped to establish was more likely to be achieved by acceding to minority demands than by force. The leaders of most of the new states were not extremists and they might have eventually come to see the economic and political benefits of some sort of loose association with Russia in the event of a White victory, just as many of them have, to a limited extent, done so today. And, in the final analysis, Denikin should have taken a page from Lenin's Brest-Litovsk book and recognized that a truncated Russia ruled in accordance with the principles he advocated was infinitely preferable to a rejuvenated Russian empire under the domination of his enemies. The former, he might have recognized, was much more likely to be achieved if the Whites could have brought themselves to recognize the independence of the new nations.

If there is anything to be said for Denikin's position it is that he was at least honest about it. As Richard Luckett points out:

> At more or less any point in the history of the Volunteer Army Denikin could have enlisted considerable additional support by the simple expedient of recognising the independence of the Don, the Ukraine, and the break-away provinces of the extreme southern, Georgia and Azerbaijan. When he had achieved his object, the conquest of central Russia, he could then have repudiated his promise and reduced the new republics one by one.[177]

This, in fact, was more or less the strategy adopted by the Bolsheviks, who were able to secure at least the neutrality of most of the non-Russian states until such time as they were ready to reconquer them. But Denikin was not sufficiently cynical to adopt such an expedient, even though the Allied military missions and even some of his own Russian advisers were constantly urging him to recognize the independence of the new states. "He was therefore," in the words of Winston Churchill, "the foe of his own allies in the war against the Soviets."[178]

But, as Churchill also argued, a share of the responsibility for the nationalities fiasco must rest with the Western Allies. For had they been more involved in the Civil War, they would have had greater leverage over the Whites, which they could have used to force some sort of compromise between them and the non-Russian states. "Could not the statesmen who had assembled at Paris have pursued their task more coherently?" Churchill asked. "Could they not have said to Koltchak and Denikin: 'Not another cartridge unless you make terms with the Border States recognizing their independence or autonomy as may be decided.' And having applied this superior compulsion to the Russian leaders, could they not have used their whole influence to combine the operations of all the States at war with Soviet Russia?"[179] Churchill himself did what he could to persuade Denikin to accommodate minority demands.[180] He also tried hard to persuade Lloyd George and the other Allied leaders to put pressure on the non-Russian states to cooperate with the Whites against the Bolsheviks.[181] But his efforts were not enough; to have a chance of success, he needed the full support of at least his own government or—better still— that of the Allies as a whole. And such aid was not forthcoming.

In sum, it is certainly true that the political failures of the Whites hurt their cause. It is even likely that a better conceived political strategy would have allowed the Whites to defeat the Bolsheviks without any more Allied support than they actually had. Certainly, the accession of the substantial Finnish, Ukrainian, and Baltic State armies to the White forces would have insured an overwhelming military superiority over the Red Army. However, it is not correct to say that their political failures doomed the Whites to defeat. For each of them was offset by equal or greater shortcomings on the part of the Bolsheviks. They too managed to alienate most of the population, probably more so than the Whites. They too clashed repeatedly with the non-Russian nationalities. Only in the field of consolidating their authority in the territories under their rule did the Reds have a clear relative advantage. They were able to mobilize the nation's resources for war to a considerably greater extent than their enemies. But it is difficult to believe that this advantage was necessarily decisive, particularly since many of the Whites' supply needs could be met by shipments from the West, as, thanks primarily to the British, they partially were.

It should also be said that the political disadvantages of the Whites were partially offset by several important strengths. For obvious reasons, the Whites had the firm support of the Russian Orthodox Church, still an important influence in the countryside and one of the few institutions of civil society which continued to function with some regularity during the war. They also had the backing of most of the middle and professional classes. This latter group had important technical and administrative expertise which the Whites badly needed for both civil and military purposes. While the Reds made a major effort to recruit "bourgeois specialists" for their own war needs, they still found it more difficult to attract such people than did the Whites. Moreover, the Bolsheviks could hardly rely on the loyalty of those they did attract; most were bound only by the threat of cutting their food rations or retaliation against their families. Here, as elsewhere, the Bolsheviks were often able to rely on coercion to take the place of freely given cooperation. But specialists bound to their positions by such means were hardly likely to work as effectively as those who served the Whites voluntarily. It is difficult to estimate the benefits the Whites derived from the support of the Church and the middle classes. But it is likely that they were at least somewhat significant.

If the political failings of the Whites were not great enough to make defeat inevitable, then what of purely military factors? In recent years, several scholars dissatisfied with the traditional "political" interpretation of the Civil War's outcome have gone to the opposite extreme and claimed that the result was largely predetermined by military and geostrategic factors.[182]

Two major Bolshevik military advantages are stressed by advocates of the new military-oriented historiography. First, the Bolsheviks controlled the center of Russia, where the bulk of the nation's population and industry was concentrated. They were therefore able to put considerably more troops into the field than their enemies, usually outnumbering the Whites by margins of three to two or more.[183] Second, their geographic position also allowed the Reds to operate on interior lines of communication and concentrate their forces as they saw fit. Thus, in the spring of 1919, they were able to transfer large numbers of troops from Denikin's front in order to beat Kolchak. In the fall, when Kolchak's army had been driven back, the opposite maneuver helped seal Denikin's own doom. By contrast, the major White armies were always separated from each other by many hundreds of miles and they had great difficulty coordinating operations.

These advantages were undeniably important. But in placing so much emphasis on them, the new Civil War historiography tends to neglect important countervailing strengths of the Whites. Perhaps the most important of these was the advantage which they enjoyed in troop quality throughout much of the war. After all, the core of White support was among military officers of the old Imperial Army. So it was understandable that the Whites found it easier to attract professional soldiers to their cause. While the Reds, under the direction of War Commissar Leon Trotsky, made enormous efforts to recruit former tsarist officers, they were never able to completely overcome the advantages of the Whites in this respect. The Whites also often had better common soldiers. The repeated victories of the Volunteer Army over numerically superior Bolshevik forces throughout most of 1918 and 1919 highlight the extent to which White quality could often offset Red quantity.

The Whites also had a crucial advantage in the vital cavalry arm. The Russian Civil War was the last major conflict in which cavalry played a decisive role.[184] Russian Civil War commanders used cavalry in much the same way as Second World War generals would one day use tanks and tactical aircraft. In fact, Denikin's troops were sometimes able to successfully use their cavalry forces in direct conjunction with the small British tank and aircraft units in southern Russia.[185]

The advantage of the Whites in cavalry stemmed from their alliance with the Cossacks, who had provided the bulk of the mounted units in the old Imperial Army. While these troops had been of little use against the well-trained, well-equipped German Army during World War I, their superior discipline and mobility were extremely effective against the much less dependable infantry of the Red Army. As a result of the Cossack contribution, particularly to Denikin's forces, the Whites enjoyed both a quantitative and a qualitative advantage in cavalry throughout most of the war. As late as October 1919, after a major effort by Trotsky to strengthen the Red cavalry, Denikin still had almost twice as many horsemen as the Red forces could field against him—48,000 versus 26,000.[186] The White superiority in cavalry tended to offset their overall numerical inferiority, since a given number of mounted troops were usually more potent than a like quantity of infantry. Thus, Red numerical superiority was not nearly as overwhelming as undifferentiated figures would suggest.

While relations between White command and the Cossacks were always somewhat tenuous, owing to the parochial attitudes and continued demands for greater autonomy of the latter and the occasional insensitivity of the former,[187] the alliance between the two groups largely held firm, to the great benefit of both sides. Unlike many of the non-Russian leaders, the Cossacks clearly understood that they would be far worse off under the Bolsheviks than under the Whites, since the communists had made it perfectly clear that they intended to abolish Cossackdom as soon as possible.

If the Red superiority in overall numbers was partially offset by the White superiority in cavalry, their advantage of operating on interior lines has also been overemphasized. For the down side to having a central position between one's enemies is vulnerability on multiple fronts. It was this factor that ultimately defeated Nazi Germany in World War II and also prevented the Germans from winning World War I in 1914–17. While the Reds certainly derived benefits from being able to transfer troops from one point to another, they had to pay a price for doing so. When Bolshevik forces were transferred from Denikin's front to Kolchak's in the spring of 1919, this allowed the Volunteer Army to make major gains. In the fall, the concentration of forces required to defend Petrograd against Yudenich also served to weaken the forces facing Denikin.

The Whites would have been able to exploit the advantage of multiple points of attack much more fully if their various armies had been better able to coordinate their operations.[188] As it was, the poor state of communications between the different White fronts made such coordination almost impossible. Messages between Kolchak and Denikin, for example, had to be carried either by brave individual officers attempting to slip through the Red lines or by steamship around almost the entire continent of Asia.[189] Needless to say, both methods were extremely slow, taking weeks or even months. The former system was also unreliable, since the couriers risked capture by the Bolsheviks. In consequence, there was very little cooperation between the two main White armies beyond a broad general agreement that both should converge on Moscow.

The strategy of converging on Moscow was undoubtedly correct in and of itself. The Whites were right to believe that central Russia was the heart of Bolshevik power and that the Communists could not hope to win without retaining control of this area. Their desire to capture Moscow was not an irrational obsession but a correct appreciation of their enemy's strengths and weaknesses.[190] Unfortunately, their sound overall strategy was often hampered by a lack of coordination brought on by poor communications facilities.

There was little the Whites themselves could do to change this state of affairs. But the Allies, with their access to wireless communications, might well have been able to help had they chosen to do so. Yet no one on the

Allied side seems to have recognized the opportunities inherent in this relatively cheap and simple form of intervention.

The White inferiority in numbers might also have been remedied by Allied action. As pointed out in chapter 2, the hundreds of thousands of Russian prisoners of war in Germany constituted a vast potential reservoir of trained manpower for the Whites. Had the Allies, as Churchill and Marshal Foch suggested, equipped only a small proportion of these men and sent them to the aid of Denikin, this step alone might have radically altered the outcome of the war. Thus, the military disadvantages which the Whites faced were not as great as is sometimes argued. Moreover, the Allies, if they so chose, had the ability to largely negate them at little cost to themselves.

This chapter is by no means an exhaustive analysis of the White movement—that would require a major study in and of itself.[191] Hopefully, however, enough has been said to make the case that the Whites, despite many shortcomings, were far preferable to the Bolsheviks and not incapable of winning. Even with the very modest Allied intervention that actually occurred, they came close to winning on several occasions, particularly in the summer of 1918 and during Denikin's great offensive. Certainly, the Bolshevik leaders, despite their belief in Marxist historical inevitability, were anything but convinced that their victory was assured. The fear they felt at the time of the Czech rebellion and the initial Allied intervention, and, later, during the offensives of Kolchak, Yudenich, and Denikin, testifies to this fact. And even the worst possible White regime, a reactionary military dictatorship, would still have been unlikely to commit mass murder on anything approaching the scale of the communists. Nor would such a regime have led to the total suppression of the free market and civil society, as communism did.

Moreover, a reactionary dictatorship would have been subject to all the same pressures for reform that had led to extensive liberalization over the last fifty years of tsarist rule. While the tsarist Russia of 1914 still probably deserved its stereotypical image as the most oppressive and backward society in Europe, it should not be forgotten that the country had made immense progress since the abolition of serfdom in 1861. The impressive growth of the middle class, the establishment of numerous active reformist political parties, the rise of civil society, the rapid development of industry after the 1890s, and the rudimentary beginnings of parliamentary institutions and the rule of law, all testified to the nation's potential for positive development.[192] Within a span of fifty years, Russia had passed through a series of historical stages that had taken centuries in most Western European states. There is no reason to believe that the impetus for liberalization would have been any less under a right-wing White dictatorship, particularly since the experience of the February Revolution had raised the expectations of the people and turned them against reaction.

Even more optimistically, a White victory might have led to the outright establishment of a liberal democratic government. This was probably the most likely outcome had the Bolsheviks been overthrown in the summer or fall of 1918, when the Allies had their best opportunity to intervene successfully. But, even after this time, it is not impossible that Denikin and Kolchak could have restrained their reactionary colleagues and forced them to accept the convening of a new Constituent Assembly. Allied pressure might have helped them to achieve this goal. In any case, the one thing that can be said with near-certainty about a White victory is that it would have resulted in a far better Russia—and a far better world—than that which actually came into being after the triumph of the Bolsheviks.

The Whites were the first political movement to fight a major war against a totalitarian enemy. They made numerous mistakes, mistakes that lessened their chances of victory and diminished the force of their claim to moral rectitude. Our justifiable revulsion at the horrors of Bolshevism should not blind us to the errors and sins of the Whites. Yet there were many among them who had a genuine concern for the future of Russia, who truly hoped that it might become a free democratic society. They deserved a better fate than what they got.

Notes

1. Denikin, *ORS*, vol. 2, p. 199.
2. Lloyd George, *War Memoirs*, vol. 6, p. 147.
3. Luckett, *White Generals*, p. xviii.
4. See, e.g., ibid.; Kenez, *Volunteer Army*; Kenez, *Defeat of the Whites*; Brovkin, *Behind the Front Lines of the Civil War*, esp. ch. 3, ch. 6, pp. 409–10.
5. See, esp., Brovkin, ch. 6.
6. Kenez, *Defeat of the Whites*, pp. 166–77.
7. Ibid., p. 176.
8. Moshe Lewin, "The Civil War: Dynamics and Legacy," in Diane Koenker, William Rosenberg, and Ronald Grigor Suny, eds., *Party, State, and Society, in the Russian Civil War*, (Bloomington: Indiana University Press, 1989), p. 401.
9. I.I. Vatsetis to Lenin, April 23, 1919, in Meijer, ed., vol. 1, p. 354.
10. See Pipes, *Bolshevik Regime*, pp. 9–13; Mawdsley, pp. 213–14.
11. Pipes, *Bolshevik Regime*, p. 10.

12. Kenez, *Defeat of the Whites*, p. xiii; See also Luckett, esp. p. 388.
13. Luckett, p. 388.
14. See, esp., Kenez, *Defeat of the Whites*.
15. See the discussions of Bolshevik reactions to Kolchak's and Denikin's offensives and to the initial Allied intervention in the summer of 1918 in chapters 2 and 3 above.
16. See Kenez, *Defeat of the Whites*; Brovkin, pp. 204-206, 226-32; W.H. Chamberlin, *The Russian Revolution*, vol. 2, pp. 80-81.
17. Unfortunately, the exact number is extremely difficult to estimate because of the highly decentralized and unofficial nature of White repression.
18. See ch. 1 above.
19. See Gerson, *The Secret Police in Lenin's Russia*; Melgounov, *The Red Terror in Russia*; Leggett, *Cheka*.
20. See works cited in ibid.
21. Brovkin, p. 211.
22. Ibid., p. 207.
23. See, generally, ibid., esp. ch. 4; Pipes, *Russian Revolution*, ch. 16.
24. See Pipes, *Russian Revolution*, ch. 16.
25. See, generally, ibid.
26. Quoted in ibid., p. 722.
27. Lenin, "Freedom to Trade in Grain," August 1919, in *Collected Works*, vol. 29, p. 570.
28. Ibid., p. 567.
29. See, generally, Brovkin, op. cit.
30. Ibid., esp. p. 131; See also my analysis of Antonov-Ovseenko's report to Lenin on the Tambov uprising, below.
31. Kenez, *Defeat of the Whites*, p. 100.
32. Ibid., p. 99; Kenez' unsupported assertion (ibid.) that the populace was "no doubt wrong" to draw this conclusion testifies more to his understanding of economics than to the perceptiveness of the Russian people. The relationship between price controls and shortages is a basic principle of economic theory flowing directly from the law of demand, as can be learned by reading any introductory economics textbook. For a broad historical analysis providing extensive empirical support for this proposition, see Robert L. Schuettinger and Eamon Butler, *Four Thousand Years of Wage and Price Controls*, (Washington, D.C.: Heritage Foundation, 1979).
33. Pipes, *Bolshevik Regime*, p. 509.
34. Pipes, *Russian Revolution*, p. 685.
35. Ibid., p. 687.
36. Kenez, *Defeat of the Whites*, pp. 95-96.
37. Ibid.
38. This position is well argued in Paul Craig Roberts, "'War Communism,' Product of Marxian Ideas," ch. 2 of Roberts, *Alienation and the Soviet Economy*, (Albuquerque: University of New Mexico Press, 1971).
39. See Bunyan, *Origin of Forced Labor in the Soviet State*.
40. See, generally, Pipes, *Russian Revolution*, ch. 15.
41. See, e.g., Fitzpatrick, *The Russian Revolution*, pp. 70-72.
42. Lenin, "Ten Theses on Soviet Power," March 9, 1918, in Lenin, *Collected Works*, vol. 27, p. 156.
43. Ibid.
44. Ibid.

45. Quoted in Pipes, *Russian Revolution,* p. 689; I have corrected a few minor stylistic flaws in Pipes' translation of this passage.
46. This issue is well covered in Pipes, *Bolshevik Regime,* ch. 8.
47. Ibid., p. 712.
48. This program, neglected in most of the historical literature, is surveyed in Pipes, *Bolshevik Regime,* ch. 7.
49. Kenez, *Volunteer Army,* p. 20.
50. See, ibid., pp. 30-34, for a reprise of the standard argument to the effect that Kornilov intended to establish a reactionary military dictatorship. But see also, Pipes, *Russian Revolution,* pp. 448-64 for a strong assertion of the view that Kornilov was not attempting a coup.
51. Dimitry Lehovich, *White Against Red: The Life of General Anton Denikin,* (New York: Norton, 1974), p. 36.
52. Ibid., pp. 35-36.
53. Denikin, *ORS,* vol. 5, pp. 157-62.
54. Ibid., pp. 158-59.
55. Kenez, *Volunteer Army,* p. 198.
56. Ibid., pp. 193-94; Denikin, *ORS,* vol. 3, p. 266.
57. "Provisional Statute for the Administration of Regions Occupied by the Volunteer Army," reprinted in Denikin, *ORS,* vol. 3, p. 267.
58. Ibid.
59. Ibid; The importance of the latter provision is rightly stressed in Kenez, *Volunteer Army,* pp. 195-96.
60. Denikin, *ORS,* vol. 3, p. 270.
61. Ibid.
62. See, generally, Kenez, *Defeat of the Whites,* though, in my view, Kenez somewhat overstates the case.
63. Footman, *Civil War in Russia,* pp. 187, 195-96.
64. Luckett, p. 203.
65. Ibid., pp. 203-4.
66. Quoted in ibid., p. 204.
67. Mawdsley, *Russian Civil War,* p. 135.
68. Ibid.
69. Kenez, *Defeat of the Whites,* p. 170.
70. The best analysis of the causes of the pogroms is Pipes, *Bolshevik Regime,* pp. 99-114.
71. Kenez, *Defeat of the Whites,* p. 172.
72. Pipes, *Bolshevik Regime,* p. 104; Denikin, *ORS,* vol. 5, p. 145.
73. Pipes, *Bolshevik Regime,* p. 104.
74. Ibid.
75. On this government, see Kenez, *Defeat of the Whites,* pp. 192-98.
76. Denikin, *ORS,* vol. 5, pp. 145-46.
77. Kenez, *Defeat of the Whites,* pp. 174-75.
78. Denikin, *ORS,* vol. 5, p. 146.
79. Cited in Pipes, *Bolshevik Regime,* p. 110; The study, conducted for the *YIVO Annual of Jewish Social Science,* reviewed 1236 incidents, of which 887 were categorized as full-fledged pogroms, with the balance counted as "excesses" which did not assume a mass character.
80. Denikin, *ORS,* vol. 5, p. 146.
81. Pipes, *Bolshevik Regime,* p. 110.

82. Ibid., p. 111; Lehovich, pp. 328-29; Denikin, *ORS*, vol. 5, pp. 149-50.
83. Denikin, *ORS*, vol. 5, p. 149; Pipes, *Bolshevik Regime*, p. 111.
84. Lehovich, p. 330.
85. Quoted in ibid., pp. 328-29.
86. Denikin, *ORS*, vol. 5, pp. 145-50.
87. Ibid., p. 147; Denikin also notes (ibid., pp. 147-48) the importance of popular revulsion against Jewish Bolsheviks.
88. Kenez, *Defeat of the Whites*, p. 174: Kenez (p. 174), citing Denikin, *ORS*, vol. 5, p. 145, does argue that the general forbade "Jews [from] buying land on the Black Sea hoping to combat speculation." However, it is clear from the text which Kenez cites that Denikin had intended to issue a general order banning "speculation" which the local White military governor had exploited to target the Jews specifically. When Denikin heard of this incident, he issued a clarification of his original command in which he made clear that speculation must be punished "irrespective of the nationality of the perpetrators"; Denikin, *ORS*, vol. 5, p. 145. While Denikin was thus not motivated by anti-Semitic prejudice, his order can still legitimately be criticized on economic grounds, in that restrictions on the sale of land prevented its rational use and exacerbated the economic crisis of the times.
89. See Churchill, *Aftermath*, p. 255.
90. Denikin, *ORS*, vol. 5, p. 150.
91. Ibid., p. 150.
92. Ibid.
93. Kenez, *Defeat of the Whites*, p. 175.
94. Lehovich, p. 329.
95. Denikin, *ORS*, vol. 5, p. 146.
96. Pipes, *Bolshevik Regime*, p. 49.
97. Brovkin, p. 206.
98. Pipes, *Bolshevik Regime*, p. 49.
99. Chamberlin, *Russian Revolution*, vol. 2, p. 163.
100. Volkogonov, *Lenin*, pp. 203-4.
101. Ibid., p. 204.
102. Quoted in Pipes, *Bolshevik Regime*, p. 103.
103. Ibid., p. 104.
104. Quoted in ibid.
105. Ibid., p. 111.
106. Lenin, "Anti-Jewish Pogroms," March 1919, in *Collected Works*, vol. 29, p. 252.
107. Ibid.
108. On this latter point, see Melgounov, *Red Terror in Russia*.
109. See, esp., Pipes, *Bolshevik Regime*; Mawdsley, op. cit.
110. Kenez, *Defeat of the Whites*, p. xvii; See also Luckett, op. cit.
111. See Brovkin, op. cit., esp. pp. 192-93; Brovkin does not argue, however, that the Reds had the support of the people, merely that popular uprisings behind the lines disproportionately tended to benefit them against the Whites in the latter stages of the war, even though the peasant rebels had no such intention. However, he does not explain why the larger scale of the uprisings in the Red areas should not have led to the opposite effect.
112. Malia, *Soviet Tragedy*, p. 122.
113. Carl von Clausewitz, *On War*, trans. Peter Paret and Michael Howard, indexed ed., (Princeton: Princeton University Press, 1984), p. 596.
114. Ullman, vol. 2, p. 351.

115. Interestingly, Secretary of State Lansing was fond using the precedent of the U.S. Civil War to argue against Wilson's notion of a universal right of self-determination; see Lansing, *Peace Negotiations,* pp. 100-1.

116. This is the general conclusion of what is probably the best recent history of the Civil War; see James McPherson, *Battle Cry of Freedom: The Civil War Era,* (New York: Oxford University Press, 1988).

117. This point is stressed by Pipes, *Bolshevik Regime,* pp. 135-38.

118. See Brovkin, esp. ch. 4, for the most thorough analysis of the Greens; see also Oliver Radkey, *The Unknown Civil War in Soviet Russia: A Study of the Green Movement in the Tambov Region, 1920–21,* (Stanford: Hoover Institution Press, 1976).

119. Brovkin, p. 161.

120. Ibid., pp. 146-48, 197-99.

121. Ibid, p. 146.

122. The postwar Bolshevik struggle against the Greens is described in Pipes, *Bolshevik Regime,* pp. 374-78, 386-88 and Brovkin, ch. 11.

123. Brovkin, 385-88.

124. Vladimir Antonov-Ovseenko, "On the Bandit Movement in Tambov Province," July 20, 1921, in Meijer, ed., *Trotsky Papers,* vol. 2, p. 552.

125. Ibid., p. 530.

126. Brovkin, p. 184.

127. Unfortunately, there is no major historical study of the impact of famine on the popularity of the Bolshevik regime during the Civil War period, though many have pointed to its importance in stimulating the peasant revolts of 1920-21.

128. See, e.g., Kenez, *Defeat of the Whites,* pp. 7-8.

129. Brovkin, p. 313.

130. Quoted in ibid.

131. Ibid., pp. 106-108, 161.

132. Pipes, *Bolshevik Regime,* p. 136.

133. Fitzpatrick, p. 70.

134. Pipes, *Russian Revolution,* p. 543.

135. Brovkin, ch. 2.

136. Ibid., pp. 63-82.

137. Ibid., p. 93.

138. Kenez, *Defeat of the Whites,* p. 104.

139. Ibid., pp. 107-8.

140. Ibid., 107.

141. Pipes, *Russian Revolution,* p. 542.

142. Ibid.

143. Technically, the Bolsheviks published no official platform at all (ibid., p. 541). However, their public statements expressed support for the positions described below.

144. Lenin, "Fear of the Collapse of the Old and the Fight for the New," December 24-27, 1917 (old-style calendar), published in January, 1918, in Lenin, *Collected Works,* vol. 26, p. 401.

145. On disputes within the Bolshevik Party during the Civil War period, See Robert V. Daniels, *Conscience of the Revolution: Communist Opposition in Soviet Russia,* (Cambridge: Harvard University Press, 1960).

146. Pipes, *Russian Revolution,* p. 540.

147. Pipes, *Bolshevik Regime,* p. 138.

148. Ibid., p. 25.
149. Ibid.
150. Ibid., pp. 23–26.
151. Kolchak to Denikin, December 28, 1918 (old-style date), excerpted in Lehovich, p. 300.
152. Quoted in ibid., p. 215.
153. Denikin, *ORS*, vol. 4, p. 210.
154. Ibid., vol. 3, p. 132.
155. Kolchak, speech at Ekaterinburg, April 19, 1919, in Wade, ed., vol. 1, p. 349; Denikin, *ORS*, vol. 4, pp. 211–14, 222–24.
156. Kolchak to Denikin, October 23, 1919 (old style date), in Denikin, *ORS*, vol. 4, pp. 223–24.
157. Ibid., p. 212.
158. Lehovich, p. 331.
159. Declaration reprinted in Denikin, *ORS*, vol. 4, p. 214n.1.
160. On Wrangel's land program see Kenez, *Defeat of the Whites*, pp. 279–88; Brinkley, *Volunteer Army and Allied Intervention in South Russia*, pp. 246–47; General Baron Peter Wrangel, *Vospominanya* [Memoirs], (Frankfurt: Possev-Verlag, 1969), Part 2, ch. 3 and pp. 244–61.
161. See, generally, Brovkin, op. cit., esp. chs. 3, 6, pp. 409–10; Kenez, *Defeat of the Whites*, chs. 3–4.
162. Morris to Lansing, July 27, 1919, in FRUS, 1919, p. 400.
163. Denikin, *ORS*, vol. 4, p. 95.
164. George Orwell, "Looking Back on the Spanish War," in Orwell, *A Collection of Essays*, (New York: Harcourt Brace Jovanovich, 1953), p. 191.
165. See, e.g., description of parliamentary debate on the pogroms in Gilbert, p. 355.
166. Quoted in Chamberlin, vol. 2, p. 322.
167. Mawdsley, p. 213.
168. Kolchak, speech at Ekaterinburg, April 19, 1919, in Wade, ed., vol. 1, p. 349.
169. Denikin, *ORS*, vol. 5, p. 138.
170. See chapter 2.
171. Churchill, *Aftermath*, p. 254; Brinkley, pp. 199–200.
172. Brinkley, pp. 165–66.
173. The Cossack-White relationship is analyzed in Kenez, *Defeat of the Whites*, ch. 5.
174. On the Bolsheviks' ruthless campaign to suppress Cossackdom, see Brovkin, pp. 103–5.
175. Denikin, *ORS*, vol. 5, p. 139.
176. Ibid., vol. 4, p. 244.
177. Luckett, pp. 175–76; In the Amherst College Library copy of Luckett's book, this entire passage has been underlined by a previous reader. Written in the margin is the single word "Yes!" However, it is not entirely clear why Luckett includes "the Don" among the states which Denikin should have recognized, since the Don Cossacks had accepted the arrangement under which they enjoyed autonomy under the aegis of the Volunteer Army.
178. Churchill, *Aftermath*, p. 254.
179. Ibid.; A similar argument was retrospectively advanced by the Finnish leader, General Mannerheim; see Mannerheim, *Memoirs*, p. 237.
180. Ibid., p. 255.
181. See chapter 2.
182. See, esp., Pipes, *Bolshevik Regime*, pp. 9–13; Mawdsley, pp. 272–85.

183. Mawdsley's estimate of "ten to one" numerical superiority (Mawdsley, p. 281) is a gross overestimate based on paper strengths of the armies, as his own figures for the numbers of troops actually at the front at various key points make clear. See, e.g., his figures for troop strengths on Denikin's front in the fall of 1919 (ibid., p. 214).

184. This point is stressed in Luckett, p. 275.

185. Ibid., p. 276.

186. Kenez, *Defeat of the Whites*, p. 216.

187. Ibid., ch. 5.

188. This point is well developed by Brinkley, pp. 190-92.

189. Lehovich, pp. 301-2.

190. For an opposing view, see Luckett, op. cit., pp. 252-53, 262. Luckett however does not make much of a systematic argument to justify his view. He contents himself with calling the drive on Moscow (p. 262) the "great, simple, and delusory idea that lay behind so many White actions." Great and simple it may have been, but there is little reason to believe that it was necessarily delusory.

191. There are, in fact, very few books devoted to the White movement as a whole, although there exist a number of studies of individual armies and fronts. Almost the only recent work with an all-Russian focus is Luckett, *White Generals*.

192. For a more pessimistic view of late tsarist Russia's chances of evolving into a liberal democracy, see Malia, pp. 83-87.

5

Lost Triumphs:
The Possibilities of Intervention

*"Not by taking things the easy way—using
superior strength to filch some province, preferring the security of this minor conquest to
great success—but by constantly seeking out the
center of his power, by daring all to win all, will
one really defeat the enemy."*[1]

—Carl von Clausewitz, *On War*

*"It stands to reason that if the Entente had used
but a fraction of the gigantic armies that were
released after the defeat of Germany.... in a
proper manner against the Russian Soviet
Republic we should not, of course, have been
able to hold out."*[2]

—Vladimir I. Lenin, December 2, 1919

*"We...committed the unbelievable folly of
landing at Archangel with fewer than twelve
hundred men."*[3]

—R.H. Bruce Lockhart

During the course of 1918-1919, the leaders of Britain and the United
States repeatedly squandered excellent opportunities to successfully intervene in the Russian Civil War and insure the destruction of the Bolshevik regime. Many of these have already been discussed in detail in the
preceding chapters. But it would be useful to go through them all together,
so that the full magnitude of the Allied folly will become more clear.

Probably the first mistake that the Allies committed was in their failure to act at all during the eight months from December 1917 to July 1918.

179

During this period, the Bolshevik regime was extremely weak and even a small intervention force could probably have overthrown it with little difficulty. With the creation of the Cheka in December 1917 and the dispersal of the Constituent Assembly in January 1918, the nature and purposes of the Bolshevik regime should have been clear. Indeed, such Western observers as Secretary of State Robert Lansing and Maddin Summers, the U.S. consul in Moscow, did understand Bolshevism relatively clearly. Lansing's December 2, 1917 memorandum on Russia, analyzed in chapter 3, is perhaps the finest early Western appraisal of Bolshevism. By December, Lansing and others also recognized that there was no chance that the Bolsheviks would continue the war against Germany. The British willingness to be deluded by Lockhart's reports was based on crude wishful thinking divorced from both the ideological and the geostrategic position of the Bolsheviks. Such British officials as Sir William Wiseman, who had no special knowledge of Russia and spent most of 1917 and 1918 in the United States, clearly recognized this fact.

American leaders such as Lansing and President Wilson generally did not allow themselves to be influenced by the mirage of intervention by Bolshevik invitation, despite the pleas of Raymond Robins and other American apologists for the Soviet regime; indeed, they were unwilling to countenance a full-fledged anti-German alliance with the Bolsheviks even if it *were* possible. But they too failed to see the possibilities of intervention, in spite of the arguments of George Kennan and a number of American officials stationed in Russia.

The lengthy dithering of the Allies notwithstanding, there was still a golden opportunity for victory available in July 1918, when the British and American governments finally made the decision to intervene. Both Allied officials stationed in Russia and the Bolshevik leaders themselves were convinced that a modest Allied expeditionary force of two or three divisions could easily have captured Petrograd and Moscow and overthrown the Bolshevik regime. Such an effort would not have been a significant drain on the Western Front, where each side had well over 150 divisions.

Yet not only did the British and Americans fail to send large enough forces to accomplish this task, they did not even really decide to fight the Bolsheviks at all. Neither the British forces in northern Russia nor the Americans in Siberia had any orders to advance inland and engage Bolshevik forces in battle. To be sure, it could be argued that the main purpose of British intervention at this time was to reestablish an Eastern Front against Germany, while the Americans hoped merely to aid the Czech Legion and provide inspiration for indigenous Russian resistance to the Germans. From the point of view of these goals, fighting the Bolsheviks might be seen as unnecessary, or even counterproductive. Lloyd George and Wilson always took care to emphasize these points.

But the British and American policy-makers should not be allowed to get off the hook so easily. For, even if we consider the intervention solely from the standpoint of its professed goals, it would *still* have been more advantageous to seek the overthrow of the Bolsheviks than to adopt the course actually chosen. After all, it was simply impossible to reestablish any kind of Eastern Front against Germany so long as the Bolsheviks controlled the heart of Russia, with its industries and manpower reserves. If there was to be any hope whatsoever of building up a new Russian army to oppose the Central Powers, these areas simply *had* to be taken. Even if they were then immediately occupied by the Germans, the Allies would still have come out ahead because of the diversion of troops from the West such a move would have entailed.

It is not at all clear that an Eastern Front could have been reestablished under any conceivable circumstances. Certainly, it could not have been re-formed on anything approaching the scale of 1914–17. But an intervention which succeeded in overthrowing the Bolshevik regime and thereby stimulating some semblance of Russian resistance to the Germans might at least have led to the diversion of a significant number of German and/or Austrian troops to the East.

A similar analysis applies to the American goals of aiding the Czechs and stimulating Russian support for the Allied cause. For the quickest and most effective way of ensuring the Legion's safety would have been to eliminate the Bolshevik forces that threatened it. Similarly, indigenous Russian support for the Allies would surely have been greater if the latter showed a willingness to remove the Bolshevik regime and end its abuses once and for all—not to mention the fact that the presence of a more substantial Allied contingent would have lessened Russian fears of opposing the Germans. As Lockhart astutely pointed out, "the support we would receive from the Russians would be in direct proportion to the number of troops we sent ourselves"[4]—and he might have added, to the willingness of the Allied governments to use those troops against the Bolsheviks.

An even more fundamental criticism of the Anglo-American stance at this stage is that they should have sought the overthrow of Bolshevism as a goal in its own right. By the summer of 1918, the domestic and foreign policy agenda of the communist regime was reasonably clear; the Red Terror, the Bolshevik economic program, and efforts to foment revolution abroad were all well underway. And it was an agenda that was deeply inimical to the sort of international system that the Allies hoped to establish after the defeat of Germany. In addition to meeting the demands of the war, British and American leaders had an obligation to consider those of the peace. This was particularly the case after July 1918, when the failure of the last great German offensive in the West made it clear that the Allies would probably emerge victorious in the end, though no one at that time foresaw the swift German collapse that eventually occurred in October and November.

Perhaps the closest historical analogy to the opportunity which the Allies lost in the summer of 1918 was the failure of the British and French to oppose Hitler in the crisis precipitated by Germany's 1936 reoccupation of the Rhineland in violation of the Treaty of Versailles. In both cases, a nascent totalitarian regime could easily have been thwarted at little cost, yet the Western powers failed to grasp the importance of the opportunity with which they were presented. It is unlikely that Hitler's government could have survived a defeat in the Rhineland or that he could successfully oppose the British and French if they chose to act decisively, as he himself was well aware. Similarly, Lenin and his colleagues realized in 1918 that they could not hope to stand against a determined Allied intervention. Both totalitarian dictators counted on the short-sightedness and disunity of their enemies and both turned out to be right.[5]

The failure to seize the opportunity presented to them in July-August 1918 was by no means the last of the Allies' follies, even if it was the greatest. In September 1918, as we saw in chapter 3, the United States had a good chance of saving the White and Czech position in the Volga region, yet chose not to do so, in spite of pleas from the Russians, the Czechs, and the European Allies. Had the Americans made a different choice, the Bolshevik regime might not have fallen immediately. But the Whites would have been able to start their great offensive in the spring of 1919 from a position much closer to Moscow. And the control of the populous Volga region would have provided them with significant additional manpower reserves while simultaneously denying these resources to the Reds.

The end of World War I both helped and hindered the cause of Allied intervention in Russia. On the one hand, it made vast new resources potentially available for this purpose. But on the other, it removed the original anti-German impetus of intervention and thereby destroyed the best incentive the Allies had to finish the job. In retrospect, Winston Churchill concluded that "[t]he Armistice proved to be the death knell of the Russian national [White] cause."[6] For those British and American leaders who did not see the overthrow of the Bolsheviks as an important end in and of itself were no longer willing to provide assistance to the Whites on a large enough scale to insure victory. If, however, "the Great War had been prolonged into 1919, intervention, which was gathering momentum every week, must have been military successful."[7] For the Allies would surely have made new and stronger efforts to reestablish the Eastern Front, efforts which could hardly help but result in the overthrow of the Bolsheviks, without which no new Eastern Front could be viable.

Yet the end of the war did not destroy all hope for intervention, even if it did eliminate the possibility—never very likely anyway—of sending extremely large Allied forces to Russia. The next important opportunity arose in January and February of 1919, when Marshal Foch, the supreme commander of the Allied armies, and Winston Churchill, the British war minister, proposed to aid the Whites by providing them with specialized volunteer detachments from the Allied armies and by sending them the Russian prisoners of war still held in Germany. As the impressive performance of the few British tanks and aircraft actually sent to southern Russia demonstrated, the deployment of such weapons against the Red Army in large numbers might have had a major effect on the outcome of the war.

The dispatch of limited numbers of regular Allied forces composed of volunteers might also have been a great blow to the Bolsheviks. Given the poor quality of the Red Army, "twenty or thirty thousand resolute, comprehending, well-armed Europeans," wrote Churchill, "could, without any serious difficulty or loss, have made their way very swiftly along any of the great railroads which converged on Moscow; and brought to the hard ordeal of battle any force that stood against them."[8] Certainly, a force of this size, operating on an important front in conjunction with the Russian Whites might have had made an enormous impact. The example of the Czech Legion's achievements in May-August 1918 showed that the Red Army had great difficulty dealing with even a relatively small, poorly equipped, and widely dispersed force of high-quality troops. And, furthermore, it is extremely difficult to believe that twenty or thirty thousand volunteers could not be found among the millions of men about to be demobilized by the American and British armies. Woodrow Wilson was not very convincing when he claimed at the Paris Peace Conference that "volunteers probably could not be obtained."[9] Churchill, after all, had little trouble finding 8000 men to reinforce the strategically insignificant British contingent in northern Russia, where conditions were far more unpleasant than they would have been with Denikin's forces in the southern or, somewhat later, Yudenich's near Petrograd; because of the strategic importance of these two fronts and their easy access to British naval transport, they were the most logical sites for a determined intervention.

The transfer of Russian war prisoners to the Whites would have been an even cheaper and less risky operation than the despatch of volunteers. The arms and equipment for these men would have cost little, since the Allies could have used the vast arsenals captured from the Central Powers or their own enormous surplus stocks. As we saw in chapter 2, even a small fraction of these prisoners would have been enough to remedy the numerical imbalance between Denikin's forces and those of the Reds on his front. Given equal numbers, the qualitatively superior forces of the Whites would likely have prevailed. Instead, the Russian prisoners were repatriated to Bolshevik Russia. And, as if to add insult to injury, the entire issue of the prisoners is barely even mentioned in most Western studies of the intervention.

Even as the Allied leaders in Paris were in the process of rejecting Churchill's pleas for a more systematic anti-Bolshevik effort, the White army of Admiral Kolchak was making impressive advances. While Kolchak was provided with substantial quantities of British and French equipment, the Americans, suspicious of his possible "reactionary" tendencies, did almost nothing. And even the British and French shipments did not include the kinds of specialized weapons—tanks and aircraft—which might have made a major impact totally disproportionate to their numbers. The default of the Americans was critical, for they had the greatest available resources and were closest to Siberia. Only in June did the Council of Four finally decide to partially recognize Kolchak and offer him increased assistance. And by that time, it was too late to do anything more than perhaps preserve the Admiral's position in Siberia. His chance to capture Moscow was irrevocably lost.

Meanwhile the Allies refused to provide the necessary logistical and financial support to make viable the efforts of Serbia, Rumania, and Bulgaria to provide arms and troops to Denikin in the spring of 1919.[10] These offers, particularly the Serbian proposal to send a 30,000-man expeditionary force to fight alongside the Volunteer Army, were large enough to have significantly affected the outcome of the fighting in southern Russia.

The Allied failure to take advantage of the Eastern Europeans' offers was part of a broader failure to combine the efforts of all the anti-Bolshevik states bordering Russia. At various times, the leaders of Poland, Finland, Serbia, the Baltic states, and a number of other nations carved out of the old Russian Empire all expressed a willingness to help the Whites fight the Bolsheviks provided that the Allies gave them financial assistance and political guarantees of their independence. Most of them actually did fight the Bolsheviks at various times, though usually only intermittently and without committing their full power. Combined with the White armies, the forces of these states would almost surely have succeeded in crushing Bolshevism once and for all. During much of 1919, the large Polish and Finnish armies would probably have been enough to defeat the Bolsheviks in and of themselves.[11] But despite Churchill's repeated pleas to take advantage of this state of affairs and "use...their whole influence to combine the operations of all the States at war with Soviet Russia,"[12] the leaders of Britain and the United States consistently refused to make any serious efforts to bring this about. As we saw in chapter 2, Lord Curzon actually *discouraged* the Finns from helping Yudenich take Petrograd in the summer and fall of 1919.

The period of Denikin's great drive on Moscow, July-October 1919, was the last great opportunity the Allies had to overthrow the Bolshevik regime. By this point, there was little the British could do to aid Denikin directly beyond what they were doing already, although the transfer of additional tanks and aircraft to his army might still have had a substantial effect. However, there was a great deal they and, to a lesser extent, the Americans, could have done for the Whites indirectly, by urging the Eastern European states bordering Russia to join in the anti-Bolshevik struggle. It was during this period that the British frittered away opportunities to involve Finland and Poland in the war.

Denikin might also have had a better chance of overthrowing the Bolsheviks if the Wilson administration had accepted Ambassador Morris' proposals for increasing assistance to Admiral Kolchak. While Kolchak's forces were no longer capable of sustained offensive action, it is possible that their position could have been stabilized, thus preventing the Bolsheviks from transferring large numbers of troops from Kolchak's front to Denikin's. But Wilson and Lansing rejected Morris' proposals, and American aid to Kolchak remained insignificant, even in the wake of the June 1919 Council of Four decision to grant him partial recognition and increased material assistance.

With the failure of Denikin's offensive in October-November 1919, there was no longer any chance of overthrowing the Bolshevik regime without a massive influx of Western troops. Yet the Allies might yet have been able to preserve White rule in some of the territories the latter still occupied. Russia might have been partitioned between the Whites and the Reds, as the terms the Bolsheviks offered to Bullitt in March had stipulated. In November 1919, Churchill urged precisely this option on the British government. "We do not want to see Denikin broken up as Kolchak was," he contended, "...Denikin has an enormous area of immense value, and if that were consolidated after a suspension of hostilities it would be much better than the complete triumph of the Bolshevik empire."[13] Churchill argued for the continuation of British aid to Denikin and hoped that it would be "possible to make terms which enable at any rate a large portion of Russia to be saved from ruin."[14]

But Lloyd George, who had decided to end British support to the Whites as early as August, when Denikin was still winning, chose to ignore Churchill's advice. The cutoff of British assistance was a major moral and material blow to the White cause which, as both Russian and British observers believed, surely hastened the collapse of Denikin's forces,[15] although it would be wrong to minimize the impact of such other factors as the overextension of the White armies and the disorganized state of their rear areas.

The last chance for a division of Russia came when Wrangel reorganized and consolidated the remnants of the Volunteer forces in the Crimea in early 1920. By all accounts, Wrangel's political and military leadership was the most competent of all the White leaders. He quickly restored the army's morale and fighting power while simultaneously creating an effective civil government.[16] Wrangel soon had a highly capable army of some 40,000 men and an orderly and surprisingly liberal administration.[17]

The Crimean peninsula is linked to the mainland by only by two narrow strips of land which could easily be dominated by naval gunfire. In fact, British naval units in the Black Sea had covered the initial White evacuation to the Crimea and prevented Red forces from intervening. They continued to give fire support to Wrangel's forces in the first few months of his command.[18] Lloyd George, however, was determined to sever ties to the Whites and come to a trade and diplomatic agreement with the Bolsheviks. Churchill's continued advocacy of support for Wrangel had little or no effect. In June 1920, the British naval commander in the Black Sea was warned that "British Naval forces are to afford no, repeat no, support to Wrangel in offence or defence."[19]

For a few months, Wrangel was able to hold out, even launching a successful offensive to capture territory on the mainland in the summer. Much of this success was due to the ongoing Soviet-Polish War, which diverted the Red Army away from his front. But the end of the Soviet-Polish War in the fall spelled Wrangel's doom. By November, he was forced to evacuate his forces from the Crimea and give up the struggle. Most of his men ended up as exiles in the West.

It is quite possible, though by no means certain, that a determined British effort could have preserved Denikin's authority over large sections of southern Russia. Such a success would have saved millions of people from Bolshevism and also prevented the Soviet government from posing nearly as great a threat to the world as it eventually did. The White regime in southern Russia would have been a constant thorn in the communist side, inhibiting them from foreign policy adventures. As Denikin's memoirs and Wrangel's policies in the Crimea indicate, the Whites had learned a great deal from their political and military mistakes of 1918-19. Given time, they might have put their newfound enlightenment to good use as rulers of an anti-Bolshevik southern Russian state. It is difficult to say how viable such a state would have been. But the lessons learned by the Whites from their earlier failures and the provision of Western aid might well have allowed them to pursue a sufficiently skillfull policy to enable them to survive. A White state in southern Russia might not have been a liberal democracy, though Denikin himself would have been sympathetic to such an outcome. But it would surely have provided more freedom and greater economic welfare to its people than did Bolshevism.

Once Wrangel had retreated to the Crimea, the possibility of creating a really powerful White counterweight to the Bolsheviks was gone. However, it was almost certainly well within the power of the British fleet to save the Crimea itself. Had Wrangel been able to retain control of the peninsula, a stable White state would likely have emerged. It might well have had a relationship to Bolshevik Russia similar to that of Taiwan and Communist China. In fact, there are numerous interesting parallels between the policies of military reorganization, land reform, and economic liberalization implemented by Wrangel in the Crimea and those later adopted by the Kuomintang in its early years on Taiwan.[20] Both Wrangel and Chiang Kai-shek were conservative in political orientation; yet both also came to understand the need for liberal reform to sustain their regimes. While any conclusions about the ultimate fate of a White Crimean state are necessarily speculative, it is not unreasonable to suggest that its economic prosperity and increasingly large middle class—which was already exceptionally large by Russian standards in 1919—would eventually have led to political democratization, just as it did in Taiwan. On the other hand, it is at best questionable whether the Soviets could have been permanently prevented from conquering the Crimea by force.

The entire issue of a possible effort to achieve the partition of Russia between the Reds and the Whites has been even more thoroughly ignored by Western historians than the other opportunities for successful intervention available to the Allies.[21] It is ignored even in Richard Ullman's immense three-volume study of British policy during the Russian Civil War, though Ullman finds room for detailed consideration of far more minor issues.[22] The only extended consideration of such a possibility that I have been able to find is *Ostrov Krim* (Island of Crimea), a novel by the Russian emigre writer Vasily Aksyonov.[23]

Next to the failure to send forces large enough to do the job, the most important shortcoming of British and American policy was the maldistribution of the forces they did send. Instead of using their troops to help in the drive on Moscow, the heart of Bolshevik power, they sent most of them to secondary theaters where their impact on the outcome of the war was minimal—northern Russia and eastern Siberia. The Anglo-American leaders thus ignored Clausewitz's warning against "using superior strength to filch some [outlying] province, preferring the security of this minor conquest to great success."[24] In this way, much of the effort they did make largely went to waste.

In addition to the particular circumstances of specific opportunities, it is important to reconsider several more general arguments raised against intervention at the time and since. Four of these are especially significant: the argument that intervention was too costly, the claim that it lacked adequate public support in the West, the belief that it would merely serve to strengthen Bolshevism by stimulating a nationalistic backlash in Russian, and the contention that anti-Bolshevik intervention was immoral because it somehow violated principles of "self-determination." Let us consider each of these issues in turn.

The cost argument was always a favorite of Lloyd George's. "We cannot afford the burden...," he wrote in February 1919, "if we are committed to a war against a continent like Russia it is the direct road to bankruptcy and Bolshevism in these islands."[25] Throughout 1919, he repeatedly used it against Churchill's proposals. But would intervention in Russia of the kind proposed by Churchill really have cost so much? The exact expenditures are difficult to calculate, but it is doubtful that they would really have been crushing. Most of them would have consisted of the transfer of surplus military stores to the Whites and to the Eastern European states that Churchill hoped to enlist in the anti-Bolshevik cause. And these munitions were, as Churchill himself pointed out, "only an unmarketable surplus of the Great War, to which no money value can be assigned."[26] In fact, Churchill noted, the transfer of these munitions to the Whites could actually *save* at least some money, by eliminating "charges for storage, care and maintenance."[27] In addition to their own substantial stores, the Allies also controlled the vast arsenals of Germany, Austria, Turkey, and Bulgaria. These too were serving little purpose where they were and could easily have been put to use against the Bolsheviks.

Additional expenses would have been involved in the deployment of volunteer forces to Russia and in the transportation of the troops and weapons earmarked for intervention. However, the cost would not have been anywhere near large enough to lead to the "bankruptcy" of Britain. Moreover, some of it could have been offset by withdrawing the 20,000 British troops stationed in the Caucasus, as Churchill advocated. These forces were doing little good, since the independence of the Caucasian republics could not be preserved if the Bolsheviks won in Russia in any case. Even transportation expenses would not have been such a problem, since the Allies had come out of World War I with immense excess shipping capacity, built up for convoy duty on North Atlantic sealanes threatened by German submarines.

Cost issues were even less a problem for the United States than for Britain. Indeed, cost did not figure among the principal arguments raised against intervention there. Unlike those of Britain and the other European Allies, U.S. resources had not been heavily taxed by the war. The United States had come out of the conflict as the world's chief creditor and its military production was just beginning to peak at the time of the Armistice. Had the Americans chosen to give Kolchak five or even ten times more than they did, it would not have represented a significant drain on their resources.

In sum, the cost of a broader intervention would hardly have been prohibitive. But there is a still deeper point to be made against Lloyd George's argument. For arguments about costs are often really arguments over values. Lloyd George and Churchill did not disagree over the issue of intervention because of cost, although the debate between them sometimes took this form on a superficial level; they disagreed because Churchill believed that the anticipated results were *worth* the cost and Lloyd George did not.

In truth, the debate over costs was a debate over priorities. Fundamentally, Churchill believed that no other object on which the British defense and foreign policy budget in 1919 could have been spent was more valuable than the destruction of Bolshevism in Russia, with the possible exception of the occupation of Germany. Hindsight suggests that he was almost certainly right. Such projects as the suppression of terrorism in Ireland, the consolidation of the new British empire in the Middle East, and so forth, could not have delivered anything like the magnitude of benefit to Britain and the world that would have flowed from the destruction of Soviet communism. They could not save millions of lives, nor could they rid the world of an immense new threat. The same analysis applies to American military expenditures—and to many British and American domestic programs as well. In the words of a December 1918 *New York Times* article on intervention in Russia, "[i]t is not the means but the will that is wanting."[28]

It is often alleged that broader intervention was impossible because it lacked public support in Britain and the Unites States. But, before the end of the World War in November 1918, intervention could easily have been justified to the public as an anti-German war measure, particularly since the cause of the Allies really would have benefited from the overthrow of the Bolsheviks.

After the Armistice, it is fair to say, the war-weary peoples of the West would not have sanctioned a full-scale war against the Bolsheviks involving hundreds of thousands of troops. But no such war was required in order to pursue the options advocated by Churchill and other defenders of intervention. In both Britain and the United States, anti-Bolshevik sentiment was very strong, fueled by reports of communist atrocities and by anger at Lenin and Trotsky for having taken Russia out of the war against Germany. In Britain, most opposition to intervention was not so much opposition to intervention per se as opposition to the possible use of conscript troops,[29] something advocates of intervention had no intention of doing in any case. As long as intervention stopped short of the commitment of large numbers of conscript troops, it would have enjoyed broad support from both Parliament and the public. In the 1918 election, Lloyd George's Liberal-Conservative Coalition government had, in the words of one of his biographers, won "the most incredible majority that had ever been known" in British politics, capturing 534 seats in the House of Commons as against 173 for all other parties combined.[30] And Churchill's views on Russia were supported by "virtually the whole of the Coalition ranks in the House of Commons"—particularly the Conservative backbenchers who formed the bulk of the government's support.[31]

Only the opposition of Lloyd George and other key ministers in the cabinet prevented Churchill's agenda from being adopted. The cabinet's tight control over the majority party in the British parliamentary system insured that its views would prevail. Even so, Lloyd George was often forced to moderate his anti-interventionist stance in the face of strong opposition by his parliamentary supporters and by the general public.[32] It was for this reason, for example, that he chose to reject the peace proposals brought back by the Bullitt mission, proposals with which he was otherwise at least somewhat in sympathy.[33]

It is true, of course, that intervention of any kind was strongly opposed by the Labor Party and its associated trade unions. But Labor had only sixty-one seats in the House of Commons and its leaders had little popularity outside their core constituency.[34] Most of the hard-core Labor supporters who objected to intervention on principle would have been likely to vote against Lloyd George and the Coalition in any case. What counts in electoral politics is not what people think about a given issue but how many of them are willing to change their votes over it. Thus, opposition to intervention from Labor could not significantly damage Lloyd George's political prospects. To be sure, there was always the threat that Labor would use its influence with the trade unions to organize strikes in opposition to intervention. But, as a secret January 1919 cabinet report pointed out, the unions were unlikely to do "anything drastic...to stop conscription and intervention, for drastic action means the loss of wages for themselves."[35] Furthermore, a series of economically debilitating strikes in opposition to intervention might actually have served to arouse the wrath of public opinion against the Labor Party, which would have been blamed for stifling the tenuous postwar economic recovery, already a major public concern. And even if intervention really were unpopular, Lloyd George's overwhelming parliamentary majority and immense personal popularity could probably have sustained the blow. Certainly, a strong argument can be made that the issue was important enough to justify some political sacrifices.

In the United States, anti-Bolshevik sentiment was at least as strong as in Britain. After all, 1919 was the year of the first Red Scare. Much of the press, led by the *New York Times,* was strongly in favor of firm anti-Bolshevik intervention.[36] In Congress, intervention was firmly backed by Senator Henry Cabot Lodge of Massachusetts, the most important leader of the Republican Party.[37] Thus, Wilson would have been largely insulated from partisan criticism had he chosen to escalate the intervention. Obviously, intervention was opposed by hard-core isolationists and by the most left-wing liberals, two groups which often overlapped, as in the case of Senator William Borah, leader of the "Irreconcilable" faction of Republican isolationists in the Senate. But these factions were heavily outnumbered by the moderate liberals prepared to follow Wilson's lead and by the Lodge Republicans. In the Senate, for example, there were only fifteen "Irreconcilables" among the forty-nine Republican senators.[38] Most of the rest of the Republicans were Lodge supporters. Contrary to popular belief, the Treaty of Versailles was defeated not by hard-core isolationists but by "reservationists," senators who believed that the Treaty in its unamended form would have unduly restricted American freedom of action. They were not isolationists but unilateralists, to use current parlance.[39] In fact, Wilson might well have derived considerable political advantage from a forceful intervention because it would have driven a wedge between the isolationist and internationalist wings of the Republican Party. As it was, Borah and Lodge only avoided a falling out because of the Wilson's insistence that the Treaty of Versailles be passed without any reservations whatsoever, a shortsighted stance which drove the reservationists into the arms of the Irreconcilables.[40] Most of the forty-seven Democrats in the Senate were reliable Wilsonians who could be depended on to follow the president's lead on foreign policy issues. Like the British Labor Party with its opposition to Lloyd George, the Republican "Irreconcilables" could be expected to oppose Wilson regardless of what he did on Russia. They were hostile to his entire foreign policy as a whole. Thus, there was little political cost involved in flouting their views on intervention.

Nonetheless, criticism of U.S. policy in Siberia did indeed arise in Congress and in the press. But, as during the early stages of the Vietnam War, much of it was directed not at intervention per se but at the weakness and indeterminacy of the administration's stance.[41] Many of Wilson's critics would have preferred a firm intervention to the policy actually adopted. "The complaint which I make," said Senator Charles Thomas of Colorado in January 1919, "is that the force which we sent to Russia was insufficient."[42] An unequivocal pro-interventionist stance by the administration would have silenced much of this criticism, as well as creating a temporary "rally-around-the-flag" effect that would have inhibited opposition long enough to insure the overthrow of the weak Bolshevik regime.

A final important point related to the issue of popular support for intervention is the great moral authority of President Wilson as the recognized leader of liberal opinion, both in America and throughout the world. This influence both flowed from and transcended the great buildup of American military and economic power which had occurred under his administration. In the words of N. Gordon Levin,

> Wilson's great influence rested...not only on American power. It rested, paradoxically perhaps, even more on the President's denial of the legitimacy of power politics; on the assumption by Wilson of the leadership for liberal reform of the world political system. To millions around the world Wilson offered the hope of a New Diplomacy designed to banish the Old Diplomacy of alliances, power balances and traditional imperialism. It was just because he represented a fusion of seeming opposites—emergent American power and the New Diplomacy—that Wilson's postwar influence was so vast.[43]

If the full force of this moral authority had been deployed in support of anti-Bolshevik intervention, if Wilson had clearly stated that a world order based on the New Diplomacy was incompatible with the continued existence of a communist despotism in Russia, left-liberal opposition to intervention would have been largely swept away, both in the United States and elsewhere. It would have been the functional equivalent of President Nixon's opening to China; conservative opposition to the move was largely ineffectual because Nixon himself had for so long been the primary conservative spokesman on foreign policy issues. And even those liberals who remained unconvinced would have had little alternative to supporting Wilson. After all, most non-Wilsonian politicians in America were to the right of him. For all these reasons, the main obstacle to a full-fledged intervention was not in "isolationist" public opinion, it was in the mind of Woodrow Wilson. The man who had so eloquently articulated a liberal vision of the world did not understand what had to be done to bring that vision closer to reality.

Among the objections to intervention raised in 1918–19, one of those that had the most currency was that intervention actually helped the Bolsheviks by causing a nationalist backlash in their favor. As we saw in chapters 2 and 3, both Lloyd George and Wilson fully subscribed to this notion. Most Western historians have agreed. George F. Kennan is an especially vehement, but nonetheless representative advocate of the orthodox position. Intervention, he firmly believed,

> served everywhere to compromise the enemies of the Bolsheviki and to strengthen the Communists themselves. So important was this factor that I think it may well be questioned whether Bolshevism would ever have prevailed throughout Russia had the Western governments not aided its progress by this ill-conceived interference.[44]

Unfortunately, the immense prestige and undoubted moral fervor of the proponents of this view cannot substitute for an almost total absence of evidence. To put it simply, *no one has ever been able to identify any important group of Russians who came to support the Bolsheviks as a result of the intervention, but would otherwise have opposed them.* It is true that those opposition parties who supported the Bolsheviks in the Civil War—principally the Mensheviks and some of the S-Rs—cited intervention as one of their reasons for doing so. But these factions had opposed the use of force against Bolshevism long before there was any intervention at all. Intervention was an additional excuse for their stance, not the main reason for it.

A second important reason to reject the view that intervention helped the Bolsheviks is that the Bolsheviks themselves clearly believed otherwise. In their response to the Bullitt mission, they expressed a willingness to make sweeping concessions to the Allies in exchange for an end to intervention. It is difficult to believe that they would have done so had they been convinced that it was really in their interest. Throughout the Civil War period, Lenin, Trotsky, and other top Bolshevik leaders continually emphasized the fact that intervention posed a serious threat to Russian communism, not just in public propaganda statements but in secret communications and speeches.[45] Lenin well understood that "[a] very small part of the armies at the disposal of the Entente would have been enough to crush us," as he said in December 1919.[46]

Finally, even if intervention did cause some sort of nationalist backlash, the Bolsheviks were hardly in a position to exploit it. For they themselves were heavily dependent on non-Russian troops. Up to the fall of 1918, these actually constituted the majority of the Red Army.[47] And even afterwards, they formed a disproportionate percentage of its units, particularly the most reliable ones.[48] The Latvian Rifle regiments, for example, were always the elite strike force of the Bolshevik forces, "the Pretorian Guard of the Soviet Government," to use R.H. Bruce Lockhart's phrase;[49] Colonel Vatsetis, the commander in chief of the Red Army during most of the war was himself a Latvian. "In fact," as the Russian emigre historians Mikhail Heller and Aleksandr Nekrich note, "the number of foreigners fighting on the side of the Red Army greatly exceeded the number of foreign 'interventionists.'"[50] Even more fundamentally, the Bolsheviks themselves were an inherently antinationalist party, with a leadership composed disproportionately of non-Russians and an essentially alien ideology that held up the irrelevance of national distinctions as one of its cardinal tenets. In light of these facts, any propaganda advantage which the Bolsheviks were able to derive from intervention could have been easily countered by Allied and White propaganda stressing the composition of the Red Army and pointing to the very nature of the Communist party. After all, the effectiveness of propaganda is not always inversely proportional to its truth.

In any case, even if the Bolsheviks did manage to get some sort of net propaganda advantage from a broader intervention, this shortcoming would surely have been outweighed by the immense military advantages which effective intervention could have given to the Whites. As we saw in chapter 4, popularity does matter in civil wars, but it is by no means necessarily decisive.

All in all, there is every reason to believe that intervention could have been made effective. But was it right? Were the Allies morally entitled to impose their will on the outcome of the Russian Civil War? Was not intervention a violation of the right to self-determination?

Certainly, such an argument was often deployed by critics of intervention at the time. "The Russian people," said Senator William Borah, one of the leading Congressional opponents of intervention, "have the same right to establish a socialistic state as we have to establish a republic."[51] Secretary of War Newton D. Baker urged Wilson to withdraw U.S. troops from Siberia on the grounds "that if the Russians... like...[Bolshevism], they are entitled to have it and...it does not lie with us to say that only ten percent of the Russian people are Bolsheviks and that therefore we will assist the other ninety percent in resisting it."[52]

A related but nonetheless distinct argument is the view of Wilson and Lloyd George, which held that a given side in a civil war only deserves to prevail if it has popular support and that the presence of popular support will necessarily insure victory. This position has a long history in the moral theory of international relations. The classic statement of the doctrine is John Stuart Mill's 1859 essay, "A Few Words on Non-Intervention."[53] According to Mill, there is no justification for interventions intended to help a people overthrow an oppressive regime which is a "purely native government." In his view, "the only test possessing any real value, of a people's being fit for popular institutions, is that they, or a sufficient portion of them to prevail in the contest, are willing to brave labour and danger for their liberation.... [I]f they have not sufficient love of liberty to be able to wrest it from merely domestic oppressors, the liberty which is bestowed on them by other hands than their own will have nothing real, nothing permanent."[54] Lloyd George applied almost the exact same reasoning to the Russian Civil War:

> Our principle ought to be 'Russia must save herself.' Nothing else would be of the slightest use to her. If she is saved by outside intervention she is not really saved. That kind of parasitic liberty is a sham and in this case would be a very costly one for the Powers.[55]

This line of argument is endorsed and extended by Professor Michael Walzer, arguably the most influential recent theorist of the justice of intervention:

> [A] government that receives economic and technical aid, military supply, strategic and tactical advice, and is still unable to reduce its subjects to obedience is clearly an illegitimate government. Whether legitimacy is defined sociologically or morally, such a government fails to meet the most minimal standards.[56]

Although Walzer had in mind the South Vietnamese government aided by the U.S. in the 1960s and 1970s, his argument clearly applies to the various White Russian governments equally well; they too received substantial amounts of the sorts of assistance that he mentions—though not as much as the Saigon regime—and they too could not prevail with such aid alone. Lloyd George likewise believed that limited grants of supplies and technical assistance was all that the Whites were entitled to.

It is important to note that the arguments of Mill, Lloyd George, and Walzer are not merely pragmatic—intervention will be ineffective—but moral—the intervention is considered wrong *even if it succeeds*. Thus, Mill held that a people unable to defend their own liberties against domestic oppression is not "fit for popular government"—morally unworthy to be free. Similarly, Walzer considers the Saigon government and others in a similar position to be "clearly...illegitimate."

What can be said against these arguments? One line of response is to outflank them entirely. For the Bolshevik regime was not just a threat to its own people, but, potentially, to the whole world. Its leaders freely admitted this themselves. As Lenin said in 1920,

> Bolshevism aims at world revolution. We have never made a secret of the fact that our revolution is only the beginning, that its victorious end will come only when we have lit up the whole world with these same fires of revolution.[57]

Nor was this mere rhetoric, for the Bolsheviks consistently backed up their words with deeds. Thus, they repeatedly tried to conquer Finland, the Baltic States, and other non-Russian territories of the old empire during the Civil War. They also hoped to stimulate communist uprisings in Western and Central Europe, particularly Germany. In 1920, after the failure of the Polish attack on the Ukraine, they even tried to subdue Poland. The purpose of the attack was not just to counter the earlier Polish invasion but to pave the way for Bolshevik-sponsored takeovers in other nations. "We are striving towards the West," said Leon Trotsky at the height of the Polish-Soviet War, "towards the European proletariat, which knows that we can meet it only over the corpse of White-Guard Poland."[58] The "destruction of Poland," he believed, was merely "[o]ur next step on the path to world victory."[59] In addition to their efforts to conquer contiguous nations, the Bolsheviks also sent agents to promote communist coups in Germany, Hungary, Austria, and a host of other states. Their "internationalism" was no mere ideological posturing.

The international dimension of Russian Bolshevism was continually stressed by Churchill and other defenders of intervention. In their view, it was both dangerous and wrong to allow an inherently expansionist ideology like communism to control the resources of a major nation. The risk was not just to the Russian people but to the world as a whole. Morality and prudence require that a regime which declares itself the enemy of all other existing governments and acts as if it means it should be taken at its word and treated accordingly.

Moreover, it should be noted that both Mill and Walzer agreed that their arguments for non-intervention do not apply to "a native tyranny upheld by foreign arms."[60] Such a situation, Mill contended, could not be a true test of a people's fitness for liberty, and third parties were fully justified in intervening.[61] And, as we have seen, the Bolshevik regime was clearly dependent on the large-scale use of foreign troops. In particular, it is highly unlikely that it could have won the Civil War without the Latvian Rifles, who were its only reliable troops in the first months of its rule. As we saw in chapter 2, the Bolsheviks had also seized large quantities of Allied military supplies originally sent to Russia for the purpose of fighting Germany. To be sure, Mill and Walzer had in mind tyrannies supported by the intervention of foreign *governments* rather than merely by troops of foreign nationality. But the principle is the same. For the touchstone of the Mill-Walzer standard is whether the regime's power is based on indigenous forces, not whether its foreign troops were sent by their governments or came of their own volition. Otherwise, any government wealthy enough to hire large numbers of foreign mercenaries would be completely immune from counterintervention, a state of affairs that neither Mill nor Walzer would likely have considered legitimate.

Therefore, even if we completely accept the standard moral criticisms of intervention, the Allies would still have been justified in seeking the destruction of the Bolshevik regime because of the threat that it posed to others and—according to the Mill-Walzer theory—because of its dependence on foreign troops and arms. No right to *self*-determination can justify a regime which by its very nature seeks to make determinations for others by means of force. But it is, we maintain, possible to go further than this—to justify anti-Bolshevik intervention *even if the Bolsheviks intended to oppress no one but their own people.*

Let us look closely at the notion of "self-determination" which Senator Borah, Newton Baker, and other contemporary leftist and liberal critics of intervention used to justify their position. This principle can have two possible meanings. On the first construction, it might mean that a people has the right to choose its own government in free elections, or by some other method which ensures that the rulers of a country have the consent of the governed. Clearly, the Bolshevik regime did not meet this first definition, for it had little popular support and had deliberately suppressed the Constituent Assembly which had been chosen by popular vote.

The second definition of self-determination, the one which seemed to be implied in Baker's statement that the U.S. had no right to intervene in support of the ninety percent of the Russian people opposed to Bolshevism, is that a government is legitimate so long as its power rests solely on the efforts of indigenous forces, whether or not these forces have the consent of the majority of the people. This second definition underlies much contemporary left-liberal opposition to American intervention abroad.[62] "[O]nce a community is effectively divided [by civil war]," writes Walzer, perhaps the best known of the liberal theorists, "foreign powers can hardly serve the cause of self-determination by acting militarily within its borders."[63]

In actuality, the standard of self-determination set up by Baker and Walzer was not met by the Bolshevik government because of its dependence on non-Russian troops. But even if it was, it would not serve to dejustify intervention. For there is no reason to believe that a tyranny is necessarily legitimate simply because the tyrants and the people they victimize happen to be of the same nationality. Whatever the nationality of a despot, he is still ruling them without their consent. Thus, they do not have *self*-determination, their government is still imposed on them by *others*. Was Hitler's seizure of power legitimate simply because he was German? Or perhaps we are entitled to object to it solely on the grounds that, though a German citizen, he was born in Austria? The case against the definition of self-determination advanced by Baker and by many contemporary liberals is effectively summarized by moral theorist Hadley Arkes:

> '[S]elf-determination' was intelligible as a moral concern only as it represented another way of saying 'self-government' or the right of human beings to be ruled only with their consent.... And so it would simply be incoherent to insist that a coup d'état or the seizure of power by guerrillas must be taken as an exercise of self-determination so long as it occurs locally, through the efforts of the natives alone. An outside power that intervened to prevent such a coup and to preserve...a government of consent could not then be violating the principle of self-determination.[64]

In addition to this argument, a strong case could be made that the Allies would have been justified in intervening to support the Whites against

the Bolsheviks even if the latter could somehow meet the first, more re-
strictive and more valid, definition of self-determination. The principle
of government by consent is certainly an important moral precept. But it
does not exist in a vacuum; for it cannot be separated from the broader
liberal political tradition from which it stems, from the principles of respect for life, liberty, and property. Thus, a truly legitimate government
must not only have popular support, it must show at least a modicum of
respect for the individual rights of its people. It must refrain from slaugh-
tering its citizens by the millions, from suppressing freedom of speech
and religion, from the massive use of forced labor, from expropriating all
property for the use of the state. And, on all of these criteria, the various
White regimes, despite their many shortcomings, had the Bolsheviks
beaten hands down.[65] Indeed, the Bolshevik regime was easily the most
oppressive, most illiberal government up to its time. The number of those
who died as a direct result of its policies in 1917–20 is approximately
equal to the death toll of the Holocaust.[66]

Under such circumstances, it would be reasonable to argue that the
right of self-determination should be overridden by other, moral fundamental, moral considerations. Even Michael Walzer is willing to grant
that intervention is legitimate when aimed at "governments and armies
engaged in massacres,"[67] though it is not easy to see how this claim can
be logically reconciled with the rest of his theory. We might even contend, as does Arkes, that no right to self-determination is involved in such
cases at all, for there can be no right to choose a regime which is inherently evil.[68] I am not sure that I would go so far. But whether the right to
self-determination is wholly absent in such cases or merely overridden
by other moral considerations, the practical conclusion is the same: governments as fundamentally unjust as the Bolshevik regime have no right
to exist, and it makes no moral difference whether they are removed by
indigenous forces or by foreigners. And this remains the case whether
they have popular support or not. After all, few would argue that the fact
that Hitler had the support of the overwhelming majority of Germans
meant that the Allies were required to refrain from insisting on the removal of his regime as a condition for ending World War II.

But what of the Mill-Walzer claim that the inability of the Whites to
prevail without outside intervention meant that they were unworthy of
winning? To the extent that this argument rests on the assumption that
the losing party to a civil war necessarily has less popular support than its

enemies, it has been adequately refuted in chapter 4. But Mill and Walzer, particularly the former, seem to go further than this. For Mill contends that a people is not "fit for popular institutions" if it cannot defend its own freedom against native tyrants. This argument suggests that intervention is unjustified even in a case where the losing party to be helped *does* have popular support. A similar conclusion is implied in Walzer's argument that a government which cannot prevail without the help of foreign troops is "clearly...illegitimate." It is not clear whether Walzer would hold to this view even in the case of a government which had popular support, but the logic of his position suggests that he would.

Several criticisms can be lodged against Walzer and Mill. First, they fail to distinguish between different *degrees* of "illegitimacy." Even if we assume, with Mill, that a people unable to defend its own liberties can never be truly free, it does not follow that all of the possible despotic regimes which might arise to dominate it are equally malign. For some despots are less despotic than others. In the particular case at hand, the relatively mild authoritarianism of, say, Wrangel's rule in the Crimea, was clearly morally preferable to the massive oppression of Bolshevism. The former, while certainly flawed, provided incomparably more freedom and well-being to the people than the latter. In addition, it would probably have taken much less time, and a much less painful transition period, to give way to democracy. For these reasons, the fact that a civil war may be a contest between two undemocratic and/or illiberal governments does not necessarily imply that outsiders should be indifferent to the outcome. If one side is clearly much less repressive than the other, intervention is just as legitimate as it would be in support of a liberal democracy.[69]

But there is a second, and theoretically deeper, reason to reject the view that a people unable to defend its own liberties is unworthy of being defended by others. For, as Professor Arkes points out in his critique of Walzer's stance, such a position unwittingly buys into the ancient fallacy that the strong have an inherent right to rule. "[T]he mere success of some people in seizing and holding power," he points out, " could not itself justify that power, as though Might were indeed the source of Right."[70] The fallacy inherent in the Mill-Walzer argument becomes clearly evident when we apply similar reasoning to other social situations. For example, are laws against rape unjustifiable because most women lack the strength to defend their freedom and bodily integrity against male assailants?[71] Are women therefore to be considered "unfit" to exercise control over their bodies?

The mere fact that a people may lack the will, the courage, or the military prowess to defeat its oppressors does not in any way prove that they have no right to their freedom or even that they would be incapable of running a liberal democratic government if given the chance. The peoples of Germany and Japan, for example, were clearly unable, not to mention unwilling, to overthrow their fascist governments in the 1940s. Yet, as the results of the Allied occupation of those nations proved, that did not mean that they were unworthy of freedom or unable to function under a democratic regime.

The same analysis that applies to a people's rights also applies to the relative moral worthiness of regimes contending for power in civil conflicts. A government less potent than its adversaries may nonetheless be morally superior to them. And, as we saw in chapter 4, this was surely the case with even the worst possible regime that might have been established by the Whites. Much as we may wish that it could be otherwise, success in war—including civil war—is not an automatic sign of virtue, nor is defeat always the consequence of vice.

The primary concern of the present work is to draw attention to the many opportunities for successful intervention that the Allies squandered. By its very nature, the thrust of our analysis suggests that the intervention which actually took place was a miserable failure. Certainly, it would be hard to doubt the general validity of such a conclusion. And, indeed, the existing historical literature is nearly unanimous in agreeing that "Allied intervention policy proved a fiasco from which ultimately no one benefited."[72] Nonetheless, there is reason to believe that the failure was not a complete one, that at least some good was accomplished by the policies of the Allies, however much that good pales in comparison with what might have been achieved by a more determined effort.

Viewed from the perspective of the goal of countering Germany, which was after all its primary purpose, the original intervention was not wholly ineffective. In his memoirs, Lloyd George cites Erich Ludendorff, the German chief of staff to demonstrate that the British effort was not entirely fruitless. "[B]y garrisoning the [Trans-Siberian] railway," Ludendorff wrote after the war, "the Entente prevented the return of our prisoners of war from Siberia. This was unquestionably a serious loss for us."[73] While it is not clear, given the poor state of transportation in European Russia, how many German and Austrian prisoners could have been repatriated in any event—and how quickly—this point does have a measure of validity. Lloyd George also argued that intervention "contributed materially to their [the Germans'] failure to exploit the resources of Russia."[74] Again, it is difficult to say whether very much "exploitation" could have been accomplished in any event, given the chaos prevalent in Russia at the time. But there may have been some small effect of this kind.

The benefits cited by Lloyd George are minor. They certainly did not amount to the full-scale reestablishment of an Eastern Front, as the Anglo-French planners had originally hoped. On the other hand, their magnitude was commensurate with the size and quality of the Allied forces sent to Russia. A small effort resulted in small gains.

The post-Armistice intervention cannot readily be defended on anti-German grounds. Even Winston Churchill, the great defender of intervention, was led to conclude that "all the efforts made by the Allies in Russia after the Revolution and after the Armistice fall under a common condemnation," though he continued to believe that the Allies were to be blamed for doing too little rather than too much.[75] It is certainly wrong to claim that "Churchill pronounced British policy toward Russian in 1919 a great success."[76] Nonetheless, he did point to two benefits of the intervention. First, he contended that intervention allowed the British government to make good its "moral" debt to "the Russian forces who were loyal to the Allies."[77] This claim is difficult to evaluate, and I will not take up its ethical foundations here.

Churchill's second argument was much more weighty. By tying down Bolshevik forces for some two years in fighting the Whites, the intervention forestalled a Soviet attack on the Eastern European nations until such time as the latter had built up the means necessary to repel it. In this way,

> [a] breathing space of inestimable importance was afforded to the whole line of newly liberated countries which stood along the western borders of Russia.... Finland, Esthonia, Latvia, Lithuania, and above all Poland, were able during 1919 to establish the structure of civilized States and to organize the strength of patriotic armies. By the end of 1920 the 'Sanitary Cordon' which protected Europe from the Bolshevik infection was formed by living national organisms vigorous in themselves, hostile to the disease and immune through experience against its ravages.[78]

Here, clearly, was an important achievement. To be sure, it was to be reversed by the outcome of World War II. But, before that point was reached, the Allies had to make a whole series of additional mistakes in relation to both Germany and the USSR; thus, the statesmen of 1919 cannot really be held responsible for the eventual communist hegemony in eastern Europe, though they did help set the stage for it by allowing the Bolshevik regime to survive.

John M. Thompson is one of the very few historians to take Churchill's claim seriously. He disputes it on two grounds, arguing that the Bolsheviks were unlikely to invade the border states because they "had enough problems at home to keep them more than busy."[79] Even if they did, Thompson contends that "the Allies would have then intervened actively to stop them, and the line demarcating Bolshevism from Europe would have probably remained at about the place where it was finally delimited in 1921."[80]

It is undeniably true that the Bolsheviks faced enormous domestic problems, but there is little reason to believe that these would have prevented them from seeking to expand their revolution westward. After all, they did not prevent them from attempting to conquer the Baltic States and Finland during the Civil War. Nor did they stop the Bolsheviks from subduing the Caucasian and Central Asian republics afterwards. Nor, finally, did internal crises prevent them from making a major bid to conquer Poland in 1920. The Bolshevik commitment to the expansion of communism was so great that they were quite prepared to pursue it even at the expense of domestic needs. In fact, they believed that Russia's domestic development could only truly come to fruition after Marxist revolution had triumphed in the West.

As to Thompson's belief that the Allies would necessarily have intervened in earnest to stop Bolshevik expansion, this is not the impression one gets from their relatively tepid response to the invasion of Poland in 1920. In the absence of strong armies deployed by the border states themselves or by the Whites, only a truly massive Allied intervention would have been sufficient to throw the Bolsheviks back. And it is difficult to believe that public opinion in the West would have tolerated a major war on that scale merely for the sake of saving Lithuania, or even Poland. In any case, intervention in Russia clearly allowed these countries to be saved at much lower cost to the West than would otherwise have been the case.

Anglo-American intervention was therefore not entirely fruitless. *Some* good was accomplished. And yet, one cannot help feeling that these gains were miniscule compared to what might have been achieved. At one of the great turning points of history, the leaders of Britain and the United States missed a priceless opportunity to change the course of events for the better. The world has paid a staggering price for their lack of foresight, a price we continue to pay even unto this very day.

Notes

1. Clausewitz, *On War*, p. 596.
2. Lenin, "Political Report of the Central Committee," 8th Congress of the Russian Communist Party, December 2, 1919, in Lenin, *Collected Works*, vol. 30, pp. 171–72.
3. Lockhart, *British Agent*, p. 308.
4. Lockhart, p. 308.
5. The classic account of the Anglo-French failure in the Rhineland crisis is, appropriately for the theme of the present analysis, Winston Churchill, *The Gathering Storm*, (Boston: Houghton Mifflin, 1948), ch. 11.
6. Churchill, *Aftermath*, p. 273.
7. Ibid.
8. Ibid., p. 234.
9. FRUS, *Peace Conference*, vol. 3, p. 1043
10. Brinkley, *Volunteer Army and Allied Intervention in South Russia*, pp. 210–13.
11. While, as many historians have pointed out, the Polish leader Joseph Pilsudski was deeply suspicious of the Whites, he nonetheless expressed a willingness to fight the Reds in exchange for Allied assistance; see Brinkley, pp. 207–8.
12. Churchill, *Aftermath*, p. 254.
13. Churchill to General H. C. Holman, November 19, 1919, in Gilbert, *Churchill: The Stricken World*, p. 359.
14. Ibid.
15. See ch. 2.
16. See Luckett, ch. 17; Ullman, vol. 3, ch. II; Kenez, *Defeat of the Whites*, ch. 9; George P. Stewart, *The White Armies of Russia: A Chronicle of Counter-Revolution and Allied Intervention*, (New York: Macmillan, 1933), ch. 15; Wrangel, *Vospominanya*
17. Stewart, p. 369.
18. Ullman, vol. 3, p. 87.
19. Quoted in ibid.
20. A study of these parallels would be an interesting subject for future research.
21. Gilbert, p. 359, merely notes Churchill's advocacy of such a position without any attempt to analyze its practicality or desirability.
22. See, generally, Ullman, op. cit., esp. vol. 3.
23. Vasily Aksyonov, *Ostrov Krim*, (New York: Ardis, 1980). Aksyonov postulates that the Crimea was an island rather than a peninsula, a circumstance which allows the British navy to seal it off from Bolshevik attack and leads to the establishment of a Taiwan-like anti-communist state, the later fate of which is the subject of the novel.
24. Clausewitz, p. 596.
25. Lloyd George to Philip Kerr February 1919, in Lloyd George, *Peace Conference*, p. 243.
26. Churchill, *Aftermath*, p. 275.
27. Ibid.
28. *New York Times*, December 22, 1918, quoted in Leonid I. Strakhovsky, *American Opinion about Russia, 1917–20*, (Toronto: University of Toronto Press, 1961), p. 92.
29. Ullman, vol. 2, pp. 130–33.
30. Rowland, *Lloyd George*, p. 474; as Rowland points out (ibid.), 73 of the opposition M.P.s belonged to the Irish nationalist Sinn Fein party, which refused to allow

its victorious candidates to take their seats in Westminister. Thus, the real size of the government's majority was even greater than the undifferentiated figures showed. The Labor party, which was the main opponent of intervention, had only sixty-one seats.

31. Ullman, vol. 2, p. 297. The Conservative Party held 384 of the Coalition's 534 seats, as opposed to 136 for the Liberals and 24 for miscellaneous minor parties allied to the government (Rowland, p. 474).

32. Ullman, vol. 2, pp. 297-98; Thompson, *Russia, Bolshevism and the Versailles Peace*, pp. 242-44.

33. Thompson, pp. 242-43.

34. Rowland, p. 474.

35. Sir Basil Thomson, "Fortnightly Report on Revolutionary Organizations in the United Kingdom," January 28, 1919, reprinted in Ullman, vol. 2, p. 132.

36. See, generally, Strakhovsky, op. cit.

37. Lasch, *American Liberals and the Russian Revolution*, p. xii.

38. George and George, *Woodrow Wilson and Colonel House*, p. 278.

39. See ibid., ch. 14; George and George also argue (pp. 268-70) that Lodge was motivated by personal and political animosity towards Wilson. This claim may well be valid, but it is largely irrelevant to the argument developed here.

40. See ibid., ch. 14.

41. Unterberger, *Expedition*, pp. 136-39; Strakhovsky, ch. 9.

42. Quoted in Strakhovsky, p. 95.

43. N. Gordon Levin, "Introduction," in N. Gordon Levin, ed., *Woodrow Wilson and the Paris Peace Conference*, 2nd ed., (Lexington: D.C. Heath, 1972), p. viii.

44. Kennan, *Russia and the West*, p. 114; See also, e.g., John Bradley, *Allied Intervention in Russia*, (London: Weidenfeld & Nicolson, 1968), p. 214; like Kennan, Bradley also fails to cite any proof for this claim.

45. See, e.g., the quote from a private letter by Chicherin in ch. 3, emphasizing the need to come to terms with the Allies lest the latter up the scale of intervention.

46. Lenin, "Political Report of the Central Committee," 8th Congress of the Russian Communist Party, December 2, 1919, in Lenin, *Collected Works*, vol. 30, p. 174.

47. Mikhail Heller and Aleksandr Nekrich, *Utopia in Power: The History of the Soviet Union From 1917 to the Present*, trans. Phyllis Carlos, (New York: Summit Books, 1986), p. 92.

48. Ibid.

49. Lockhart, p. 312.

50. Heller and Nekrich, pp. 91-92; Heller and Nekrich nonetheless endorse (p. 91) the traditional view that intervention "gave a formidable weapon to the Soviet propagandists." But they give no evidence to support this claim.

51. Quoted in Strakhovsky, p. 95.

52. Baker to Wilson, November 27, 1918, in *PWW*, vol. 53, p. 228.

53. John Stuart Mill, "A Few Words on Non-Intervention," [1859], in John Robson, ed., *The Collected Works of John Stuart Mill*, vol. 21, (Toronto: University of Toronto Press, 1984).

54. Ibid., p. 122.

55. Lloyd George to Philip Kerr, February 19, 1919, in Lloyd George, *Peace Conference*, pp. 246-47.

56. Michael Walzer, *Just and Unjust Wars*, (New York: Basic Books, 1977), pp. 98-99.

57. Lenin, speech to the First All-Russian Congress of Working Cossacks, March 1, 1920, in Lenin, *Collected Works*, vol. 30, pp. 382-83.

58. Quoted in Mawdsley, *Russian Civil War,* p. 261.
59. Quoted in Churchill, *Aftermath,* p. 262.
60. Mill, p. 123; see also Walzer, p. 100.
61. Mill, pp. 123-24.
62. See, e.g., Richard J. Barnet, *Intervention and Revolution*; William A. Williams, *The Tragedy of American Diplomacy,* 2nd rev. ed., (New York: Dell, 1972), esp. pp. 104-6.
63. Walzer, p. 96.
64. Hadley Arkes, *First Things: An Inquiry into the First Principles of Morals and Justice,* (Princeton: Princeton University Press, 1986), p. 267.
65. See ch. 4 above.
66. See figures cited in ch. 1.
67. Walzer, p. 106.
68. See Arkes, op. cit., esp. p. 267.
69. In fact, the legitimacy of the intervention must be directly proportional to the size of the moral gap between the contending the parties. For this reason, it may sometimes actually be *more* legitimate to intervene in support of an authoritarian faction which is far superior to its adversary than a democratic party contending with opponents who are only moderately worse than they are. The magnitude of the wrong forestalled by intervention in the former case is greater than in the latter.
70. Arkes, p. 270.
71. For the sake of argument, we set aside the case of homosexual rape.
72. Bradley, p. 214.
73. Quoted in Lloyd George, *War Memoirs*, vol. 6, pp. 169-70.
74. Ibid., p. 170.
75. Churchill, *Aftermath,* p. 272.
76. Gardner, *Safe for Democracy,* p. 262.
77. Churchill, *Aftermath,* p. 275.
78. Ibid., p. 276.
79. Thompson, p. 397.
80. Ibid.

Epilogue:
Conclusions and Implications

*"The ultimate aims of the Bolsheviki are
hostile to all existing governments and any
apparent compromise which they make with
these governments is vitiated by their
avowed opportunism. "*[1]

—Robert Lansing, 1919

*"[W]e are fighting not only for ourselves...
but for the victory of Soviet power all over
the world. "*[2]

—Vladimir I. Lenin, 1919

Perhaps no other great transformative event in world history was less inevitable than the triumph of Bolshevism in Russia. As late as the spring of 1917, the Bolshevik party was little more than the minority faction of the Russian Social Democratic Party, itself a relatively weak faction on the far left of the Russian political spectrum. They were the fringe of a fringe group. And yet, by means of skillfull strategy and the use of coercion and terror on a scale unparalleled up to that time, they managed to seize power and then retain it against a host of enemies.

As we saw in earlier chapters, the Bolshevik leaders themselves fully realized that they had many close calls and that their enemies had squandered numerous opportunities to destroy them. They knew that a truly determined intervention would most likely spell their doom. The purpose of the present work has been to bring out this point.

If British and American policymakers had so many good chances to crush Bolshevism, why did they so consistently fritter them away? The answer cannot lie in ignorance, although ignorance of Russian conditions did occasionally mislead them. For, in each case, there were important officials and advisers who carefully explained the available opportuni-

209

ties to Prime Minister Lloyd George and President Wilson. In Britain, the main such adviser and advocate of intervention was Winston Churchill, whose views were shared by the majority of British officials stationed in Russia. On the American side, U.S. diplomats in Russia were also generally supportive of intervention. They were joined by the elder George Kennan, then generally considered the leading American authority on Russian affairs.

To be sure, Lloyd George, Wilson, and Lansing sometimes made narrowly technical errors in judging the information they received. The best example is probably Wilson and Lansing's belief, in the fall of 1918, that the United States had no means of sending troops and supplies to the Czech and White forces in the Volga region. However, such errors cannot explain a consistent pattern of lost opportunities throughout virtually the entire intervention period, even though they might account for some isolated individual mistakes.

In chapter 5, we argued that public opinion in Britain and the United States was not a significant constraint on intervention. Though it would have ruled out a full-scale war against Bolshevism, it certainly left open numerous options for much more vigorous action than was actually taken. Thus, it would be wrong to look there for an explanation of the failure of intervention. If anything, public opinion, especially in Britain, might well have been more supportive of a firm policy of intervention than of the policy actually adopted.

If neither the constraints of public opinion, nor case-specific errors, nor the other external factors analyzed in chapter 5, can explain the shortcomings of Anglo-American policy towards Russia in 1918–20, then the search for causes leads inexorably to the attitudes and worldviews of the leaders who formulated that policy. And, indeed, it was the ideological attitudes to foreign policy of men like Lloyd George, Curzon, Wilson, Lansing, and House which led them to misunderstand the situation they were dealing with in Russia.

In some ways, Lloyd George and Wilson were not that far apart ideologically from Churchill, the elder Kennan, and others who understood the Soviet regime correctly and realized the potential effectiveness of intervention. Both sides were strong adherents of liberal democracy. Both believed that the international system had to be substantially altered in order to prevent a recurrence of World War I, although Wilson was prepared to go further in this respect than Lloyd George, who in turn was more radical than Churchill. Unlike Raymond Robins and William C. Bullitt, President Wilson never accepted the view that Bolshevik power represented Russia's right of self-determination.[3] It is not *unimaginable* that Lloyd George and Wilson could have been won over to a more Churchillian viewpoint, as it would have been in the case of leftists such as Bullitt or Robins or the leaders of the British Labor Party. Churchill and Lloyd George had in fact been close political allies for a number of years, working together on a wide range of issues.

Ultimately, however, no such conversion took place. For Lloyd George and Wilson were too strongly wedded to certain ideas about the nature of revolution, intervention, and the efficacy of force in the international arena. These ideas have been discussed individually in preceding chapters, but it would be helpful to draw them together.

First, Lloyd George and Wilson generally accepted the view that victory in a civil war was primarily dependent on obtaining popular support and that, conversely, the side that seemed to be winning at any given time probably had more backing from the people. Lloyd George was considerably more dogmatic about this view than Wilson, but the American leader was not free of this delusion either, as his comments at the Paris Peace Conference show.[4] Thus, the two leaders created a moral bind for themselves: if the Whites had popular support, they should win even without the aid of intervention; if they didn't, they would not deserve to win because such a victory would be a violation of the right of self-determination. Neither Wilson nor Lloyd George ever grasped the point that intervention may be justified even in cases where popular support was lacking, because of the foreign policy agenda of the government in question or because of its violation of numerous liberal values other than the principle of government by consent. To a considerable extent, this idea was understood by men like Churchill, Lansing, and the elder George Kennan; but they were never able to convert their superiors to their views.

The second great mistake made by Wilson and Lloyd George was in ignoring the differences between Bolshevik foreign policy ambitions and those of traditional autocratic and imperialistic states. While the latter generally sought merely to carve out a sphere of influence for themselves, however large, the Bolsheviks sought to conquer the whole world for their ideology, or at least as much of it as they could. In addition, they would not stop at merely controlling a neighboring state's trade and foreign policy, as traditional imperialists would do, but sought to control every aspect of the state's government and society, as they showed by their policies in the Ukraine, the Caucasus states, Central Asia, Mongolia, and all the other non-Russian areas conquered during Lenin's years in power. Because of the vast sweep of its ambitions, Bolshevism posed a greater long-term menace to the West than any previous enemy. This was understood by Churchill and Lansing, both of whom saw Bolshevism as an even worse threat than the recently defeated Germans.

The president and the prime minister erred also in underestimating the importance of military power in a civil war. To the average lay person, the idea that wars are won primarily by superior military power seems intuitively obvious. But Wilson and Lloyd George, under the influence of the emerging liberal view of international relations, held that the key to victory was popular support, and that foreign intervention in a civil conflict would merely stimulate a nationalist backlash. The lack of evidence to support this view did not prevent them from sticking to it throughout the Russian Civil War. Ideology triumphed over fact.

So far, we have dealt with errors stemming from the liberal view of international relations, of which President Wilson was the foremost advocate. This view downplayed the importance of military power in the international system and tended to overestimate the importance of the danger from residual reactionary elements relative to that stemming from adversaries on the left. The liberal outlook completely dominated Wilson's mindset and was an important influence on Lloyd George as well. It also informed the world-views of men such as Hoover and Lansing, who understood the nature of Bolshevism but could not bring themselves to sanction full-fledged intervention against it. But, among the British policymakers, there was also a second ideological source of misconception.

This latter was what we today call the "realist" theory. Realism holds that the internal political structure of states does not significantly influence their foreign policy, which is largely determined by "objective" factors such as the state's size, population, economic and military power, and geographic location.[5] Within the British government, the leading advocate of this position was Lord Curzon, who believed that a White victory might pose a greater threat to British interests than a Red one because it could lead to a stronger, more united Russia. Fundamentally, Curzon believed that any Russian government would behave in largely the same way as any other, depending on the amount of territory and resources it was able to control. Realist views also sometimes influenced Lloyd

George, particularly in his suspicious attitude towards Denikin and his advocacy of breaking up Russia.

In a sense, the liberal and realist positions erred in opposite directions. While liberals tended to underestimate the role of force in international relations, realists made physical power the be all and end all of their outlook, ignoring the importance of the values and goals by which the use of that power was guided.

In both Britain and the United States, there were those who combined the liberal understanding of the importance of ideological factors in foreign policy with a realist appreciation for the power of force. Thus, Churchill understood that Bolshevism was an ideological challenge rather than a purely military one, just as the liberals did. But it was precisely his understanding of Bolshevik ideology that led him to advocate the suppression of Bolshevism by force; for he realized, as the liberals did not, that the values of the Bolsheviks were such that this was the only way to end their pursuit of totalitarianism at home and expansion abroad. In the words of Robert Conquest, "Churchill...understood, as Lloyd George and most others did not, that Leninism's dominating principle was unappeasable conflict, struggle to the death with the non-communist regimes."[6] Churchill fought hard to put his ideas into practice. But, trapped between the illiberal liberalism of Lloyd George and the unrealistic realism of Curzon, he failed to carry the day. Anglo-American policy continued to be dominated by the illusions fostered by liberalism and realism, with tragic results that we are only now beginning to overcome.

How grave were the consequences of Wilson's and Lloyd George's mistakes? The world that would have come into being in the event of a successful Allied intervention is likely to have been so different from the one that actually existed that we can only speculate about its nature. The only thing that can be said with anything approaching certainty is that it would have been a much better world than the one which emerged as a result of the triumph of Bolshevism.

In the first place, a White victory would surely have prevented the slaughter of millions by the Bolshevik regime in Russia itself, saving both those killed under Lenin and the still greater number of victims of Stalin. No imaginable White regime would have been so brutal. The Whites, even in their worst incarnations, would also not have suppressed civil liberties, freedom of religion, and property rights on anything like the scale that the Bolsheviks did.

In the foreign policy realm, it is possible that the Whites, particularly the more authoritarian elements among them, would have pursued a policy of traditional imperialist expansionism. But their ambition and ruthlessness was nowhere near as great as that of the Bolsheviks. They did not seek to dominate the world or even to completely control the lives of those neighboring peoples whom they wished to subject to Russian control. Even under the late tsarist regime, nations such as Poland and the Baltic States enjoyed considerably more autonomy than they eventually would in the Soviet scheme of things.

In the long run, a White victory would surely have spared the West all of the vast expense it incurred in combating Soviet expansionism over the years, though this expense only became as high as it did because of a second series of Western foreign policy errors in the 1930s and 1940s. More immediately, the absence of a communist government in Russia might have forestalled the rise of Nazi Germany. For Hitler learned a great deal from the methods of the Russian Bolsheviks and also benefited from their victory directly in two ways: first, he was able to use fear of communism to galvanize support for himself among many Germans; second, the division between the communists and his other opponents, brought on by Moscow's dogmatic hatred of liberals and social democrats, hindered efforts to oppose him. Even if Hitler had been able to take power anyway, the Western democracies would surely have found it easier to form an alliance against him with almost any Russian government other than one led by the communists.

The failure to destroy Russian communism was one of the two great errors which severely impaired the Versailles system of international relations at its very conception. The second great mistake was the antagonizing of Germany by extremely harsh peace terms, including the imposition of foreign rule on Germans living in territories allocated to Poland, Czechoslovakia, and other new states, and ridiculously high reparations payments. Winston Churchill became the leading critic of both these errors at the time they occurred, though he opposed the transfer of ethnic German territory to other states only in the case of Silesia.[7] "Since the armistice," he wrote to Lloyd George in March 1920, "my policy w[oul]d have been 'Peace with the German people, war on the Bolshevik tyranny.' Willingly or unavoidably, you have followed something v[er]y near the reverse."[8] But Churchill's counsel, as this letter suggests, largely fell on deaf ears.

This is not to minimize the significance of the later mistakes of 1930s appeasement. Had Churchill's advice been heeded *then,* the tragedy of the Second World War might yet have been avoided. But, though the failures of 1918–1919 did not make World War II inevitable, they certainly made it more likely. Had they not occurred, there might have been a real chance to create the kind of liberal international system envisioned by Woodrow Wilson, or at least bring it much closer to realization than would have been possible otherwise. Moreover, the combination of liberal and realist fallacies which doomed the cause of intervention in Russia would also prevent the development of an effective response to Nazi Germany.

Although we cannot take back the errors of Woodrow Wilson, David Lloyd George, and their minions, we can at least learn from them. The first, and philosophically most important, lesson is that neither the liberal nor the realist visions of international relations are adequate, even though these two theories, along with the Marxist, have dominated Western thought over the last two centuries. We must realize, as Churchill did, that the liberal belief in the importance of ideology as a determinant of policy must be combined with a realist understanding of the utility of force. Only thus can a reasonably sound view of the world be constructed.

On a more directly practical level, the great lesson to be derived from the failure of intervention, as well as from Western experience with Nazi Germany in the 1930s is that totalitarian regimes must, as much as possible, be destroyed while they are still in their infancy. If liberal democratic powers instead wait to deploy their power until such time as a major threat has actually materialized, they will be faced with a much more difficult struggle, if, indeed, they are still in a position to fully remedy their earlier oversight at all.

The implementation of this principle is a complicated and difficult matter. In some cases, for example, democracies may simply be unable to intervene with sufficient force to fully vanquish the enemy. In others, it may be necessary to ally with one totalitarian force to combat another, as in the World War II alliance with the Soviet Union against Hitler. Moreover, totalitarian regimes may, as in the case of Nazi Germany, arise on the right as well as the left, and it is not always as easy as in the case of the Bolsheviks to tell them apart from ordinary despotisms. In a few cases, as recently in Rwanda, a nontotalitarian regime may commit crimes on a scale comparable to those of totalitarian states, thus partly weakening the moral distinction between the two categories.[9] To fully discuss these difficulties would require a whole other study at least as long as this one. For present purposes, it is enough to suggest the general validity of the idea of intervention against totalitarianism. For once our analysis of particular cases takes place within a sound overall framework, we are much more likely to come up with the correct answers, even if such an outcome can never be guaranteed.

And even if we conclude, in any given situation, that liberation is unfeasible and we must therefore resort to containment, it is important to keep in mind that the latter policy can only be a compromise brought on by necessity while the former remains the ideal to strive for. Unlike George F. Kennan in his later years, we must not fall prey to the idea that containment can be considered an end in itself. For if a force is so malignant that great sacrifices can legitimately be incurred to limit its extent, then surely the world would be better off if the evil could not only be contained but destroyed.

In addition to the lessons which can be derived from the intervention itself, there is also much to be learned from its treatment at the hands of Western scholars. The present study is the first extended analysis to seriously consider the possibility that a larger effort might have been successful and that such an outcome would have been to the good. Almost all of the existing literature, as we saw in chapter 1, ignores this possibility entirely. The idea that a bigger intervention leading to the destruction of the Bolshevik regime might have led to a better world is not even argued against; it is simply discounted. For, as we have seen, most historians simply assume, with little or no argument, that anti-Bolshevik intervention was necessarily wrong. In their minds, the major salient question is whether the intervention that did occur was really anti-Bolshevik in nature or not.

In part, their mistake may be the consequence of specific errors in the analysis of particular events. Such errors are inevitable in scholarly research; they are surely present in this study as well. But no random pattern of *specific* errors can account for the broad, *general* neglect of the entire issue of lost opportunities to intervene more effectively. Nor can it be explained by a reluctance to consider "counterfactual" issues, since many of the same scholars who neglect the possibility of a larger intervention are keen on attempting to demonstrate that a more accommodating policy on the part of the West might have led to better Western-Soviet relations in the long run.

The most likely explanation for such a trend is the ideological orientation of the scholars working in the field. While it would be wrong to portray the many outstanding analysts who have taken up the subject of the intervention as a monolithic group, it is nonetheless correct to say that virtually all of them are, broadly speaking, liberal or radical in political orientation. As such, they have tended to sympathize either with Wilson and Lloyd George themselves or, as in the case of William Appleman Williams, with their critics on the left. These sympathies seem to be the most likely explanation for their reluctance to consider the issues highlighted here. As was argued in chapter 1, a strong ideological perspective is not necessarily incompatible with good scholarship. But when it leads us not just to *reject* opposing views on the basis of argument but to *ignore* them, it can have a debilitating effect on the quality of research. And to the extent that the work of professional historians and other intellectuals eventually comes to shape the views of the broader population, that debilitating effect may have important consequences indeed.

The failure to consider important aspects of the intervention is just one part of the general failure of Western intellectuals to fully face up to the evils of communism and other movements of the far left. As sociologist Paul Hollander has argued, the response of educated American opinion to the crimes of Soviet communism has been completely incommensurate with the massive soul-searching engendered by those of the Nazis, even though the victims of the former greatly outnumber those of the latter.[10] This trend has continued long after the reality and magnitude of the Soviet crimes had been demonstrated beyond all reasonable doubt.[11] Even today, after the fall of Soviet communism, there is relatively little public awareness of its crimes. Much of the general public is ignorant even of the crimes of Stalin. And the fact that Lenin's policies in the first years of Soviet rule imposed a death toll as great as that of the Holocaust is known only to specialists.

But perhaps the Russian victims of communism should not complain unduly. For there is even less Western public awareness of the equally great atrocities of communist governments in non-European nations such as China, North Korea, Vietnam, and Ethiopia. In each of these countries, hundreds of thousands or millions of people were slaughtered to a chorus of silence in the Western intellectual world. Only the mass murders of the Pol Pot regime in Cambodia have drawn commensurate attention in the West. And even here, the connection between the murders and communist ideology is generally neglected. Instead, the deaths are usually attributed to some special depravity of the Khmer Rouge or, among radicals, to backlash against U.S. intervention in Indochina. In any case, no communist regime has ever become the kind of symbol of evil in Western discourse is represented by the Nazis.

Symptomatic of the contrast has been the response to Holocaust denial as compared to that accorded to efforts to minimize the magnitude of Soviet crimes.[12] The attempts of a small number of marginal anti-Semitic cranks to "prove" that the Holocaust never occurred have been met by a spate of books and articles by leading scholars denouncing this phenomenon.[13] Holocaust denial is—rightly—seen as outside the bounds of reasonable intellectual discourse. But there has been no such denunciation of those scholars, notably Jerry Hough and J. Arch Getty, who have sought to minimize the scale of Soviet atrocities,[14] even though the advocacy of absurd views by respected academics should logically be a much greater cause for alarm than similar efforts by fringe elements in the netherworld of society. While, in light of overwhelming evidence to the contrary, few specialists now agree with Hough's and Getty's views, these views are not considered beyond the pale of reasonable argument and their purveyors continue to occupy respected positions in the intellectual world.

What is true for the intellectual response to Soviet crimes is, if anything, even more the case for the scholarly community's view of the failures of Western policy in opposing the Soviet Union. The possibility of a successful intervention in 1918–19 is only one of the most important of a large number of other similarly neglected issues. For example, the return, by the U.S. and British governments, of some 2 million Soviet prisoners of war to almost certain death in the U.S.SR at the end World War II[15] has been largely ignored by historians and other scholars, in striking contrast to the vast literature on the internment of Japanese-Americans during roughly the same period.[16]

While clearly inexcusable from a moral point of view, the latter policy merely entailed the deportation and confinement to camps of some 110,000 people; conditions in these camps, while hardly pleasant, were neither unsanitary nor unsafe. And the inmates were not required to perform crippling physical labor. The return of the Soviet prisoners, on the other hand, resulted in the death of many hundreds of thousands of people in Siberian Gulags. Even those who survived had to undergo years of hard labor under extraordinarily poor living conditions. All in all, a strong argument can be made that the return of the prisoners was a considerably greater evil than the Japanese internment; indeed, it was arguably one of the greatest humans rights violations in which the U.S. government has been complicit since the end of slavery. Yet it has received little attention from scholars and has hardly registered at all among the general public. Ironically, the exiled White General Denikin spent the last year of his life in a futile effort to persuade U.S. officials to desist from the policy of returning the prisoners.[17]

Likewise, there has been little effort by serious scholars—as opposed to the McCarthyite Red-baiters of the early 1950s—to examine the failures of the U.S. to adequately oppose Soviet expansionism during and immediately after World War II.[18] For that matter, the same could be said for scholarly studies of the entire history of U.S. policy towards the Soviet Union in the Cold War period. As in the case of the intervention, most scholarly opinion on these issues is divided between those who believe that U.S. policy was too hard on the Soviets and those who argue that it was reasonably balanced. There is little room in this framework for the argument that American policy was often not tough enough. In recent years, this trend has exhibited itself in the reluctance of many intellectuals to believe that Western pressure had anything to do with the collapse of the Soviet Union.[19] Hopefully, the collapse of communism will stimulate new scholarship on these issues, just as it has led to a reexamination of the Soviet regime's domestic policies.[20] So far, however, there have been few signs of such a development.[21]

The fall of the Soviet Union has, in some respects, obviated the urgency of correcting these errors. But it would be a grave mistake to conclude that they are now only of academic interest. To take one obvious point, there are still several communist regimes left in the world, notably those in China, Cuba, North Korea, and Vietnam. Our policy towards these states will be, in considerable part, determined by our view of communism in general, and of past U.S. policy towards communist nations. The contrast between the Clinton administration's treatment of the authoritarian regime in Haiti and the Cuban communist government of Castro speaks volumes about the extent to which Woodrow Wilson's double standard between reaction and radicalism continues to persist in our thinking.

Furthermore, we cannot be entirely certain that communism, or some other ideology of the far left, will never again prevail in a major nation. When and if that time comes, we must be prepared—not just by maintaining appropriate military capabilities, but by having a proper intellectual framework for approaching the problem.

On a more immediate level, the Western failure to come to grips with the evils of communism may be having a deleterious effect on the course of reform efforts in the former Soviet bloc states. These reforms have encountered many difficulties, some inherent in the admittedly difficult situation which the new governments face and others stemming from the mistakes of reformist policymakers. But surely a strong argument can be made that at least some of the shortcomings of reform efforts thus far have been due to a failure to pursue a policy of de-communization with the same thoroughness and moral will as de-Nazification was implemented in post-World War II Germany. After all, much of the opposition to political and economic reform comes from real and perceived beneficiaries of the communist regimes' policies. To the extent that many Eastern Europeans often take their intellectual and moral cues from the Western intellectual community, our unduly forgiving view of communism has been a disservice to them and an additional obstacle to the already difficult process of postcommunist reform.

With the exception of the trials of a few former East German officials, there has been no equivalent to the Nuremberg Trials in the former communist states. Nor has educated Western opinion seen fit to call for such trials. As a result, numerous communist officials responsible for the massive atrocities remain at large. Some even continue to hold positions in government. In addition to allowing heinous criminals to go free, our failure in this area has helped legitimate efforts to resist reform on the basis of communist and socialist ideological assumptions. A complete examination of the links between the inadequate Western condemnation of communism and the difficulties encountered by reformers in Russia and Eastern Europe is outside the scope of this work. However, the entire issue is an interesting, not to mention disturbing, example of the extent to which the ideological fallacies which led to the failure of intervention continue to influence the course of history.

The entire world has paid a horrifying price for the mistakes of 1918. At this late date, we cannot possibly hope to make up for them. But we can at least make an effort to understand their causes, and to insure that they are never repeated. One century dominated by the expansion of totalitarianism should be enough. Human civilization would be hard-pressed to survive a second.

Notes

1. Lansing to Ambassador in Great Britain, December 4, 1919, in FRUS, 1919, p. 129.
2. Lenin, "Report on the Domestic and Foreign Policy Situation of the Soviet Republic," April 3, 1919, in Lenin, *Collected Works*, vol. 29, p. 269.
3. See ch. 3.
4. See ch. 3.
5. The classic modern defense of realism is Kenneth Waltz, *Man, the State, and War,* (New York: Columbia University Press, 1959).
6. Conquest, "Reds," p. 4.
7. See Churchill, *Aftermath*, pp. 153–56, 208–14; for Churchill's post-World War II reflections on the German reparations payments, see Churchill, *The Gathering Storm*, ch. 1.
8. Churchill to Lloyd George, March 24, 1920, reprinted in Gilbert, p. 384.
9. However, even the Rwandan government, as heinous as its internal crimes were, did not pose the kind of threat to its neighbors as totalitarian states usually do. Furthermore, its massive genocidal massacres seem to have been a comparatively isolated incident rather than a core element of the regime's very nature, although smaller massacres had occurred in earlier years.
10. See Paul Hollander, "Soviet Terror, American Amnesia," *National Review,* May 2, 1994.
11. Ibid., pp. 29–30.
12. A similar point is made in ibid., p. 34.
13. See, e.g., Deborah Lipstadt, *Denying the Holocaust: The Growing Assault on Truth and Memory,* (New York: Free Press, 1993); Kenneth Stern, *Holocaust Denial,* (New York: American Jewish Committee, 1993).
14. See, e.g., J. Arch Getty and Roberta Manning, eds., *Stalinist Terror: New Perspectives,* (New York: Cambridge University Press, 1993); see also critique of Getty in Hollander, "Soviet Terror," pp. 33–34, which perceptively points out that Getty seeks not only to minimize the scope of the terror but to demonstrate that Stalin and other Soviet leaders were not really personally responsible for it.
15. As a matter of policy, the Soviet government under Stalin considered all prisoners captured by the Germans to be "traitors." As such, the prisoners were immediately sent to Gulags in Siberia upon their arrival in the Soviet Union. Most died there.
16. For rare exceptions, see Nikolai Tolstoy, *The Great Betrayal,* (New York: Scribner's, 1978); Nicholas Bethell, *The Last Secret: The Delivery to Stalin of Over 2 Million Russians,* (New York: Basic Books, 1974).
17. See Lehovich, *White Against Red,* pp. 485–87.
18. This gap has been partly filled by two recent books: Amos Perlmutter, *Roosevelt and Stalin: The Not so Grand Alliance,* (Columbia: University of Missouri Press, 1993); Patrick Glynn, *Closing Pandora's Box: Arms Races, Arms Control, and the History of the Cold War,* (New York: Basic Books, 1992), ch. 3; the former work, unfortunately, tends to overstate its case. I attempted to address some of these issues myself in Ilya Somin, "Soviet Opportunism and the Origins of the Cold War," *Concord Review,* Fall 1990. While this article was necessarily inadequate on some points—it originated as a high school term paper—I still endorse its major conclusions. There is, however, one important exception, and I would like to take this opportunity to repudiate my earlier view that Stalin's foreign policy was moti-

vated primarily by a desire for imperial expansion rather than the spread of Communist ideology. The ideological factor, I now believe, was a more important influence on policy than traditional balance of power calculations throughout almost the whole of the Soviet era.

19. I have examined some of the ways in which Western pressure may have stimulated Soviet leaders to undertake the reforms which led to the collapse of the USSR in Ilya Somin, "Riddles, Mysteries, and Enigmas: Unanswered Questions of Communism's Collapse," *Policy Review,* Fall 1994.

20. The outstanding new works in this field are Malia, *Soviet Tragedy,* and Pipes, *Bolshevik Regime.*

21. For an important exception, see, generally, Glynn, op. cit.

Bibliography

Aksyonov, Vasily, *Ostrov Krim,* (New York: Ardis, 1980).

Arkes, Hadley, *First Things: An Inquiry into the First Principles of Morals and Justice,* (Princeton: Princeton University Press, 1986).

Bradley, John, *Allied Intervention in Russia,* (London: Weidenfeld & Nicolson, 1968).

Brinkley, George, *The Volunteer Army and Allied Intervention in South Russia, 1917–21,* (Notre Dame: University of Notre Dame Press, 1966).

Brovkin, Vladimir, *Behind the Front Lines of the Civil War: Political Parties and Social Movements in Russia, 1918–22,* (Princeton: Princeton University Press, 1994).

Brzezinski, Zbigniew, *The Grand Failure: The Birth and Death of Communism in the Twentieth Century,* (New York: Macmillan, 1989).

Buchanan, Sir George, *My Mission to Russia and Other Diplomatic Memories,* vol. 2, (Boston: Little Brown, 1923).

Bunyan, James, *Intervention, Revolution, and Civil War in Russia, April-December 1918: Documents and Materials,* (Baltimore: Johns Hopkins Press, 1936).

_____, *The Origin of Forced Labor in the Soviet State, 1917–21,* (Baltimore: Johns Hopkins Press, 1967).

Chamberlin, W.H., *The Russian Revolution,* vol. 2, (New York: Macmillan, 1935).

Churchill, Winston, *The Aftermath,* (London: Thornton Butterworth, 1929).

_____, *The Gathering Storm,* (Boston: Houghton Mifflin, 1948).

Clausewitz, Carl von, *On War,* Trans. Michael Howard and Peter Paret, indexed ed., (Princeton: Princeton University Press, 1984).

Conquest, Robert, *The Human Cost of Soviet Communism,* (Washington, D.C: Government Printing Office, 1970).

_____, "Reds," *New York Review of Books,* July 14, 1994.

Cumming, C.K., and Pettit, Walter, eds., *Russian-American Relations, 1917–20: Documents and Papers,* (New York: Harcourt, Brace, and Howe, 1920).

Denikin, General Anton I., *Ocherki Russkoi Smuty* [Notes on the Russian Turmoil], 5 vols., (Paris and Berlin: Povolozky and Russkoe Slovo, 1921–26).

Deutscher, Isaac, *The Prophet Armed: Trotsky, 1879–1921,* (New York: Oxford University Press, 1954).

Eudin, Xenia and Fisher, Harold H., eds., *Soviet Russia and the West, 1920–27: A Documentary Survey,* (Stanford: Stanford University Press, 1957).

Fainsod, Merle, *How Russia is Ruled,* 2nd ed., (Cambridge: Harvard University Press, 1963).

Farnsworth, Patricia, *William C. Bullitt and the Soviet Union,* (Bloomington: Indiana University Press, 1967).

Fitzpatrick, Sheila, *The Russian Revolution, 1917–32,* (New York: Oxford University Press, 1982).

Fleming, Peter, *The Fate of Admiral Kolchak,* (New York: Harcourt, Brace, & Howe, 1963).

Footman, David, *Civil War in Russia,* (London: Faber and Faber, 1961).

Foreign Relations of the United States, 1918, *Russia,* 3 vols., (Washington, D.C.: Government Printing Office, 1931–32).

_____, 1919, *Russia,* (Washington, D.C.: Government Printing Office, 1937).

_____, *The Lansing Papers, 1914–20,* vol. 2, (Washington, D.C.: Government Printing Office, 1940).

_____, *The Paris Peace Conference, 1919,* 13 vols., (Washington, D.C.: Government Printing Office, 1942–47).

Gabriel, Christopher C., "Colonel House and the Development of American Peace Policy, 1918," unpublished M.Phil. thesis, New College, Oxford University, 1993.

Gaddis, John Lewis, *Russia, the Soviet Union and the United States,* 2nd ed., (New York: McGraw-Hill, 1990).

Gardner, Lloyd C., *Safe for Democracy: The Anglo-American Response to Revolution, 1913–23,* (New York: Oxford University Press, 1984).

George, Alexander L. and George, Juliette L., *Woodrow Wilson and Colonel House: A Personality Study,* corrected ed., (New York: Dover, 1964).

Gerson, Leonard, *The Secret Police in Lenin's Russia,* (Philadelphia: Temple University Press, 1976).

Gilbert, Martin, *Winston S. Churchill: The Stricken World, 1916–22,* (Boston: Houghton Mifflin, 1975).

Glynn, Patrick, *Closing Pandora's Box: Arms Races, Arms Control, and the History of the Cold War,* (New York: Basic Books, 1992).

Goldin, Vyacheslav I., "Interventy ili Soyuzniki? Murmanskii 'Uzel' v Marte-Iiune 1918 Goda," ["Interventionists or Allies? The Murmansk 'Knot' in March-June 1918,"], *Otechestvennaya Istoriya,* January-February 1994.

Graves, General William S., *America's Siberian Adventure, 1918–20,* (New York: Jonathan Cape, 1931).

Gregory, Ross, *The Origins of American Intervention in the First World War,* (New York: Norton, 1971).

Heller, Mikhail and Nekrich, Aleksandr, *Utopia in Power: The History of the Soviet Union From 1917 to the Present,* trans. Phyllis Carlos, (New York: Summit Books, 1986).

Hollander, Paul, *Political Pilgrims*, (New York: Oxford University Press, 1981).

_____, "Soviet Terror, American Amnesia," *National Review*, May 2, 1994.

Hoover, Herbert, *The Ordeal of Woodrow Wilson*, (New York: McGraw-Hill, 1958).

James, Robert Rhodes, ed., *Winston S. Churchill: His Complete Speeches*, vol. III, 1914-22, (London: Chelsea House, 1974).

Kenez, Peter, *Civil War in South Russia, 1918: The First Year of the Volunteer Army*, (Berkeley: University of California Press, 1971).

_____, *Civil War in South Russia, 1919-20: The Defeat of the Whites*, (Berkeley: University of California Press, 1977).

Kennan, George F., *American Diplomacy, 1900-1950*, (Chicago: University of Chicago Press, 1951).

_____, *Soviet-American Relations, 1917-20*, vol. 1, *Russia Leaves the War*, (Princeton: Princeton University Press, 1956).

_____, vol. 2, *The Decision to Intervene*, (Princeton: Princeton University Press, 1958).

_____, *Russia and the West Under Lenin and Stalin*, (New York: Mentor, 1961).

_____, *Soviet Foreign Policy, 1917-41*, (Princeton: Van Nostrand, 1960).

_____, "American Troops in Russia," *Atlantic Monthly*, January 1959.

_____, "The United States and the Soviet Union, 1917-76," *Foreign Affairs*, July 1976.

Kissinger, Henry, *Diplomacy*, (New York: Simon & Schuster, 1994).

Koenker, Diane, Rosenberg, William, & Suny, Ronald, eds., *Party, State, and Society in the Russian Civil War*, (Bloomington: Indiana University Press, 1989).

Lansing, Robert, *The Peace Negotiations: A Personal Narrative*, (Boston: Houghton Mifflin, 1921).

_____, *War Memoirs of Robert Lansing*, (New York: Bobbs-Merrill, 1935).

Lasch, Christopher, *The American Liberals and the Russian Revolution*, (New York: Columbia University Press, 1962).

_____, "American Intervention in Siberia: A Reinterpretation," *Political Science Quarterly*, June 1962.

Leggett, George, *The Cheka: Lenin's Political Police*, (Oxford: Clarendon Press, 1981).

Lehovich, Dimitry, *White Against Red: The Life of General Anton Denikin*, (New York: Norton, 1974).

Lenin, Vladimir I. *Collected Works*, vols. 25-32, (Moscow: Progress Publishers, 1965). Other editions of Lenin's works used as supplements.

Levin, N. Gordon, Jr., *Woodrow Wilson and World Politics*, (New York: Oxford University Press, 1968).

_____,ed., *Woodrow Wilson and the Paris Peace Conference*, 2nd ed., (Lexington: D.C. Heath, 1972).

_____, "The Open Door Thesis Reconsidered," *Reviews in American History,* December 1974.

Lincoln, W. Bruce, *Red Victory: A History of the Russian Civil War,* (New York: Simon & Schuster, 1989).

Link, Arthur S., *Wilson the Diplomatist: A Look at His Major Foreign Policies,* 2nd ed., (Chicago: Quadrangle, 1965).

_____, ed., *The Papers of Woodrow Wilson,* vols. 45-61, (Princeton: Princeton University Press, 1966-94).

_____, ed., *The Deliberations of the Council of Four,* 2 vols., (Princeton: Princeton University Press, 1992).

Lloyd George, David, *War Memoirs of David Lloyd George,* vols. 5-6, (Boston: Little Brown, 1936-37).

_____, *Memoirs of the Peace Conference,* [British ed. title: *The Truth About the Peace Treaties*], 2 vols., (New Haven: Yale University Press, 1939).

Lockhart, R.H. Bruce, *British Agent,* (New York: G.P. Putnam's Sons, 1933).

Luckett, Richard, *The White Generals: An Account of the White Movement and the Russian Civil War,* (New York: Viking, 1971).

Malia, Martin, *The Soviet Tragedy,* (New York: Free Press, 1994).

Mannerheim, Marshal Carl Gustaf, *The Memoirs of Marshal Mannerheim,* trans. Count Eric Lewenhaupt, (London: Cassell and Co., Ltd., 1953).

Mawdsley, Evan, *The Russian Civil War,* (London: Allen & Unwin, 1987).

Mayer, Arno, *Political Origins of the New Diplomacy,* (New Haven: Yale University Press, 1959).

_____, *Politics and Diplomacy of Peace-Making, 1918–19,* (New York: Knopf, 1967).

Meijer, Jan, ed., *The Trotsky Papers,* vol. 1, 1917-19, (London: Mouton & Co., 1964).

_____, vol. 2, 1920-22, (London: Mouton & Co., 1971).

Melgounov, Sergei, *The Red Terror in Russia,* trans. anonymous, (London: J.M. Dent & Sons, 1925).

Miliukov, Pavel, *Russia To-day and To-morrow,* (New York: Macmillan, 1922).

Mill, John Stuart, "A Few Words on Non-Intervention, " [1859], in John Robson, ed., *The Collected Works of John Stuart Mill,* vol. 16, (Toronto: University of Toronto Press, 1984).

Morley, William J., *The Japanese Thrust into Siberia, 1918,* (New York: Columbia University Press, 1957).

Pipes, Richard, *The Russian Revolution,* (New York: Knopf, 1990).

_____, *Russia Under the Bolshevik Regime,* (New York: Knopf, 1993).

_____, "1917 and the Revisionists," *National Interest,* Spring 1993.

Radkey, Oliver H., *The Unknown Civil War in Soviet Russia: A Study of the Green Movement in the Tambov Region,* (Stanford: Hoover Institution Press, 1976).

Roberts, Paul Craig, *Alienation and the Soviet Economy,* (Albuquerque: University of New Mexico Press, 1971).

Rowland, Peter, *David Lloyd George: A Biography,* (New York: Macmillan, 1975).

Seymour, Charles, ed., *The Intimate Papers of Colonel House,* vols. 3-4, (Boston: Houghton Mifflin, 1928).

Silverlight, John, *The Victors' Dilemma: Allied Intervention in the Russian Civil War,* (New York: Weybright & Talley, 1970).

Somin, Ilya, "Soviet Opportunism and the Origins of the Cold War," *Concord Review,* Fall 1990.

_____, "Riddles, Mysteries, and Enigmas: Unanswered Questions of Communism's Collapse," *Policy Review,* Fall 1994.

Stewart, George, *The White Armies of Russia: A Chronicle of Counter-Revolution and Allied Intervention,* (New York: Macmillan, 1933).

Strakhovsky, Leonid I., *American Opinion About Russia, 1917-20,* (Toronto: University of Toronto Press, 1961).

Thompson, John M., *Russia, Bolshevism, and the Versailles Peace,* (Princeton: Princeton University Press, 1966).

Trotsky, Leon, *The History of the Russian Revolution,* vol. 3, *The Triumph of the Soviets,* trans. Max Eastman, (New York: Simon & Schuster, 1932).

Tucker, Robert C., ed., *The Lenin Anthology,* (New York: Norton, 1975).

Ulam, Adam, *The Bolsheviks,* (New York: Macmillan, 1965).

_____, *Expansion and Coexistence: Soviet Foreign Policy, 1917-73,* 2nd ed., (New York: Praeger, 1974).

Ullman, Richard H. *Anglo-Soviet Relations, 1917-21,* vol. 1, *Intervention and the War,* (Princeton: Princeton University Press, 1961).

_____, vol. 2, *Britain and the Russian Civil War,* (Princeton: Princeton University Press, 1968).

_____, vol. 3, *The Anglo-Soviet Accord,* (Princeton: Princeton University Press, 1973).

Unterberger, Betty Miller, *America's Siberian Expedition, 1918-20,* (Durham: Duke University Press, 1956).

_____, ed., *American Intervention in the Russian Civil War,* (Lexington: D.C. Heath, 1969).

_____, "Woodrow Wilson and the Russian Revolution," in Arthur S. Link, ed., *Woodrow Wilson and a Revolutionary World, 1913-21,* (Chapel Hill: University of North Carolina Press, 1982).

_____, *The United States, Revolutionary Russia, and the Rise of Czechoslovakia,* (Chapel Hill: University of North Carolina Press, 1989).

Varneck, Elena, and Fisher, H.H., eds., *The Testimony of Admiral Kolchak and Other Siberian Materials,* (Stanford: Stanford University Press, 1935).

Volkogonov, Dmitri, *Lenin: A New Biography,* trans. Harold Shukman, (New York: Free Press, 1994).

Walzer, Michael, *Just and Unjust Wars*, (New York: Basic Books, 1977).

Weinberg, Gerhard, *A World at Arms: A Global History of World War II*, (Cambridge: Cambridge University Press, 1994).

White, John Albert, *The Siberian Intervention*, (Princeton: Princeton University Press, 1950).

Williams, William A., *American-Russian Relations, 1781–1947*, (New York: Rinehart & Co., 1952).

_____, "American Intervention in Russia, 1917–20, II," *Studies on the Left*, Winter 1964.

_____,*The Tragedy of American Diplomacy*, 2nd rev. ed., (New York: Dell, 1972).

Woodward, E.L., and Butler, Rohan, eds., *Documents on British Foreign Policy, 1919–1939*, series 1, vol. III, (London: His Majesty's Stationery Office, 1949).

Wade, Rex A., ed., *Documents of Soviet History*, vol. 1, *The Triumph of Bolshevism, 1917–19*, (Gulf Breeze: Academic International Press, 1991).

Wrangel, General Baron Peter N., *Vospominanya* [Memoirs], (Frankfurt: Possev-Verlag, 1969).

_____, *Always with Honor*, (New York: Robert Speller & Sons, 1957).

Index

aircraft, provided to Whites by British, 57-58, 183
Aksyonov, Vasily, 188, 205n23
Alekseev, General Mikhail, 42, 142, 145, 146-47
Alexander, Prince of Serbia, 54
American Relief Administration, 3, 119
anti-Semitism, see Jews, pogroms
Antonov-Ovseenko, Vladimir, 153
Archangel, Allied intervention in, 18, 19, 33, 37, 39, 91, 100-101; arms stockpiled in, 34
Arkes, Hadley, 199, 201
Armed Forces of Southern Russia, see Volunteer Army
Armenia, 165
Astrov, Nikolai, 158, 159
Azerbaidjan, 43

Baker, Newton D., 101, 108, 196, 198, 199
Bakhmetev, Boris, 120
Balfour, Arthur, Lord, 30, 40, 47, 52, 68, 81; hopes for intervention by Bolshevik invitation, 18, 33; urges cooperation with Bolsheviks against Germans, 28-29; on impossibility of politically neutral intervention, 37; opposes reestablishment of tsarism in Russia, 38; sets out limited program for intervention after end of World War I, 43-44
Bolsheviks, 1; famine caused by, 2, 117-19, 138-39; deaths caused by policies of, 2-3, 4-5; totalitarianism of, 3-4; arming of German and Austrian prisoners by, 12, 36; support of by Germans, 12-13, 89-90, 96; seek separate peace with Central Powers, 27-28; legitimacy of not recognized

by British, 29-30; unwilling to cooperate with Allies to oppose Germans, 31-32; fear large Allied intervention, 39, 115-16; popularity of relative to Whites, 44, 152-53, 155-56; response of to Prinkipo proposal, 50; fear White victory in spring 1919, 60; express fear of Denikin's advance in fall 1919, 63; fear White capture of Petrograd, 66; reject terms of Hoover-Nansen Plan, 119; agricultural policy of, 138-39; inflation policy of, 140; economic policies of, 140-41; and campaign against religion, 141; expansionism of, 142, 197-98, 211-12; and pogroms, 149-50
Borah, Senator William, 192, 195-96, 198
Brest-Litovsk, Treaty of, 12, 30, 31, 87, 166; and non-Russian minorities, 165-66; military advantages and disadvantages of, 168-71; reject nationalist backlash theory, 194-95; rely on non-Russian troops, 195
Brzezinski, Zbigniew, 23n27
Bukharin, Nikolai, 2
Bulgaria, 185, 189
Bullitt, William C., 113-16, 117, 122, 131n250, 186, 211

calendars (Russian Orthodox vs. Western), 25n63
Castro, Fidel, 219
casualties, of British forces in Russia, 59
Caucasus states, 43, 47, see also Georgia, Armenia, Azerbaidjan
cavalry, 169
Cecil, Lord Robert, 70n11
Chaikovsky, Nikolai V., 39, 60, 118-19, 138, 144, 163

Cheka, 3, 22n13, 137, 146, 155, 163, 180
Chelyabinsk, 36
Chiang Kai-shek, 188
Chicherin, Georgi, 25n76, 115
Churchill, Winston, 6, 10, 19, 27, 54, 56, 111, 210, 214; on dangers of Bolshevik victory in Russia, 1; view of Bolshevik totalitarianism and ideology of, 4, 45–46, 80, 213; advocates intervention in Russia, 9, 18, 44–47, 51–53; disagreements with Curzon, 9; disagreements with Lloyd George, 9, 214; predicts Soviet-German alliance, 10; on Red Army, 36; on opportunities presented by Czech uprising, 36–37; criticizes inconsistency of British policy, 44, 70 ; sees Bolsheviks as minority in Russia, 45; fears Bolshevik expansionism, 46, 197–98; fears Bolshevik-German-Japanese alliance, 46; seeks to mobilize border states against Bolsheviks, 46–47, 51–52, 64, 185; advocates withdrawal of British forces from the Caucasus, 47, 189; criticizes Curzon, 48–49; seeks to use aid as lever to moderate White attitudes on independence of minority nationalities, 49, 166–67; predicts failure of Prinkipo proposal, 50–51; advocates using Russian prisoners held in Germany against Bolsheviks, 51, 171, 183; proposes sending volunteer contingents to Russia, 51, 183; at Paris Peace Conference, 51–52, 112; opposes early withdrawal of German troops from Ukraine, 52; on cost of British aid to Whites, 57, 76n214; advocates sending tanks and aircraft to Whites, 57–58, 183; raises volunteer force to aid British troops in northern Russia, 58–59, 184; seeks to effect juncture between Kolchak and north Russia Whites, 59; advocates increased assistance to Kolchak, 60; believes decision to recognize Kolchak taken too late, 62; advocates support of Denikin in summer and fall of 1919, 62–64; overoptimistic about Denikin's prospects, 64; favors united Russia, 67,

123; unable to win Cabinet support for his views, 68–69; personal style of, 69; on Siberian intervention, 100; seeks to curb White atrocities, 162; claims end of World War I doomed intervention, 183; supports aid to Denikin even after his defeat, 186; advocates aid to Wrangel, 187; on costs of intervention, 189–90; on failure of British intervention of policy, 203; on benefits of intervention in containing Bolsheviks, 203–204
Civil War, American, 151
Civil War, British, 151
Civil War, Spanish, 151, 162
Clark, Representative Frank, 83
Clausewitz, Carl von, 151, 179
Clemenceau, Georges, 8, 49, 51, 116
Committee of the Constituent Assembly (Komuch), 36, 41, 156–57
communications, military, 170–71
communism, see Bolsheviks
Conquest, Robert, 3, 5, 213
Conservative Party, 191
Constituent Assembly, 4, 39, 44, 61, 136, 144, 155–56, 157, 158, 160, 166, 172, 180, 199
Constitutional Democratic (Kadet) Party, 98, 143, 145, 147, 162
Cossacks, 29, 42, 102, 147, 169–70; see also Don Cossacks, Kuban Cossacks
costs, of intervention, 188–90
Council of Four, 56, 186
counterfactualism, 20–21, 216
Crimea, 68, 186–88
Cromwell, Oliver, 151
Curzon, George Nathaniel, Lord, 67, 68, 123, 142, 210; realism of, 9, 212; disagreements with Churchill, 9, 47–49; concern of with British interests in Caucasus, 47–48; supports only very limited intervention in Russia, 48; personally suspicious of Churchill, 49; opposes Finnish attack on Petrograd, 65, 185; fears "reactionary tendencies" of Yudenich, 65
Czech Legion, 12–13, 35–37, 39–40, 41, 59, 72n66, 92–95, 98, 101, 104, 105–106, 121, 124, 145, 155, 181, 183–84

deaths, number of, resulting from Bolshevik policies, 2-3, 4-5, 137-38, 213
Democratic Party, 192-93
Denikin, General Anton I., 9, 18, 43, 47, 49, 54, 59, 61, 78n298, 113, 121, 135, 140, 145, 158, 168, 169, 170, 171, 172, 184, 185-87, 213, 219; takes command of Volunteer Army, 42; proposes "autonomy" for non-Russian nationalities, 48, 164-65; attempts to capture Moscow in fall 1919, 52-53, 63-64; figures on British aid received by, 56-58; final defeat of, 66, 68; on Lloyd George's cutoff of aid to Whites, 67-68; replaced by Wrangel, 68; on inconsistency of British policy, 70; liberalism of, 143; on Jews, 143, 175n88; personal dictatorship of, 143-44; and pogroms, 147-49; and non-predetermination, 157-58; on causes of White misgovernment, 161; criticizes minority leaders, 165-66
Dieterichs, General M.K., 121
Disraeli, Benjamin, 67
Don Cossacks, 29, 43, 144, 165

Eastern Front, reestablishment of as motive for intervention, 37, 79, 86, 180-81
Estonia, 56, 66, 165
executions, by Cheka, 3, 22n13

famine, in Russia, caused by Bolshevik policies, 2, 117-19, 138-39, 154, 176n127
February Revolution, 79-80, 172
Finland, 56, 61, 64-66, 163, 165, 185, 196
Foch, Marshal Ferdinand, 8, 51, 53, 93-94, 107, 110, 127-28n112, 171, 183
Foglesong, David, 11n
forced labor, used by Bolsheviks, 140-41
Fourteen Points Address, 79, 84-86
France, and Allied intervention in Russia, 8-9, 39, 40, 60, 104
Francis, Ambassador David, 14, 89-90, 96, 122
French Revolution, 45

Georgia, 43

Getty, J. Arch, 218
Gins, Georgi, 158
Gladstone, William, 67
Gough, General Sir Hubert, 65
Grant, Ulysses S., 151
Graves, General William S., 101-103, 109, 124
Great Emancipation (of serfs), 154
Greens, 153
Gulag system, 142, 218
Gumberg, Alexander, 87

"Hard Times Come Again No More," 124
Harris, Ernest, L., 122
Heller, Mikhail, 195
Hitler, Adolf, 1-2, 5, 182, 199, 213, 215
Hollander, Paul, 217
Holocaust, 4, 200, 217, 218
Hong Kong, 40
Hough, Jerry, 218
House, Colonel Edward M., 83, 84, 86, 93, 96, 113, 116, 118, 122, 125n31, 210
Hoover, Herbert, 3, 23n26, 117-19, 122, 123, 132n269
Hoover-Nansen food relief plan, 23n26, 117-19, 122

Ice March, 42, 146
ideological bias, in research, 20-21
"Irreconcilables," 192-93
Ironside, General, 144

Japan, intervention of in Siberia, 8, 14-15, 24n38, 31, 40, 86, 91, 96-97, 102, 109-110
Japanese-Americans, internment of during World War II, 218
Jews, 136, 143, see pogroms

Kadet Party, see Constitutional Democratic (Kadet) Party
Kaledin, General A.M., 29, 34, 82-83
Kalmykov, General I.M., 102, 109
Karakhan, L.M., 39
Kenez, Peter, 143, 146, 148, 174n79, 175n88
Kennan, George (the elder), 97-100, 122, 180, 210-11

Kennan, George Frost, 7, 10, 12, 20, 23n34, 25n76; on Treaty of Versailles, 11; on lost opportunities for Allied-Bolshevik cooperation, 16-18, 21; on Bolshevik unwillingness to oppose Germans, 31-32; on failure of Prinkipo proposal, 50; on Robins, 87; on nationalist backlash, 194

Kerensky, Alexander, 80, 85, 144

Kerr, Philip, 52, 54

Khmer Rouge, 217

Kissinger, Henry, 69

Knox, General Alfred, 33, 61

Kolchak, Admiral Alexander, 15, 25n60, 54, 59, 102, 106, 110, 113, 116, 120-22, 124, 138, 144-45, 146, 152, 158, 161, 168, 170, 171, 172, 184, 190; becomes White "Supreme Ruler," 41-42; figures on British arms received by, 57-59; advance of in spring of 1919, 60-61; partial recognition of by Allies, 60-62, 119-20; announces liberal war aims, 61; driven back by Bolsheviks, 62; captured and executed, 62; seeks US protection against Japan, 102; criticizes General Graves, 102-103; criticizes Allied policy in Siberia, 108; anti-Semitism of, 149-50; prevents anti-Semitic outbreaks in Siberia, 149; and nonpredetermination, 157; and land reform, 159-60; and minority nationalities, 164-65

Komuch, see Committee of the Constituent Assembly

Kornilov, General Lavr, 42, 143

Krym, Solomon S., 147

Kuban Cossacks, 43, 144, 165

Labor Party, 69, 191-93, 211

land reform, 150, 153-54, 159-61

Lansing, Robert, 13, 84, 88, 93, 96, 97-98, 99, 111, 117, 123, 124n15, 129n150, 176n115, 180, 209; predicts scale of Red Terror, 5, 81; on Bolshevik-German cooperation, 14; criticizes Root Commission, 80; opposes recognition of Bolshevik regime, 80-81; takes Bolshevik ideology seriously, 80; predicts de-feat of Bolsheviks, 81; opposes aid to Whites in December 1917, 81-82; fears Bolsheviks will take Russia out of World War I, 82; proposes sending message to General Kaledin, 82-83; rejects British calls for intervention, 86; unwilling to cooperate with Bolsheviks against Germans, 88; prefers intervention in northern Russia to Siberia, 91-92; sees anti-German motives as main reason for intervention, 92; believes Bolshevism worse than autocracy, 97; opposes full-scale anti-Bolshevik intervention, 97, 122; on Kennan's proposals for intervention, 99-100; on General Graves, 102; rejects proposal for political coordination of intervention, 104; rejects open commitment to Whites, 104; fears aiding reaction in Russia, 104; opposes deployment of US troops to Volga region, 105-107, 210; suspicious of Japanese motives in Siberia, 109; rejects Morris' request for further aid for Kolchak, 122, 186; opposes division of Russia, 123

Lasch, Christopher, 12-14, 96

Latvian Rifles, 39, 195, 198

League of Nations, 1, 61

Leggett, George, 3

Lenin, Vladimir Ilyich, 3, 6-7, 13, 14, 85, 87, 152, 179, 182, 191, 194-95, 213; justifies Red Terror, 4; on Bolshevik cooperation with Germans, 13; on US-Japanese rivalry, 15; hostility of to all capitalist states, 16-17; calls for peace with Germany, 27-28; more powerful than Trotsky, 31; opposes anti-German coalition with Allies, 32; worried by Kolchak's advance in spring 1919, 60; worried by Denikin's advance in fall 1919, 63; fears White capture of Petrograd, 66; fears Western intervention in Siberia, 98; response of to Hoover-Nansen plan, 119; on agricultural policy, 138-39; on need for socialization of the economy, 140-41; and pogroms, 149-50; on necessity of class struggle

and civil war, 155-56; calls for world revolution, 196, 209
Levin, Jr., N. Gordon, 15-16, 25n70, 85-86, 95-96, 105, 193
Lewin, Moshe, 136
Liberal Party, 67, 68
liberalism, theory of international relations of, 9, 48, 212-13
Lincoln, Abraham, 113
Lloyd George, David, 5, 27, 36, 52, 64, 103, 105, 113, 115, 135, 157, 167, 181, 187, 191-92, 202-203, 210-11, 215, 217; opposes all-out intervention in Russia, 9, 45, 54-56, 69-70; disagreements with Churchill, 9, 214; liberalism of, 9, 48, 212; hopes for intervention by Bolshevik invitation, 18, 33; seeks to cooperate with Bolsheviks against Germans, 28-29; justifies aid to Whites as war measure, 29; refuses to recognize Bolsheviks as legitimate government, 29-30; on role of the Czech Legion in precipitating intervention, 37; supports establishing non-Bolshevik government in Russia, 38; seeks to reassure Americans of liberal motives behind intervention in Russia, 38; fears reestablishment of Russian tsarism, 38; urges negotiations with Bolsheviks, 44; sees Bolsheviks as commanding popular support in Russia, 44-45; fears that intervention will provoke Russian nationalist backlash, 45, 194; analogizes Russian Civil War to French Revolution, 45; on Curzon, 47; willing to recognize Bolsheviks as de facto government, 49; and Prinkipo proposal, 49-51, 110; opposes Churchill's initiatives at Paris Peace Conference, 52, 75n187; supports aid only to "maintain" White position, 55; believes popular support crucial to victory in Russian Civil War, 54-55, 196; justifies assistance to Whites only on grounds of prior obligation, 55-56; believes Bolsheviks not expansionist, 56; describes Bolsheviks as anti-militarist, 56; advocates compromise peace with Nazi Germany in 1940, 56; decides to withdraw British forces from northern Russia, 58; briefly optimistic on Kolchak, 60; agrees to partial recognition of Kolchak's government, 60-61; denounces Yudenich as reactionary, 65; announces cutoff of aid to Whites, 67-68, 186; favors division of Russia, 67, 123; criticizes Churchill's "obsession" with Russia, 69; fears costs of intervention, 189-90
Lockhart, R.H. Bruce, 44, 73n95, 87-88, 95, 98, 181, 195; selected as unofficial British envoy to Bolsheviks, 28-29; believes Bolsheviks will fight Germans, 30-33; criticizes British intervention as too small, 39-40, 179; influenced by realism, 212-13
Lodge, Senator Henry Cabot, 192
Luckett, Richard, 166, 177n177, 178n190
Luddendorf, Erich, 202-203
Lvov, Prince, 118

Makhno, Nestor, 147
Maklakoff, Vladimir, 119
Malia, Martin, 6, 151
Mannerheim, General Carl Gustaf, 64-65
Mao Zedong, 5
Mawdsley, Evan, 66, 145, 163
Mensheviks, 138, 194
Mexico, 108
Mill, John Stuart, 196-201
Miller, General Eugene K., 59-60, 144, 163
minority nationalities, of former Russian Empire, 163-67
Morris, Ambassador Roland, 107, 120-22, 185-86
Moscow, as military objective in Russian Civil War, 40, 52-53, 60, 63-64, 170
"Moscow Directive," of Denikin, 63
Murmansk, Allied intervention in, 18, 33-35, 37, 39, 91, 100; arms stockpiled in, 34
Mussolini, Benito, 1-2

nationalist backlash, allegedly caused by intervention in Russia, 45
Nansen, Fridtjof, 118

nationalist backlash, against intervention, 45, 111, 194-95
Nazism, 21, 22n13, 214; influenced and strengthened by Bolshevik victory, 1-2
Nekrich, Aleksandr, 195
New Economic Policy (NEP), 141
New York Times, 1, 190, 192
Nicholas II, 142
Nixon, Richard M., 193-94
"nonpredetermination," 157-58
northern Russia, British operations in, 58-60; see also Murmansk, Archangel

Omsk, 36, 62, 107
Omsk Directorate, 36, 41-42, 102, 108
Open Door policy, 103
Orlando, Vittorio, 49
Orwell, George, 162
Osvag, 147

Pale of Settlement, 147
Paris Peace Conference, 6, 46, 49, 110-111, 184
"Peace Offensive" (of German army), 33
Petlura, Semyon, 147
Petrograd (St. Petersburg), as military objective in Russian Civil War, 40, 48, 58, 64-66
Pilsudski, Joseph, 205n11
Pipes, Richard, 20, 136, 154, 156-57, 158
pogroms, 146-50, 174n79
Poland, 47, 51, 61, 163, 185, 196, 203-204
Pol Pot, 5, 217
Polk, Frank, 102, 103
Poole, DeWitt, 25n76
Poole, General F.C., 35, 39, 40, 100-101
popular support, role of in Russian Civil War, 44-45, 150-59, 162-63, 211
popular support, for intervention (in West), 190-94
price controls, 138-39, 154, 173n32
Princeton University, 111
Prinkipo proposal, 49-51, 110
prisoners of war, German and Austrian, armed by Bolsheviks, 36, 95-96, 202-203
prisoners of war, Russian, held in Germany, 51, 171,183-84
Protocols of the Elders of Zion, 149

Provisional Government, 30, 79, 118-19, 142-43, 144, 155-56

Radek, Karl, 149-50
Reading, Lord, 38, 91-92, 104-105
realism, theory of international relations of, 9, 48, 212-13
Red Army, 31, 36, 41, 53, 107, 155, 156, 183
Reds, see Bolsheviks
Red Scare, 87, 192
Red Terror, see Terror, Red
Reinsch, Paul, 92-93, 99
Republican Party, 192-93
"Reservationists," 192
Rhineland crisis, 182
Robertson, Colonel T.A., 41
Robins, Colonel Raymond, 31-32, 87-88, 90, 95, 117, 122, 180, 211
Romania, 47
Roosevelt, Franklin D., 69, 131n250
Root, Elihu, 80
Root Commission, 80
Rumania, 185
Russian Orthodox Church, 167-68
Russian Political Conference, 118-19, 144
Rwanda, 215

Samara, 36, 41
Sazonov, Prince
self-determination, right of, 91, 195-202
Semenov, General Grigori, 88-89, 102, 109
Serbia, 54, 185
Sherman, William T., 151
Siberia, Allied intervention in, 8, 12, 14-15, chapt. 3
Sinn Fein Party, 205-206n30
Social Democratic Party, 209
Socialist-Revolutionary (S-R) Party, 36, 98, 102, 138, 139, 155, 156-57, 194
Sokolov, K.N., 143
South Vietnam, 196-97
Stalin, Joseph, 2, 5, 87, 213
Steffens, Lincoln, 114
Stepanov, V.A., 143
Summers, Maddin, 89-90, 97, 122
Supreme War Council, 37

Talleyrand, 40
tanks, provided to Whites by British, 57–58, 183
Taiwan, 188
Terror, Red, 4–5, 23n21, 114, 137–38, 163, 182
Terror, White, 137–38
Thomas, Senator Charles, 193
Thompson, John M., 114, 204
totalitarianism, of Bolsheviks, 3–4
Trans-Siberian Railway, 36, 100, 101, 103, 106, 109
Trotsky, Leon, 6–7, 28, 31, 41, 53, 66, 85, 92, 141, 149, 169, 191, 194–95
Tsaritsyn, 57

Ullman, Richard, 18–20, 29, 40, 41, 48, 68, 151, 188
Unterberger, Betty, 7, 12, 14, 23n23, 24n35, 24n58, 85, 91, 93, 96, 133n301
upward mobility, in early years of Soviet rule, 3
Ural Mountains, 41, 60

Vatsetis, Colonel, 60, 136, 195
Versailles, Treaty of, 11, 182, 192–93
Vinnaver, Mikhail, 147
Vladivostok, Allied intervention in, 34–35, 40, 93, 100, 124; Allied arms stockpiled in, 34
Volga River, 41, 60, 105–106, 182
Volkogonov, Dmitri, 13, 149
Volunteer Army, 9, 18, 42, 53, 142, 146–47, 160, 169, 185

Walzer, Michael, 196–201
War Communism, 3, 140–41
Wardrop, Oliver, 49
Webster-Hicks report, 95–96
Whites, 11, 19, 29, 135–36; come close to victory in Civil War, 6; advocate re-establishment of Constituent Assembly, 44; popular support of relative to Bolsheviks, 44, 150–59; reject Prinkipo proposal, 50; significance of Moscow to, 63–64; refuse to recognize de jure independence of Finland, 65–66; atrocities committed by, 102, 162; misgovernment of, 102, 161–62;

resent Allied policy in Siberia, 108; oppose Hoover-Nansen Plan, 118–19; analogized to Bolsheviks, 136; and anti-Jewish pogroms, 136, 146–49; military advantages and disadvantages of, 136, 168–71; political strategy of, 137, 157–59; agricultural policies of, 139–40, 153–54, 159–61; political ideology of, 142–45, 213–14; and minority nationalities, 163–67
Williams, William Appleman, 10, 11–12, 14–16, 20, 82–83, 85–86, 89–90, 91, 105, 116, 126–27n85, 217
Wilson, General Sir Henry, 58
Wilson, Woodrow, 5, 7, 12–13, 14, 37, 79, 83, 99, 113, 115, 146, 151, 157, 181, 183, 186, 192–93, 196, 210–11, 215, 217; liberalism of, 9, 48, 212; opposes anti-Bolshevik intervention, 10–11, 89, 110–13; as symbol of liberalism, 10, 193–94; seeks to promote liberalism in Russia, 15–16; supports Lloyd George's Prinkipo proposal, 49–50, 110; opposes Churchill's plan to send volunteer units to Russia, 51, 112; agrees to partial recognition of Kolchak's government, 60–61, 119; supports Provisional Government, 79–80; endorses policy of nonrecognition and nonintervention in Russia, 82; less anti-Bolshevik than Lansing, 83; believes Bolshevism will collapse of its own accord, 84; endorses British policy of contacts with Bolsheviks and Whites, 84; proposes informal contacts with Bolsheviks, 84; and Fourteen Point Address, 84–86; rejects British calls for intervention, 86; fears Japanese intervention may discredit Allies in Russia, 86, 91–92; unwilling to cooperate with Bolsheviks against Germans, 88; asks Lansing for information on Siberian Whites, 88–89; softens anti-interventionist stance, 90–91; does not see Bolsheviks as embodiments of right to self-determination, 91, 122–23; sees anti-German motives as main reason for intervention, 91, 95; endorses Lansing's distinction between

north Russia and Siberia, 92; begins to support intervention after revolt of Czech Legion, 92–93; and July 17, 1918 aide-memoire on Siberian intervention, 94–95; uninfluenced by Kennan, 100; insists on early withdrawal of US troops in northern Russia, 100; defends General Graves, 103; rejects open commitment to Whites, 104; opposes deployment of US troops to Volga region, 105–107; undecided on Russia policy, 108–109, 116; suspicious of Japanese motives in Siberia, 109; believes Bolshevism can only be defeated by addressing root causes, 111; fears intervention will generate pro-Bolshevik backlash in Russia, 111, 194; and double standard between left- and right-wing despotisms, 111–12, 123, 219; expects Whites to lose Civil War, 113; sees popular support as key to victory in Russian Civil War, 113, 150; and Hoover-Nansen plan, 117–18; ideological hostile to Bolshevism, 123; opposes division of Russia, 123

Wiseman, Sir William, 32–33, 90–91, 108–109, 180

workers, in Russian Civil War, 154–55

Wrangel, General Baron Peter, 57, 68, 148, 160, 162–63, 186–88, 200

Yudenich, General Nikolai, 6, 48, 58, 59, 64–66, 145, 165, 170, 171, 185